The American Commonwealth

VOLUME I

The American Commonwealth

BY JAMES BRYCE

NEWLY EDITED, ABRIDGED, AND INTRODUCED BY

LOUIS M. HACKER

PROFESSOR OF ECONOMICS, COLUMBIA UNIVERSITY

IN TWO VOLUMES

Volume One

The National Government—The State Governments—
The Party System—Public Opinion (*in part*)

CAPRICORN BOOKS

G. P. PUTNAM'S SONS   NEW YORK

To my friends and colleagues
ALBERT VENN DICEY
THOMAS ERSKINE HOLLAND
(*Original dedication*)

Library of Congress Catalog
Card Number 59-11821

Contents

VOLUME I

v

25711

Contents

PART IV—PUBLIC OPINION (*in part*)

Introduction

BY LOUIS M. HACKER

JAMES BRYCE is the best foreign friend the United States has ever had and his *The American Commonwealth* is the greatest book written about this country. When it first appeared in 1888, it had at once a profound effect on Great Britain and undoubtedly paved the way toward that improvement of Anglo-American relations that has led, step by step, to our present position of mutual goodwill and firm alliance. It still stands as the outstanding analysis of the nature of the American political character and Americans can read it today with as much assurance as they did 70 years ago as a description of the weaknesses and strengths of their democratic system.

What gives Bryce's book its authority is not simply the knowledge he had of the United States—and in almost every particular it was exact and encyclopedic—but his intuitive understanding of the uniqueness of the American experiment and the soundness of its basic assumptions. These were, the easy and therefore equal access to property and educational opportunity and the determination of political decisions by consent, with majority rule and minority right both being respected. He was far closer to the truth of American stability and growth than that other great commentator Alexis de Tocqueville, writing 50 years earlier, who saw in America centrifugal rather than centripetal forces at work, elements of disunity rather than those of cohesion.

Bryce, of course, was older than Tocqueville when he wrote—he was 50 and the Frenchman was 30; he had visited the United States many times and had seen all of it, while the young Tocqueville was recording the results of a single trip and that confined almost exclusively to the New England states. More important even, Tocqueville, oppressed by the turbulences and excesses of the series of revolutions in his own land's recent history was convinced that the fundamental error of democracy, that is to say, equalitarianism, was incapable of fostering talent and assuring individual privacy and right. Bryce's tradition was different, for as a Scotsman, a Presbyterian and a Liberal—trained both in the classical tradition at Oxford and in the law at Lincoln's Inn, London—he was prepared to accept the durability of English (and American) legal and political institutions with the great weight they placed on private conscience and responsibility, the sanctity of law and the determination of decisions by discussion and accommodation. Here you had order but also mobility (he himself has risen from modest circumstances) and one could face up to change without alarm as long as the voices of men were not silenced and their talents were not unnaturally curbed by privilege or prescription.

The American Commonwealth in consequence is not only a friendly book—recording both demerits and merits honestly yet always coming out on the credit side (our state and city governments are weak and their political leaders only too frequently venal; but the federal principle is a sound one)—but it is a sanguine book. Indeed those elements of survival he saw at work in the 1880's largely exist today and the spirit of hopefulness in which he wrote still continues as a fundamental aspect of the American character.

Why would American democracy improve and America endure? Because, unlike Europe, said Bryce, of these three forces: (1) the United States was a classless country without ranks and class hatreds; (2) the general diffusion of its wealth led to a respect for and a defense of property and at the same time a dislike for concentration (Said he: "I do not think that the ruling magnates are themselves generally disliked. On the contrary, they receive that tribute of admiration which the American gladly pays to whoever has done best what everyone desires to do"); (3) the quite universal absence of chronic pauperism was an important support of political authority and social organization.

He was not unaware of powerful divisive forces at work. The new immigrants from southern and eastern Europe were alien to the Anglo-American tradition. Yet he was less concerned—and sounder—on this score than his American contemporaries. For he said in 1888 what we generally know is the case today: "The intellectual and moral atmosphere into which the settlers from Europe come has more power to assimilate them than their race qualities have power to change it; . . . the future of America will be less affected by this influx of new blood than any one who has not studied the American democracy of today can realize." He was worried about the new great growth of cities and the exhaustion of the soil and the country's other natural resources. On the other hand, America's accepted commitments would stand it in good stead: the absence of internecine struggle between capital and labor, the continued access to property, its moderate temper as regards political and social relations, and "the restraining and conciliating influence of religion." Thus safeguarded, he could end his penultimate chapter about America: "We may look forward to the future, not indeed without anxiety, when we mark the clouds that hang on the horizon, yet with a hope that is stronger than anxiety." And his final chapter: "America has still a long vista of years stretching before her in which she will enjoy conditions far more auspicious than England can count upon. And that America marks the highest level, not only of material well-being, but of intelligence and happiness, which the race has yet attained, will be the judgment of those who look not at the favored few for whose benefit the world seems hither to have framed its institutions, but at the whole body of the people."

In his description of American political institutions and attitudes, Bryce is very good indeed. He accepts the federal principle as workable but he sees the growing concentration of power in the central government; he recognizes the importance of the Supreme Court; he reports on with interest, intelligence and great discernment—indeed, he was the first political commentator to do so—the role and activities of political parties and public opinion in America. At these points, he can continue to be read profitably today.

Bryce gave a good deal of attention to state and municipal government; in fact, he made an original and painstaking analysis of state constitutions and municipal charters. In those two areas, he found the greatest weaknesses and the least political responsibility. And because the greatest changes since have occurred in them, Bryce's discussions have little for our guidance today. And the same is true of American business and of economic habits generally. He was aware of the vitality of the new American economic enterprise (he has a chapter, and a good one, on American railroads; but, curiously enough, nothing on the new industries of steel, oil, and electrical goods) and saw the leadership of these new forces in America. Yet he expressed the wistful and of course unrealized hope—here he was the European rather than the American—that: "As the pressure of the effort towards

material success is relaxed, as the number of men devoted to
science, art and learning increases, so will the dominance of what
may be called the business mind decline."

Bryce's biographer, H. A. L. Fisher, records the fact that Bryce's
friends in America and presumably at many points his informants
were men of birth, education and definite upper-class loyalties;
among them were Theodore Roosevelt, John Hay, Seth Low and
Andrew D. White. It has been said of him, in criticism, that
he was a Hamiltonian rather than a Jeffersonian in his political
sympathies. Yet never was there a man with fewer political
and social prejudices; and rarely has there been a man to
catch so unerringly the essential nature of the American spirit.
He saw the uniformity in American life but he did not cavil over
it; he saw its violence and at the same time the ready acceptance
of law; he recognized the strong property-sense of most and as
well the broad tolerance toward the interests and aspirations of
every one. Above all, its equalitarianism did not repel but it
was America's most powerful attraction and, if America had a
moral to teach Europe, it was "that the masses of the people are
wiser, fairer, and more temperate in any matter to which they
can be induced to bend their minds than most European philosophers have believed it possible for the masses of the people to be."

Bryce came to his study of America partly because of his love
for travel and partly because of his education and adult interests
as English politician, jurist and historian. He was born in 1838
in Belfast of Scotch-Presbyterian origins; his parents soon returned to Scotland; and from Scotland he went to Trinity College,
Oxford, for his education. He wrote his brilliant book *The Holy
Roman Empire* in its original form when he was only 24; he was
named to the Regius Chair of Civil Law at Oxford (having also
read for the bar while he was a fellow of Oriel College) when he
was 32; and he was elected to Parliament as a Gladstonian Liberal
ten years later. Reelected in 1885, he held his constituency (at
Aberdeen) continuously for 21 years at the same time occupying
cabinet offices. Bryce quit Parliament to become the Ambassador
to the United States (1907-1913) and on his return to England
received the title of viscount and entered the House of Lords. He
died in 1922.

During his whole lifetime he was the indefatigable traveler.
He went to Germany and France as a youth, studying for a time
at Heidelberg; he crisscrossed again and again the European continent and the Near East; he visited India, North and South
Africa, Canada, Mexico, Cuba, Jamaica, Tahiti, Hawaii, New

Zealand and Australia. His first trip to the United States was in 1870, his second in 1881, and his third during 1883-84. In America, as a result of these visits, he was able to go everywhere; he read widely; and he talked with everyone. Indeed, Fisher estimated that five-sixths of his book was based on personal conversation.

Bryce began to write *The American Commonwealth* in 1883 and it made its appearance in England in three volumes in 1888, to immediate success. It was reprinted in the United States three years later (without the famous chapter on the Tweed Ring) and Bryce himself revised the work extensively twice, in 1893 and in 1910.

This edition is based on the original English one and it includes the Tweed Ring chapter. It should be said that what is here presented is not so much an abridgment as a selection; using such a method, it has been possible to cut the original by more than half and at the same time present Bryce's essential intention. The whole work is not included, chapter by chapter, in consequence, in abridged form. This editor has left out those materials—notably those having to do with the operations of state and local governments—which clearly are obsolete as far as the modern-day reader is concerned.

On the other hand, he has kept almost entire and nearly always in their full form those sections that have to do with American political attitudes and social institutions. These are the parts Bryce calls "The Party System," "Public Opinion," "Illustrations and Reflections," and "Social Institutions." This is the Bryce that survives in relevance and interest and continues to be read as eagerly today as it was 70 years ago.

LOUIS M. HACKER

Introductory

"WHAT do you think of our institutions ?" is the question addressed to the European traveller in the United States by every chance acquaintance. The traveller finds the question natural, for if he be an observant man his own mind is full of these institutions. But he asks himself why it should be in America only that he is so interrogated. In England one does not inquire from foreigners, nor even from Americans, their views on the English laws and government; nor does the Englishman on the Continent find Frenchmen or Germans or Italians anxious to have his judgment on their politics. Presently the reason of the difference appears. The institutions of the United States are deemed by inhabitants and admitted by strangers to be a matter of more general interest than those of the not less famous nations of the Old World. They are, or are supposed to be, institutions of a new type. They form, or are supposed to form, a symmetrical whole, capable of being studied and judged all together more profitably than the less perfectly harmonized institutions of older countries. They represent an experiment in the rule of the multitude, tried on a scale unprecedentedly vast, and the results of which every one is concerned to watch. And yet they are something more than an experiment, for they are believed to disclose and display the type of institutions towards which, as by a law of fate, the rest of civilized mankind are forced to move, some with swifter, others with slower, but all with unresting feet.

When our traveller returns home he is again interrogated by the more intelligently curious of his friends. But what now strikes him is the inaptness of their questions. Thoughtful Europeans have begun to realize, whether with satisfaction or regret, the enormous and daily-increasing influence of the United

States, and the splendour of the part reserved for them in the development of civilization. But such men, unless they have themselves crossed the Atlantic, have seldom either exact or correct ideas regarding the phenomena of the New World. The social and political experiments of America constantly cited in Europe both as patterns and as warnings are hardly ever cited with due knowledge of the facts, much less with comprehension of what they teach; and where premises are misunderstood inferences must be unsound.

It is such a feeling as this, a sense of the immense curiosity of Europe regarding the social and political life of America, and of the incomparable significance of American experience, that has led and will lead so many travellers to record their impressions of the Land of the Future. Yet the very abundance of descriptions in existence seems to require the author of another to justify himself for adding it to the list.

I might plead that America changes so fast that every few years a new crop of books is needed to describe the new face which things have put on, the new problems that have appeared, the new ideas germinating among her people, the new and unexpected developments for evil as well as for good of which her established institutions have been found capable. I might observe that a new generation grows up every few years in Europe, which does not read the older books, because they are old, but may desire to read a new one. And if a further reason is asked for, let it be found in this, that during the last fifty years no author has proposed to himself the aim of portraying the whole political system of the country in its practice as well as its theory, of explaining not only the National Government but the State Governments, not only the Constitution but the party system, not only the party system but the ideas, temper, habits of the sovereign people. Much that is valuable has been written on particular parts or aspects of the subject, but no one seems to have tried to deal with it as a whole; not to add that some of the ablest writers have been either advocates, often professed advocates, or detractors of democracy.

To present such a general view of the United States both as a Government and as a Nation is the aim of the present book. But in seeking to be comprehensive it does not attempt to be exhaustive. The effort to cover the whole ground with equal minuteness, which a penetrating critic—the late Karl Hillebrand —remarked upon as a characteristic fault of English writers, is to be avoided not merely because it wearies a reader, but because it leads the writer to descant as fully upon matters he knows imperfectly as upon those with which his own tastes and knowledge qualify him to deal. I shall endeavour to omit nothing which seems necessary to make the political life and the national character and tendencies of the Americans intelligible to Europeans, and with this view shall touch upon some topics only distantly connected with government or politics. But there are also many topics, perhaps no more remote from the main subject, which I shall pass lightly over, either because they have been sufficiently handled by previous writers, or because I have no such minute acquaintance with them as would make my observations profitable. For instance, the common-school system of the United States has been so frequently and fully described in many easily accessible books that an account of it will not be expected from me. But American universities have been generally neglected by European observers, and may therefore properly claim some pages. The statistics of manufactures, agriculture, and commerce, the systems of railway finance and railway management, are full of interest, but they would need so much space to be properly set forth and commented on that it would be impossible to bring them within the present volumes, even had I the special skill and knowledge needed to distil from rows of figures the refined spirit of instruction. Moreover, although an account of these facts might be made to illustrate the features of American civilization, it is not necessary to a comprehension of American character. Observations on the state of literature and religion are necessary, and I have therefore endeavoured to convey some idea of the literary tastes and the religious habits of the people, and of the part which these play in forming and colouring the whole life of the country.

The book which it might seem natural for me to take as a model is the *Democracy in America* of Alexis de Tocqueville. It would indeed, apart from the danger of provoking a comparison with such an admirable master of style, have been an interesting and useful task to tread in his steps, and seek to do for the United States of 1888, with their sixty millions of people, what he did for the fifteen millions of 1832. But what I have actually

tried to accomplish is something different, for 1 have conceived
the subject upon quite other lines. To De Tocqueville America
was primarily a democracy, the ideal democracy, fraught with
lessons for Europe, and above all for his own France. What he
has given us is not so much a description of the country and
people as a treatise, full of fine observation and elevated thinking,
upon democracy, a treatise whose conclusions are illustrated
from America, but are founded, not so much on an analysis of
American phenomena, as on general and somewhat speculative
views of democracy which the circumstances of France had
suggested. Democratic government seems to me, with all deference to his high authority, a cause not so potent in the moral
and social sphere as he deemed it ; and my object has been less
to discuss its merits than to paint the institutions and people of
America as they are, tracing what is peculiar in them not merely
to the sovereignty of the masses, but also to the history and
traditions of the race, to its fundamental ideas, to its material
environment. I have striven to avoid the temptations of the
deductive method, and to present simply the facts of the case,
arranging and connecting them as best I can, but letting them
speak for themselves rather than pressing upon the reader my
own conclusions. The longer any one studies a vast subject,
the more cautious in inference does he become. When I first
visited America eighteen years ago, I brought home a swarm of
bold generalizations. Half of them were thrown overboard after
a second visit in 1881. Of the half that remained, some were
dropped into the Atlantic when I returned across it after a third
visit in 1883-84 : and although the two later journeys gave birth
to some new views, these views are fewer and more discreetly
cautious than their departed sisters of 1870. I can honestly say
that I shall be far better pleased if readers of a philosophic turn find
in the book matter on which they feel they can safely build theories
for themselves, than if they take from it theories ready made.

    In the effort to bring within reasonable compass a description
of the facts of to-day, I have had to resist another temptation,
that of straying off into history. The temptation has been
strong, for occasional excursions into the past might have been
used not only to enliven but to confirm and illustrate statements
the evidence for which it has sometimes been necessary to omit.
American history, of which Europeans know scarcely anything,

may be wanting in colour and romance when compared with the annals of the great states of the Old World; but it is eminently rich in political instruction. I hope that my American readers, who, if I am not mistaken, know the history of their country better than the English know that of England, will not suppose that I have ignored this instruction, but will allow for the omissions forced on me by the magnitude of the subject. Similar reasons have compelled me to deal briefly with the legal aspects of the Constitution; but this is a defect which the lay reader will probably deem a merit.

It may be thought that a subject of this great compass ought, if undertaken at all, to be undertaken by a native American. No native American has, however, undertaken it. Such a writer would doubtless have many advantages over a stranger. Yet there are two advantages which a stranger, or at least a stranger who is also an Englishman, with some practical knowledge of English politics and English law, may hope to secure. He is struck by some things which a native does not think of explaining, because they are too obvious, and whose influence on politics or society, one to whom they seem part of the order of nature forgets to estimate. And the stranger finds it easier to maintain a position of detachment, detachment not only from party prejudice, but from those prepossessions in favour of persons, groups, constitutional dogmas, national pretensions, which a citizen can scarcely escape except by falling into that attitude of impartial cynicism which sours and perverts the historical mind as much as prejudice itself. He who regards a wide landscape from a distant height sees its details imperfectly, and must unfold his map in order to make out where each village lies, and how the roads run from point to point. But he catches the true perspective of things better than if he were standing among them. The great features of the landscape, the valleys, slopes, and mountains, appear in their relative proportion : he can estimate the height of the peaks and the breadth of the plains. So one who writes of a country not his own may turn his want of familiarity with details to good account if he fixes his mind strenuously on the main characteristics of the people and their institutions, while not forgetting to fill up gaps in his knowledge by frequent reference to native authorities. My own plan has been first to write down what struck me as the salient and dominant facts, and then to test, by consulting American friends and by a further study of American books, the views which I had reached.

To be non-partisan, as I trust to have been, in describing the politics of the United States, is not difficult for a European, especially if he has the good fortune to have intimate friends in both the great American parties. To feel and show no bias in those graver and more sharply accentuated issues which divide men in Europe, the issues between absolutism, oligarchy, and democracy ; between strongly unified governments and the policy of decentralization, this is a harder task, yet a not less imperative duty. This much I can say, that no fact has been either stated or suppressed, and no opinion put forward, with the purpose of serving any English party-doctrine or party-policy, or in any way furnishing arguments for use in any English controversy. The admirers and the censors of popular government are equally likely to find in the present treatise materials suited to their wishes ; and in many cases, if I may judge from what has befallen some of my predecessors, they will draw from these materials conclusions never intended by the author.

Few things are more difficult than to use aright arguments founded on the political experience of other countries. As the chief practical use of history is to deliver us from plausible historical analogies, so a comprehension of the institutions of other nations enables us to expose sometimes the ill-grounded hopes, sometimes the idle fears, which loose reports about those nations generate. Direct inferences from the success or failure of a particular constitutional arrangement or political usage in another country are rarely sound, because the conditions differ in so many respects that there can be no certainty that what flourishes or languishes under other skies and in another soil will likewise flourish or languish in our own. Many an American institution would bear a different fruit if transplanted to England, as there is hardly an English institution which has not undergone, like the plants and animals of the Old World, some change in America. The examination and appraisement of the institutions of the United States is no doubt full of instruction for Europe, full of encouragement, full of warning; but its chief value lies in what may be called the laws of political biology which it reveals, in the new illustrations and enforcements it supplies of general truths in social and political science, truths some of which were perceived long ago by Plato and Aristotle, but might have been forgotten had not America poured a stream of new light upon them. Now and then we may directly claim transatlantic experience as accrediting or discrediting some specific constitutional device or the policy of some enactment. But even in these cases he who desires to rely on the results shown in America must first satisfy himself that there is such a parity of conditions and surroundings in respect to the particular matter as justifies him in reasoning directly from ascertained results there to probable results in his own country.

It is possible that these pages, or at least those of them which describe the party system, may produce on European readers an impression which the author neither intends nor desires. They may set before him a picture with fewer lights and deeper shadows than I have wished it to contain. Sixteen years ago I travelled in Iceland with two friends. We crossed the great Desert by a seldom trodden track, encountering, during two months of late autumn, rains, tempests, snow-storms, and other hardships too numerous to recount. But the scenery was so grand and solemn, the life so novel, the character of the people so attractive, the historic and poetic traditions so inspiring, that we returned full of delight with the marvellous isle. When we expressed this enchantment to our English friends, we were questioned about the conditions of travel, and forced to admit that we had been frozen and starved, that we had sought sleep in swamps or on rocks, that the Icelanders lived in huts scattered through a wilderness, with none of the luxuries and few even of the comforts of life. Our friends passed over the record of impressions to dwell on the record of physical experiences, and conceived a notion of the island totally different from that which we had meant to convey. We perceived too late how much easier it is to state tangible facts than to communicate impressions. If I may attempt to apply the analogy to the United States and their people, I will say that they make on the visitor an impression so strong, so deep, so fascinating, so inwoven with a hundred threads of imagination and emotion, that he cannot hope to reproduce it in words, and to pass it on undiluted to other minds. With the broad facts of politics it is otherwise. These a traveller can easily set forth, and is bound in honesty to set forth, knowing that in doing so he must state much that is sordid, much that will provoke unfavourable comment. The European reader grasps these tangible facts, and, judging them

as though they existed under European conditions, draws from
them conclusions disparaging to the country and the people.
What he probably fails to do, because this is what the writer is
most likely to fail in enabling him to do, is to realize the existence in the American people of a reserve of force and patriotism
more than sufficient to sweep away all the evils which are now
tolerated, and to make the politics of the country worthy of its
material grandeur and of the private virtues of its inhabitants.
America excites an admiration which must be felt upon the spot
to be understood. The hopefulness of her people communicates
itself to one who moves among them, and makes him perceive
that the graver faults of politics may be far less dangerous there
than they would be in Europe. A hundred times in writing this
book have I been disheartened by the facts I was stating : a
hundred times has the recollection of the abounding strength
and vitality of the nation chased away these tremors.

There are other risks to which such a book as this is necessarily exposed. There is the risk of supposing that to be
generally true which the writer has himself seen or been told,
and the risk of assuming that what is now generally true is
likely to continue so. Against the former of these dangers he
who is forewarned is forearmed : as to the latter I can but say
that whenever I have sought to trace a phenomenon to its causes
I have also sought to inquire whether these causes are likely to
be permanent, a question which it is well to ask even when no
answer can be given. I have attributed less to the influence of
democracy than most of my predecessors have done, believing
that explanations drawn from a form of government, being easy
and obvious, ought to be cautiously employed. Some one has
said that the end of philosophy is to diminish the number of
causes, as the aim of chemistry is to reduce that of the elemental
substances. But it is an end not to be hastily pursued. A close
analysis of social and political phenomena often shows us that
causes are more complex than had at first appeared, and that
that which had been deemed the main cause is active only
because some inconspicuous, but not less important, condition is
also present. The inquisition of the forces which move society
is a high matter ; and even where certainty is unattainable it is
some service to science to have determined the facts, and correctly
stated the problems, as Aristotle remarked long ago that the first
step in investigation is to ask the right questions.

I have, however, dwelt long enough upon the perils of the voyage : it is now time to put to sea. Let us begin with a survey of the national government, examining its nature and describing the authorities which compose it.

Part 1

THE NATIONAL GOVERNMENT

CHAPTER 1

The Origin of the Constitution

WHEN in the reign of George III. troubles arose between England and her North American colonists, there existed along the eastern coast of the Atlantic thirteen little communities, the largest of which (Virginia) had not more than half a million of free people, and the total population of which did not reach three millions. All owned allegiance to the British Crown, all, except Connecticut and Rhode Island, received their governors from the Crown;[1] in all, causes were carried by appeal from the colonial courts to the English Privy Council. Acts of the British Parliament ran there, as they now run in the British colonies, whenever expressed to have that effect, and could over-rule such laws as the colonies might make. But practically each colony was a self-governing commonwealth, left to manage its own affairs with scarcely any interference from home. Each had its legislature, its own statutes adding to or modifying the English common law, its local corporate life and traditions, with no small local pride in its own history and institutions, superadded to the pride of forming part of the English race and the great free British realm. Between the various colonies there was no other political connection than that which arose from their all belonging to this race and realm, so that the inhabitants of each enjoyed in every one of the others the rights and privileges of British subjects.

When the oppressive measures of the home government roused the colonies, they naturally sought to organize their resistance in common. Singly they would have been an easy prey, for it was long doubtful whether even in combination they could make head against regular armies. A congress of delegates from nine colonies held at New York in 1765 was followed by another at Philadelphia in 1774, at which twelve were represented, which

[1] In Maryland and Pennsylvania, however, the governor was, during the larger part of the colonial period, appointed by the "Proprietor."

called itself Continental (for the name American had not yet become established), and spoke in the name of "the good people of these colonies," the first assertion of a sort of national unity among the English of America. This congress, in which from 1775 onwards all the colonies were represented, was a merely revolutionary body, called into existence by the war with the mother country. But in 1776 it declared the independence of the colonies, and in 1777 it gave itself a new legal character by framing the "Articles of Confederation and Perpetual Union," whereby the thirteen States (as they now called themselves) entered into a "firm league of friendship" with each other, offensive and defensive, while declaring that "each State retains its sovereignty, freedom, and independence, and every power, jurisdiction, and right which is not by this Confederation expressly delegated to the United States in Congress assembled."

This Confederation, which was not ratified by all the States till 1781, was rather a league than a national government, for it possessed no central authority except an assembly in which every State, the largest and the smallest alike, had one vote, and this authority had no jurisdiction over the individual citizens. There was no Federal executive, no Federal judiciary, no means of raising money except by the contributions of the States, contributions which they were slow to render, no power of compelling the obedience either of States or individuals to the commands of Congress. The plan corresponded to the wishes of the colonists, who did not yet deem themselves a nation, and who in their struggle against the power of the British Crown were resolved to set over themselves no other power, not even one of their own choosing. But it worked badly even while the struggle lasted, and after the immediate danger from England had been removed by the peace of 1783, it worked still worse, and was in fact, as Washington said, no better than anarchy. The States were indifferent to Congress and their common concerns, so indifferent that it was found difficult to procure a quorum of States for weeks or even months after the day fixed for meeting. Congress was impotent, and commanded respect as little as obedience. Much distress prevailed in the trading States, and the crude attempts which some legislatures made to remedy the depression by emitting inconvertible paper, by constituting other articles than the precious metals legal tender, and by impeding the recovery of debts, aggravated the evil, and in several instances

led to seditious outbreaks.   The fortunes of the country seemed
at a lower ebb than even during the war with England.

Sad experience of their internal difficulties, and of the contempt with which foreign governments treated them, at last produced a feeling that some firmer and closer union was needed.
A convention of delegates from five States met at Annapolis in
Maryland in 1786 to discuss methods of enabling Congress to
regulate commerce, which suffered grievously from the varying
and often burdensome regulations imposed by the several States.
It drew up a report which condemned the existing state of things,
declared that reforms were necessary, and suggested a further
general convention in the following year to consider the condition
of the Union and the needed amendments in its Constitution.
Congress, to which the report had been presented, approved it,
and recommended the States to send delegates to a convention,
which should "revise the Articles of Confederation, and report to
Congress and the several legislatures such alterations and provisions therein as shall, when agreed to in Congress and confirmed by the States, render the Federal Constitution adequate
to the exigencies of government and the preservation of the
Union."

The Convention thus summoned met at Philadelphia on the
14th May 1787, became competent to proceed to business on
May 25th, when seven States were represented, and chose George
Washington to preside.   Delegates attended from every State
but Rhode Island, and these delegates, unlike those usually sent
to Congress, were the leading men of the country, influential in
their several States, and now filled with a sense of the need for
comprehensive reforms.   The instructions they had received
limited their authority to the revision of the Articles of Confederation and the proposing to Congress and the State legislatures such improvements as were required therein.   But with
admirable boldness, boldness doubly admirable in Englishmen
and lawyers, the majority ultimately resolved to disregard these
restrictions, and to prepare a wholly new Constitution, to be considered and ratified neither by Congress nor by the State legislatures, but by the peoples of the several States.

This famous assembly, which consisted of fifty-five delegates,
thirty-nine of whom signed the Constitution which it drafted, sat
nearly five months, and expended upon its work an amount of
labour and thought commensurate with the magnitude of the

task and the splendour of the result. The debates were secret, and fortunately so, for criticism from without might have imperilled a work which seemed repeatedly on the point of breaking down, so great were the difficulties encountered from the divergent sentiments and interests of different parts of the country, as well as of the larger and smaller States. The records of the Convention were left in the hands of Washington, who in 1796 deposited them in the State Department. In 1819 they were published along with the notes of the discussions kept by James Madison (afterwards twice President), who had proved himself one of the ablest and most useful members of the body. From these official records and notes the history of the Convention has been written, and may be found in the instructive volumes of Mr. G. T. Curtis and of Mr. George Bancroft, now the patriarch of American literature.

It is hard to-day, even for Americans, to realize how enormous those difficulties were. The Convention had not only to create *de novo*, on the most slender basis of pre-existing national institutions, a national government for a widely scattered people, but they had in doing so to respect the fears and jealousies and apparently irreconcilable interests of thirteen separate commonwealths, to all of whose governments it was necessary to leave a sphere of action wide enough to satisfy a deep-rooted local sentiment, yet not so wide as to imperil national unity. Well might Hamilton say : "The establishment of a Constitution, in time of profound peace, by the voluntary consent of a whole people, is a prodigy to the completion of which I look forward with trembling anxiety."

It was even a disputable point whether the colonists were already a nation or only the raw material out of which a nation might be formed. There were elements of unity, there were also elements of diversity. All spoke the same language. All, except a few descendants of Dutchmen and Swedes in New York and Delaware, some Germans in Pennsylvania, some children of French Huguenots in New England and the middle States, belonged to the same race. All, except some Roman Catholics in Maryland, professed the Protestant religion. All were governed by the same English Common Law, and prized it not only as the bulwark which had sheltered their forefathers from the oppression of the Stuart kings, but as the basis of their more recent claims of right against the encroachments of George

III. and his colonial officers. In ideas and habits of life there was less similarity, but all were republicans, managing their affairs by elective legislatures, attached to local self-government, and animated by a common pride in their successful resistance to England, which they then hated with a true family hatred, a hatred to which her contemptuous treatment of them added a sting.

On the other hand their geographical position made communication very difficult. The sea was stormy in winter, the roads were bad, it took as long to travel by land from Charleston to Boston as to cross the ocean to Europe, nor was the journey less dangerous. The wealth of some States consisted in slaves; of others in shipping; while in others there was a population of small farmers, characteristically attached to old habits. Manufactures had hardly begun to exist. The sentiment of local independence showed itself in intense suspicion of any external authority; and most parts of the country were so thinly peopled that the inhabitants had lived practically without any government, and thought that in creating one they would be forging fetters for themselves. But while these diversities and jealousies made union difficult, two dangers were absent which have beset the framers of constitutions for other nations. There were no reactionary conspirators to be feared, for every one prized liberty and equality. There were no questions between classes, no animosities against rank and wealth, for rank and wealth did not exist.

It was inevitable under such circumstances that the Constitution, while aiming at the establishment of a durable central power, should pay great regard to the existing centrifugal forces. It was and remains what its authors styled it, eminently an instrument of compromises; it is perhaps the most successful instance in history of what a judicious spirit of compromise may effect. Yet out of the points which it was for this reason obliged to leave unsettled there arose fierce controversies, which after two generations, when accumulated irritation and incurable misunderstanding had been added to the force of material interests, burst into flame in the War of Secession.

The draft Constitution was submitted, as its last article provided, to conventions of the several States (*i.e.* bodies specially chosen by the people for the purpose) for ratification. It was to come into effect as soon as nine States had ratified, the effect of which would have been, in case the remaining States, or any of them, had rejected it, to leave such States standing alone in the world, since the old Confederation was of course superseded and annihilated. Fortunately all the States did eventually ratify the new Constitution, but two of the most important, ·Virginia and New York, did not do so till the middle of 1788, after nine others had already accepted it; and two, North Carolina and Rhode Island, at first refused, and only consented to enter the new Union more than a year later, when the government it had created had already come into operation.

There was a struggle everywhere over the adoption of the Constitution, a struggle which gave birth to the two great parties that for many years divided the American people. The chief source of hostility was the belief that a strong central government endangered both the rights of the States and the liberties of the individual citizen. Freedom, it was declared, would perish, freedom rescued from George III. would perish at the hands of her own children. Consolidation (for the word centralization had not yet been invented) would extinguish the State governments and the local institutions they protected. The feeling was very bitter, and in some States, notably in Massachusetts and New York, the majorities were dangerously narrow. Had the decision been left to what is now called "the voice of the people," that is, to the mass of the citizens all over the country, voting at the polls, the voice of the people would probably have pronounced against the Constitution, and this would have been still more likely if the question had been voted on everywhere upon the same day, seeing that several doubtful States were influenced by the approval which other States had already given. But the modern "plebiscital" method of taking the popular verdict had not been invented. The question was referred to conventions in the several States. The conventions were composed of able men, who listened to weighty arguments, and were themselves influenced by the authority of their leaders. The judgment of the wise prevailed over the prepossessions of the multitude. Yet this judgment would hardly have prevailed but for a cause which is apt to be now overlooked. This was the dread of foreign powers. The United States had at that time two European monarchies, Spain and England, as its neighbours on the American continent. France had lately held territories to the north of them in Canada, and to the south and west of them in Louisiana. She had been their ally against England, she became in a few years again the owner of territories west of the Mississippi. The fear of foreign interference, the sense of weakness, both at sea and on land, against the military monarchies of Europe, was constantly before the mind of American statesmen, and made them anxious to secure at all hazards a national government capable of raising an army and navy, and of speaking with authority on behalf of the new republic. It is remarkable that the danger of European aggression or complications was far more felt in the United States from 1783 down till about 1820, than it has been during the last half century when steam has brought Europe five times nearer than it then was.

Several of the Conventions which ratified the Constitution accompanied their acceptance with an earnest recommendation of various amendments to it, amendments designed to meet the fears of those who thought that it encroached too far upon the liberties of the people. Some of these were adopted, immediately after the original instrument had come into force, by the method it prescribes, viz. a two-thirds majority in Congress and a majority in three-fourths of the States. They are the amendments of 1791, ten in number, and they constitute what the Americans, following a venerable English precedent, call a Bill or Declaration of Rights.

The Constitution of 1789 deserves the veneration with which the Americans have been accustomed to regard it. It is true that many criticisms have been passed upon its arrangement, upon its omissions, upon the artificial character of some of the institutions it creates. Recognising slavery as an institution existing in some States, and not expressly negativing the right of a State to withdraw from the Union, it has been charged with having contained the germ of civil war, though that germ took seventy years to come to maturity. And whatever success it has attained must be in large measure ascribed to the political genius, ripened by long experience, of the Anglo-American race, by whom it has been worked, and who might have managed to work even a worse drawn instrument. Yet, after all deductions, it ranks above every other written constitution for the intrinsic excellence of its scheme, its adaptation to the circumstances of the people, the simplicity, brevity, and precision of its language, its judicious mixture of definiteness in principle with elasticity

in details.   One is therefore induced to ask, before proceeding
to examine it, to what causes, over and above the capacity of
its authors, and the patient toil they bestowed upon it, these
merits are due, or in other words, what were the materials at
the command of the Philadelphia Convention for the achievement of so great an enterprise as the creation of a nation
by means of an instrument of government.   The American
Constitution is no exception to the rule that everything which
has power to win the obedience and respect of men must have
its roots deep in the past, and that the more slowly every
institution has grown, so much the more enduring is it likely
to prove.   There is little in this Constitution that is absolutely
new.   There is much that is as old as Magna Charta.

The men of the Convention had the experience of the English
Constitution.   That Constitution, very different then from what
it is now, was even then not quite what they thought it.   Their
view was tinged not only by recollections of the influence exercised by King George the Third, an influence due to transitory
causes, but which made them overrate its monarchical element,
but also by the presentation of it which they found in the work
of Mr. Justice Blackstone.   He, as was natural in a lawyer and
a man of letters, described rather its theory than its practice,
and its theory was many years behind its practice.   The powers
and functions of the cabinet, the overmastering force of the
House of Commons, the intimate connection between legislation
and administration, these which are to us now the main characteristics of the English Constitution were still far from fully developed.   But in other points of fundamental importance they
appreciated and turned to excellent account its spirit and
methods.

They had for their oracle of political philosophy the treatise
of Montesquieu on the Spirit of Laws, which, published anony-
mously at Geneva forty years before, had won its way to an
immense authority on both sides of the ocean.   Montesquieu,
contrasting the private as well as public liberties of Englishmen
with the despotism of Continental Europe, had taken the Constitution of England as his model system, and had ascribed its
merits to the division of legislative, executive, and judicial functions which he discovered in it, and to the system of checks and
balances whereby its equilibrium seemed to be preserved.   No
general principle of politics laid such hold on the constitution-

makers and statesmen of America as the dogma that the separation of these three functions is essential to freedom. It had
already been made the groundwork of several State constitutions.
It is always reappearing in their writings : it was never absent
from their thoughts. Of the supposed influence of other continental authors, such as Rousseau, or even of English thinkers
such as Burke, there are few direct traces in the Federal Constitution or in the classical contemporaneous commentary on and
defence of it [1] which we owe to the genius of Hamilton and his
hardly less famous coadjutors, Madison and Jay. But we need
only turn to the Declaration of Independence and the original
constitutions of the States, particularly the Massachusetts Constitution of 1780, to perceive that abstract theories regarding
human rights had laid firm hold on the national mind. Such
theories naturally expanded with the practice of republican
government, and have at various times been extremely potent
factors in American history. But the influence of France and
her philosophers belongs chiefly to the years succeeding 1789,
when Jefferson, who was fortunately absent in Paris during the
Constitutional Convention, headed the democratic propaganda.

Further, they had the experience of their colonial and State
governments, and especially, for this was freshest and most in
point, the experience of the working of the State Constitutions,
framed at or since the date when the colonies threw off their
English allegiance. Many of the Philadelphia delegates had
joined in preparing these instruments : all had been able to watch
and test their operation. They compared notes as to the merits,
tested by practice, of the devices which their States had respectively adopted. They had the inestimable advantage of knowing written or rigid constitutions in the concrete ; that is to say,
of comprehending how a system of government actually moves
and plays under the control of a mass of statutory provisions
defining and limiting the powers of its several organs. The so-
called Constitution of England consists largely of customs, precedents, traditions, understandings, often vague and always flexible.
It was quite a different thing, and for the purpose of making a
constitution for the American nation an even more important
thing, to have lived under and learnt to work systems determined by the hard and fast lines of a single document having the
full force of law, for this experience taught them how much
might safely be included in such a document and how far room

must be left under it for unpredictable emergencies and unavoidable development.

Lastly, they had one principle of the English common law whose importance deserves special mention, the principle that an act done by any official person or law-making body in excess of his or its legal competence is simply void. Here lay the key to the difficulties which the establishment of a variety of authorities not subordinate to one another, but each supreme in its own defined sphere, necessarily involved. The application of this principle made it possible not only to create a national government which should leave free scope for the working of the State governments, but also so to divide the powers of the national government among various persons and bodies as that none should absorb or overbear the others. By what machinery these objects were attained will sufficiently appear when we come to consider the effect of a written or rigid constitution embodying a fundamental law, and the functions of the judiciary in expounding and applying such a law.

Chapter 2

Observations on the Presidency

ALTHOUGH the President has been, not that independent good citizen whom the framers of the Constitution contemplated, but, at least during the last sixty years, a party man, seldom much above the average in character or abilities, the office has attained the main objects for which it was created. Such mistakes as have been made in foreign policy, or in the conduct of the administrative departments, have been rarely owing to the constitution of the office or to the errors of its holder. This is more than one who should review the history of Europe during the last hundred years could say of any European monarchy. Nevertheless, the faults chargeable on hereditary kingship, faults more serious than Englishmen, who have watched with admiration the wisdom of the Crown during the present reign, can easily realize, must not make us overlook certain defects incidental to the American presidency, perhaps to any plan of vesting the headship of the State in a person elected for a limited period.

In a country where there is no hereditary throne nor hereditary aristocracy, an office raised far above all other offices offers too great a stimulus to ambition. This glittering prize, always dangling before the eyes of prominent statesmen, has a power stronger than any dignity under a European crown to lure them (as it lured Clay and Webster) from the path of straight-forward consistency. One who aims at the presidency—and all prominent politicians do aim at it—has the strongest possible motives to avoid making enemies. Now a great statesman ought to be prepared to make enemies. It is one thing to try to be popular—an unpopular man will be uninfluential—it is another to seek popularity by courting every section of your party. This is the temptation of presidential aspirants.

A second defect is that the presidential election, occurring once

20

in four years, throws the country for several months into a state of turmoil, for which there may be no occasion. Perhaps there are no serious party issues to be decided, perhaps the best thing would be that the existing Administration should pursue the even tenor of its way. The Constitution, however, requires an election to be held, so the whole costly and complicated machinery of agitation is put in motion ; and if issues do not exist, they have to be created. Professional politicians who have a personal interest in the result, because it involves the gain or loss of office to themselves, conduct what is called a "campaign," and the country is forced into a factitious excitement from midsummer, when each party selects the candidate whom it will nominate, to the first week of November, when the contest is decided. There is some political education in the process, but it is bought dearly, not to add that business, and especially finance, is disturbed, and much money spent unproductively.

Again, these regularly recurring elections produce a discontinuity of policy. Even when the new President belongs to the same party as his predecessor, he usually nominates a new cabinet, having to reward his especial supporters. Many of the inferior offices are changed ; men who have learned their work make way for others who have everything to learn. If the new President belongs to the opposite party, the change of officials is far more sweeping, and involves larger changes of policy. The evil would be more serious were it not that in foreign policy, where the need for continuity is greatest, the United States have little to do, and that the co-operation of the Senate in this department prevents the divergence of the ideas of one President from those of another from being so wide as it might otherwise be.

Fourthly. The fact that he is re-eligible once, but (practically) only once, operates unfavourably on the President. He is tempted to play his cards for a re-nomination by so pandering to active sections of his own party, or so using his patronage to conciliate influential politicians, as to make them put him forward at the next election. On the other hand, if he is in his second term of office, he has no longer much motive to regard the interests of the nation at large, because he sees that his own political death is near. It may be answered that these two evils will correct one another, that the President will in his first term be anxious to win the respect of the nation, in his second he will have no motive for yielding to the unworthy pressure of party wire-pullers.

But the fact is, as has been pointed out by some foreign observers, that if he were held ineligible for the next term, but eligible for any future term, both sets of evils might be avoided, and both sets of benefits secured. The argument against such a provision would be that it makes that breach in policy which may now happen only once in eight years, necessarily happen once in four years. It would, for instance, have prevented the re-election of Abraham Lincoln in 1864. The founders of the Southern Confederacy of 1861-65 were so much impressed by the objections to the present system that they provided that their President should hold office for six years, but not be re-eligible.

Fifthly. An outgoing President is a weak President. During the four months of his stay in office after his successor has been chosen, he declines, except in cases of extreme necessity, to take any new departure, to embark on any executive policy which cannot be completed before he quits office. This is, of course, even more decidedly the case if his successor belongs to the opposite party.

Lastly. The result of an election may be doubtful, not from equality of votes, for this is provided against, but from a dispute as to the validity of votes given in or reported from the States. This difficulty arose in 1876, between Mr. Hayes and Mr. Tilden, disclosing the existence of a set of cases for which the Constitution had not provided. It will not recur in quite the same form, for provision has now been made by statute for dealing with disputed returns. But cases may arise in which the returns from a State of its electoral votes will, because notoriously obtained by fraud or force, fail to be recognized as valid by the party whose candidate they prejudice. No presidential election passes without charges of this kind, and these charges are not always unfounded. Should manifest unfairness coincide with popular excitement over a really important issue, the self-control of the people, which has hitherto restrained, as it did in 1877, the party passions of their leaders, may prove unequal to the strain such a crisis would put upon it.

Further observations on the President, as a part of the machinery of government, will be better reserved for the discussion of the relations of the executive and legislative departments. I will therefore only observe here that, even when we allow for the defects last enumerated, the presidential office, if not one of the conspicuous successes of the American Constitution, is nowise to be deemed a failure. The problem of constructing a stable executive in a democratic country is so immensely difficult that anything short of a failure deserves to be called a success. Now the President has, during ninety-nine years, carried on the internal administrative business of the nation with due efficiency. Once or twice, as when Jefferson purchased Louisiana, and Lincoln emancipated the slaves in the revolted States, he has courageously ventured on stretches of authority, held at the time to be doubtfully constitutional, yet necessary, and approved by the judgment of posterity. He has kept the machinery working quietly and steadily when Congress has been distracted by party strife, or paralyzed by the dissensions of the two Houses, or enfeebled by the want of first-rate leaders. The executive has been able, at moments of peril, to rise into a dictatorship, as during the War of Secession, and when peace returned, to sink back into its proper constitutional position. It has shown no tendency so to dwarf the other authorities of the State as to pave the way for a monarchy.

Europeans are struck by the faults of a plan which plunges the nation into a whirlpool of excitement once every four years, and commits the headship of the State to a party leader chosen for a short period. But there is another aspect in which the presidential election may be regarded, and one whose importance is better appreciated in America than in Europe. The election is a solemn periodical appeal to the nation to review its condition, the way in which its business has been carried on, the conduct of the two great parties. It stirs and rouses the nation as nothing else does, forces every one not merely to think about public affairs but to decide how he judges the parties. It is a direct expression of the will of ten millions of voters, a force before which everything must bow. It refreshes the sense of national duty ; and at great crises it intensifies national patriotism. A presidential election is sometimes, as in 1800, and as again most notably in 1860 and 1864, a turning-point in history. In form it is nothing more than the choice of an administrator who cannot influence policy otherwise than by refusing his assent to bills. In reality it is the deliverance of the mind of the people upon all such questions as they feel able to decide. A curious parallel may in this respect be drawn between it and a general election of the House of Commons in England. A general election is in form a choice of representatives, with reference primarily to their views upon various current questions. In substance it is often a national vote (what the French call a plebiscite), committing executive power to some one prominent statesman. Thus the elections of 1868, 1874, 1880, were practically votes of the nation to place Mr. Gladstone or Mr. Disraeli at the head of the government. So conversely in America, a presidential election, which purports to be merely the selection of a man, is often in reality a decision upon issues of policy, a condemnation of the course taken by one party, a mandate to the other to follow some different course.

The choice of party leaders as Presidents has in America caused far less mischief than might have been expected. Nevertheless, those who have studied the scheme of constitutional monarchy as it works in England, or Belgium, or Italy, or the reproductions of that scheme in British colonies, where the Crown-appointed governor stands outside the strife of factions as a permanent official, will, when they compare the institutions of these countries with the American presidency, be impressed by the merits of a plan which does not unite all the dignity of office with all the power of office, and which, by placing the titular chief of the executive above and apart from party, makes the civil and military services feel themselves the servants rather of the nation than of any section of the nation, and suggests to them that their labours ought to be rendered with equal heartiness to whatever party may hold the reins of government. Party government may be necessary. So far as we can see, it is necessary. But it is a necessary evil; and whatever tends to diminish its mischievous influence upon the machinery of administration, and to prevent it from obtruding itself upon foreign states ; whatever holds up a high ideal of devotion to the nation as a majestic whole, living on from century to century while parties form and dissolve and form again, strengthens and ennobles the commonwealth and all its citizens.

Such an observation of course applies only to monarchy as a political institution. Socially regarded, the American presidency deserves nothing but admiration. The President is simply the first citizen of a free nation, depending for his dignity on no title, no official dress, no insignia of state. It was originally proposed, doubtless in recollection of the English Commonwealth of the seventeenth century, to give him the style of "Highness," and "Protector of the Liberties of the United States." Others suggested "Excellency"; and Washington is said to have had leanings to the Dutch style of "High Mightiness." The head of the ruling President does not appear on coins, nor even on postage stamps. His residence at Washington called officially "the Executive Mansion," and familiarly "the White House," a building with a stucco front and a portico supported by Doric pillars, said to have been modelled upon the Duke of Leinster's house in Dublin, stands in a shrubbery, and has the air of a large suburban villa rather than of a palace. The rooms, though spacious, are not spacious enough for the crowds that attend the public receptions. The President's salary, which is only $50,000 (£10,000) a year, does not permit display, nor indeed is display expected from him.

Washington, which even so lately as the days of the war was a wilderness of mud and negroes, with a few big houses scattered here and there, has now become one of the handsomest capitals in the world, and cultivates the graces and pleasures of life with eminent success. Besides its political society and its diplomatic society, it is becoming a winter resort for men of wealth and leisure from all over the continent. It is a place where a court might be created, did any one wish to create it. No President has made the attempt; and as the earlier career of the chief magistrate and his wife has seldom qualified them to lead the world of fashion, none is likely to make it. However, the action of the wife of President Hayes, an estimable and energetic lady, whose ardent advocacy of temperance caused the formation of a great many total abstinence societies, called by her name (Lucy Webb), showed that there may be fields in which a President's consort can turn her exalted position to good account, while of course such graces or charms as she possesses will tend to increase his popularity.

To a European observer, weary of the slavish obsequiousness and lip-deep adulation with which the members of reigning families are treated on the eastern side of the Atlantic, fawned on in public and carped at in private, the social relations of an American President to his people are eminently refreshing. There is a great respect for the office, and a corresponding respect for the man as the holder of the office, if he has done nothing to degrade it.   There is no servility, no fictitious self-abasement on the part of the citizens, but a simple and hearty deference to one who represents the majesty of the nation, the sort of respect which the proudest Roman paid to the consulship, even if the particular consul was, like Cicero, a "new man." The curiosity of the visitors who throng the White House on reception days is sometimes too familiar ; but this fault tends to disappear, and Presidents have now more reason to complain of the persecutions they endure from an incessantly observant journalism.   After oscillating between the ceremonious state of George Washington, who drove to open Congress in his coach and six, with outriders and footmen in livery, and the ostentatious plainness of Citizen Jefferson, who rode up alone and hitched his horse to the post at the gate, the President has settled down into an attitude between that of the mayor of a great English town on a public occasion, and that of a European cabinet minister on a political tour.   He is followed about and fêted, and in every way treated as the first man in the company ; but the spirit of equality which rules the country has sunk too deep into every American nature for him to expect to be addressed with bated breath and whispering reverence.   He has no military guard, no chamberlains or grooms-in-waiting ; his everyday life is simple ; his wife enjoys precedence over all other ladies, but is visited and received just like other ladies ; he is surrounded by no such pomp and enforces no such etiquette as that which belongs to the governors even of second-class English colonies, not to speak of the viceroys of India and Ireland.

It begins to be remarked in Europe that monarchy, which used to be deemed politically dangerous but socially useful, has now, since its claws have been cut, become politically valuable, but of more doubtful social utility.   In the United States the most suspicious democrat—and there are democrats who complain that the office of President is too monarchical—cannot accuse the chief magistracy of having tended to form a court, much less to create those evils which thrive in the atmosphere of European courts.   No President dare violate social decorum as European sovereigns have so often done.   If he did, he would be the first to suffer.

CHAPTER 3

Why Great Men Are Not Chosen Presidents

EUROPEANS often ask, and Americans do not always explain, how it happens that this great office, the greatest in the world, unless we except the Papacy, to which any man can rise by his own merits, is not more frequently filled by great and striking men ? In America, which is beyond all other countries the country of a "career open to talents," a country, moreover, in which political life is unusually keen and political ambition widely diffused, it might be expected that the highest place would always be won by a man of brilliant gifts. But since the heroes of the Revolution died out with Jefferson and Adams and Madison some sixty years ago, no person except General Grant has reached the chair whose name would have been remembered had he not been President, and no President except Abraham Lincoln has displayed rare or striking qualities in the chair. Who now knows or cares to know anything about the personality of James K. Polk or Franklin Pierce ? The only thing remarkable about them is that being so commonplace they should have climbed so high.

Several reasons may be suggested for the fact, which Americans are themselves the first to admit.

One is that the proportion of first-rate ability drawn into politics is smaller in America than in most European countries. This is a phenomenon whose causes must be elucidated later : in the meantime it is enough to say that in France and Italy, where half-revolutionary conditions have made public life exciting and accessible ; in Germany, where an admirably-organized civil service cultivates and develops statecraft with unusual success ; in England, where many persons of wealth and leisure seek to enter the political arena, while burning questions touch the interests of all classes and make men eager observers of the

27

combatants, the total quantity of talent devoted to parliamentary
or administrative work is far larger, relatively to the population,
than in America, where much of the best ability, both for
thought and for action, for planning and for executing, rushes
into a field which is comparatively narrow in Europe, the business of developing the material resources of the country.

Another is that the methods and habits of Congress, and
indeed of political life generally, seem to give fewer opportunities
for personal distinction, fewer modes in which a man may com-
mend himself to his countrymen by eminent capacity in thought,
in speech, or in administration, than is the case in the free
countries of Europe.

A third reason is that eminent men make more enemies, and
give those enemies more assailable points, than obscure men do.
They are therefore in so far less desirable candidates. It is
true that the eminent man has also made more friends, that his
name is more widely known, and may be greeted with louder
cheers. Other things being equal, the famous man is preferable.
But other things never are equal. The famous man has probably attacked some leaders in his own party, has supplanted
others, has expressed his dislike to the crotchet of some active
section, has perhaps committed errors which are capable of being
magnified into offences. No man stands long before the public
and bears a part in great affairs without giving openings to cen-
sorious criticism. Fiercer far than the light which beats upon a
throne is the light which beats upon a presidential candidate,
searching out all the recesses of his past life. Hence, when the
choice lies between a brilliant man and a safe man, the safe man
is preferred. Party feeling, strong enough to carry in on its
back a man without conspicuous positive merits, is not always
strong enough to procure forgiveness for a man with positive
faults.

A European finds that this phenomenon needs in its turn to
be explained, for in the free countries of Europe brilliancy, be it
eloquence in speech, or some striking achievement in war or
administration, or the power through whatever means of some-
how impressing the popular imagination, is what makes a leader
triumphant. Why should it be otherwise in America ? Because
in America party loyalty and party organization have been
hitherto so perfect that any one put forward by the party will
get the full party vote if his character is good and his " record,"

as they call it, unstained. The safe candidate may not draw in quite so many votes from the moderate men of the other side as the brilliant one would, but he will not lose nearly so many from his own ranks. Even those who admit his mediocrity will vote straight when the moment for voting comes. Besides, the ordinary American voter does not object to mediocrity. He has a lower conception of the qualities requisite to make a statesman than those who direct public opinion in Europe have. He likes his candidate to be sensible, vigorous, and, above all, what he calls "magnetic," and does not value, because he sees no need for, originality or profundity, a fine culture or a wide knowledge. Candidates are selected to be run for nomination by knots of persons who, however expert as party tacticians, are usually commonplace men; and the choice between those selected for nomination is made by a very large body, an assembly of over eight hundred delegates from the local party organizations over the country, who are certainly no better than ordinary citizens. How this process works will be seen more fully when I come to speak of those Nominating Conventions which are so notable a feature in American politics.

It must also be remembered that the merits of a President are one thing and those of a candidate another thing. An eminent American is reported to have said to friends who wished to put him forward, " Gentlemen, let there be no mistake. I should make a good President, but a very bad candidate." Now to a party it is more important that its nominee should be a good candidate than that he should turn out a good President. A nearer danger is a greater danger. As Saladin says in *The Talisman*, " A wild cat in a chamber is more dangerous than a lion in a distant desert." It will be a misfortune to the party, as well as to the country, if the candidate elected should prove a bad President. But it is a greater misfortune to the party that it should be beaten in the impending election, for the evil of losing national patronage will have come four years sooner. " B " (so reason the leaders), " who is one of our possible candidates, may be an abler man than A, who is the other. But we have a better chance of winning with A than with B, while X, the candidate of our opponents, is anyhow no better than A. We must therefore run A." This reasoning is all the more forcible because the previous career of the possible candidates has generally made it easier to say who will succeed as a candi-

date than who will succeed as a President ; and because the
wire-pullers with whom the choice rests are better judges of the
former question than of the latter.

After all, too, and this is a point much less obvious to Europeans than to Americans, a President need not be a man of
brilliant intellectual gifts. Englishmen, imagining him as something like their prime minister, assume that he ought to be a
dazzling orator, able to sway legislatures or multitudes, possessed also of the constructive powers that can devise a great
policy or frame a comprehensive piece of legislation. They forget that the President does not sit in Congress, that he ought
not to address meetings, except on ornamental and (usually) non-
political occasions, that he cannot submit bills nor otherwise
influence the action of the legislature. His main duties are to be
prompt and firm in securing the due execution of the laws and
maintaining the public peace, careful and upright in the choice
of the executive officials of the country. Eloquence, whose value
is apt to be overrated in all free countries, imagination, profundity
of thought or extent of knowledge, are all in so far a gain to him
that they make him a bigger man, and help him to gain a greater
influence over the nation, an influence which, if he be a true patriot
he may use for its good. But they are not necessary for the due dis
charge in ordinary times of the duties of his post. A man may
lack them and yet make an excellent President. Four-fifths of
his work is the same in kind as that which devolves on the
chairman of a commercial company or the manager of a railway, the work of choosing good subordinates, seeing that they
attend to their business, and taking a sound practical view of
such administrative questions as require his decision. Firmness,
common sense, and most of all, honesty, an honesty above all
suspicion of personal interest, are the qualities which the country
chiefly needs in its chief magistrate.

So far we have been considering personal merits. But in the
selection of a candidate many considerations have to be regarded
besides personal merits, whether they be the merits of a candidate, or of a possible President. The chief of these considerations is the amount of support which can be secured from
different States or from different regions, or, as the Americans
say, "sections," of the Union. State feeling and sectional feeling are powerful factors in a presidential election. The North-
west, including the States from Ohio to Dakota, is now the

most populous region of the Union, and therefore counts for most in an election. It naturally conceives that its interests will be best protected by one who knows them from birth and residence. Hence *prima facie* a North-western man makes the best candidate. A large State casts a heavier vote in the election; and every State is of course more likely to be carried by one of its own children than by a stranger, because his fellow-citizens, while they feel honoured by the choice, gain also a substantial advantage, having a better prospect of such favours as the administration can bestow. Hence, *cœteris paribus*, a man from a large State is preferable as a candidate. New York casts thirty-six votes in the presidential election, Pennsylvania thirty, Ohio twenty-three, Illinois twenty-two, while Vermont and Rhode Island have but four, Delaware, Nevada, and Oregon only three votes each. It is therefore, parties being usually very evenly balanced, better worth while to have an inferior candidate from one of the larger States, who may carry the whole weight of his State with him, than a somewhat superior candidate from one of the smaller States, who will carry only three or four votes. The problem is further complicated by the fact that some States are already safe for one or other party, while others are doubtful. The North-western and New England States are most of them certain to go Republican: the Southern States are (at present) all of them certain to go Democratic. It is more important to gratify a doubtful State than one you have got already; and hence, *cœteris paribus*, a candidate from a doubtful State, such as New York or Indiana, is to be preferred.

Other minor disqualifying circumstances require less explanation. A Roman Catholic, or an avowed disbeliever in Christianity, would be an undesirable candidate. Since the close of the Civil War, any one who fought, especially if he fought with distinction, in the Northern army, has enjoyed great advantages, for the soldiers of that army, still numerous, rally to his name. The two elections of General Grant, who knew nothing of politics, and the fact that his influence survived the faults of his long administration, are evidence of the weight of this consideration. It influenced the selection both of Garfield and of his opponent Hancock. Similarly a person who fought in the Southern army would be a bad candidate, for he might alienate the North.

On a railway journey in the Far West in 1883 I fell in with two newspaper men from the State of Indiana, who were taking their holiday. The conversation turned on the next presidential election. They spoke hopefully of the chances for nomination by their party of an Indiana man, a comparatively obscure person, whose name I had never heard. I expressed some surprise that he should be thought of. They observed that he had done well in State politics, that there was nothing against him, that Indiana would work for him. "But," I rejoined, "ought you not to have a man of more commanding character. There is Senator A. Everybody tells me that he is the shrewdest and most experienced man in your party, and that he has a perfectly clean record. Why not run him?" "Why, yes," they answered, "that is all true. But you see he comes from a small State, and we have got that State already. Besides, he wasn't in the war. Our man was. Indiana's vote is worth having, and if our man is run, we can carry Indiana."

"Surely the race is not to the swift, nor the battle to the strong, neither yet bread to the wise, nor yet riches to men of understanding, nor yet favour to men of skill, but time and chance happeneth to them all."

These secondary considerations do not always prevail. Intellectual ability and force of character must influence the choice of a candidate, and their influence is sometimes decisive. They count for more when times are so critical that the need for a strong man is felt. Reformers declare that their weight will go on increasing as the disgust of good citizens with the methods of professional politicians increases. But for many generations past it is not the greatest men in the Roman Church that have been chosen Popes, nor the most brilliant men in the Anglican Church that have been appointed Archbishops of Canterbury.

Although several Presidents have survived their departure from office by many years, only one, John Quincy Adams, has played a part in politics after quitting the White House. It may be that the ex-President has not been a great leader before his accession to office ; it may be that he does not care to exert himself after he has held and dropped the great prize, and found (one may safely add) how little of a prize it is. Something, however, must also be ascribed to other features of the political system of the country. It is often hard to find a vacancy in the representation of a given State through which to re-enter Congress ; it is disagreeable to recur to the arts by which seats are secured. Past greatness is rather an encumbrance than a help to resuming a political career. Exalted power, on which the unsleeping eye of hostile critics was fixed, has probably disclosed all a President's weaknesses, and has either forced him to make enemies by disobliging adherents, or exposed him to censure for subservience to party interests. He is regarded as having had his day ; he belongs already to the past, and unless, like Grant, he is endeared to the people by the memory of some splendid service, he soon sinks into the crowd or avoids neglect by retirement. Possibly he may deserve to be forgotten ; but more frequently he is a man of sufficient ability and character to make the experience he has gained valuable to the country, could it be retained in a place where he might turn it to account. They managed things better at Rome in the days of the republic, gathering into their Senate all the fame and experience, all the wisdom and skill, of those who had ruled and fought as consuls and prætors at home and abroad.

"What shall we do with our ex-Presidents ?" is a question often put in America, but never yet answered. The position of a past chief magistrate is not a happy one. He has been a species of sovereign at home. He is received—General Grant was—with almost royal honours abroad. His private income may be insufficient to enable him to live in ease, yet he cannot without loss of dignity, the country's dignity as well as his own, go back to practice at the bar or become partner in a mercantile firm. If he tries to enter the Senate, it may happen that there is no seat vacant for his own State, or that the majority in the State legislature is against him. It has been suggested that he might be given a seat in that chamber as an extra member ; but to this plan there is the objection that it would give to the State from which he comes a third senator, and thus put other States at a disadvantage. In any case, however, it would seem only right to bestow such a pension as would relieve him from the necessity of re-entering business or a profession.

We may now answer the question from which we started. Great men are not chosen Presidents, firstly, because great men are rare in politics ; secondly, because the method of choice does not bring them to the top ; thirdly, because they are not, in quiet times, absolutely needed. I may observe that the Presidents, regarded historically, fall into three periods, the second inferior to the first, the third rather better than the second.

Down till the election of Andrew Jackson in 1828, all the

Presidents had been statesmen in the European sense of the word, men of education, of administrative experience, of a certain largeness of view and dignity of character. All except the first two had served in the great office of secretary of state ; all were well known to the nation from the part they had played. In the second period, from Jackson till the outbreak of the Civil War in 1861, the Presidents were either mere politicians, such as Van Buren, Polk, or Buchanan, or else successful soldiers, such as Harrison or Taylor, whom their party found useful as figure-heads. They were intellectual pigmies beside the real leaders of that generation—Clay, Calhoun, and Webster. A new series begins with Lincoln in 1861. He and General Grant his successor, who cover sixteen years between them, belong to the history of the world. The other less distinguished Presidents of this period contrast favourably with the Polks and Pierces of the days before the war, but they are not, like the early Presidents, the first men of the country. If we compare the eighteen Presidents who have been elected to office since 1789 with the nineteen English prime ministers of the same hundred years, there are but six of the latter, and at least eight of the former whom history calls personally insignificant, while only Washington, Jefferson, Lincoln, and Grant can claim to belong to a front rank represented in the English list by seven or possibly eight names. It would seem that the natural selection of the English parliamentary system, even as modified by the aristocratic habits of that country, has more tendency to bring the highest gifts to the highest place than the more artificial selection of America.

CHAPTER 4

General Observations on Congress

IT remains for me to make some observations which apply to both Houses and which may tend to indicate the features that distinguish them from the representative assemblies of Europe. The English reader must bear in mind three points which he may have forgotten. The first is that Congress is not like the Parliaments of England, France, and Italy, a sovereign assembly, but is subject to the Constitution, which only the people can change. The second is, that it neither appoints nor dismisses the executive government, which springs directly from popular election. The third is, that its sphere of legislative action is limited by the existence of thirty-eight governments in the several States, whose authority is just as well based as its own, and cannot be curtailed by it.

I. The choice of members of Congress is locally limited by law and by custom. Under the Constitution every representative and every senator must when elected be an inhabitant of the State whence he is elected. Moreover, State law has in many and custom practically in all States, established that a representative must be resident in the congressional district which elects him. The only exceptions to this practice occur in large cities where occasionally a man is chosen who lives in a different district of the city from that which returns him ; but such exceptions are extremely rare. This restriction surprises a European, who thinks it must be found highly inconvenient both to candidates, as restricting their field of choice in looking for a constituency, and to constituencies, as excluding persons, however eminent, who do not reside in their midst. To Americans, however, it seems so obviously reasonable that I found very few persons, even in the best educated classes, who would admit its policy to be disputable. In what are we to seek the causes of this opinion ?

First. In the existence of States, originally separate political communities, still for many purposes independent, and accustomed to consider the inhabitant of another State as almost a foreigner. A New Yorker, Pennsylvanians would say, owes allegiance to New York; he cannot feel and think as a citizen of Pennsylvania, and cannot therefore properly represent Pennsylvanian interests. This sentiment has spread by a sort of sympathy, this reasoning has been applied by a sort of analogy, to the counties, the cities, the electoral districts of the State itself. State feeling has fostered local feeling; the locality deems no man a fit representative who has not by residence in its limits, and by making it his political home, the place where he exercises his civic rights, become soaked with its own local sentiment.

Secondly. Much of the interest felt in the proceedings of Congress relates to the raising and spending of money. Changes in the tariff may affect the industries of a locality ; or a locality may petition for an appropriation of public funds to some local public work, the making of a harbour, or the improvement of the navigation of a river. In both cases it is thought that no one but an inhabitant can duly comprehend the needs or zealously advocate the demands of a neighbourhood.

Thirdly. Inasmuch as no high qualities of statesmanship are expected from a congressman, a district would think it a slur to be told that it ought to look beyond its own borders for a representative ; and as the post is a paid one, the people feel that a good thing ought to be kept for one of themselves rather than thrown away on a stranger. It is by local political work, organizing, canvassing, and haranguing, that a party is kept going : and this work must be rewarded.

A perusal of the chapter of the *Federalist,* which argues that one representative for 30,000 inhabitants will sufficiently satisfy republican needs, suggests another reflection. The writer refers to some who held a numerous representation to be a democratic institution, because it enabled every small district to make its voice heard in the national Congress. Such representation then existed in the State legislatures. Evidently the habits of the people were formed by these State legislatures, in which it was a matter of course that the people of each township or city sent one of themselves to the assembly of the State. When they came to return members to Congress, they followed the same practice. A stranger had no means of making himself known to them and would not think of offering himself. That the habits of England are different may be due, so far as the eighteenth century is concerned, to the practice of borough-mongering, under which candidates unconnected with the place were sent down by some influential person, or bought the seat from the corrupt corporation or the limited body of freemen. Thus the notion that a stranger might do well enough for a borough grew up, while in counties it remained, till 1885, a maxim that a candidate ought to own land in the county —the old law required a freehold qualification somewhere—or ought to live in, or ought at the very least (as I once heard a candidate, whose house lay just outside the county for which he was standing, allege on his own behalf) to look into the county from his window while shaving in the morning. The English practice might thus seem to be an exception due to special causes, and the American practice that which is natural to a free country, where local self-government is fully developed and rooted in the habits of the people. It is from their local government that the political ideas of the American people have been formed : and they have applied to their State assemblies and their national assembly the customs which grew up in the smaller area.

These are the best explanations I can give of a phenomenon which strikes Europeans all the more because it exists among a population more unsettled and migratory than any in the Old World. But they leave me still surprised at this strength of local feeling, a feeling not less marked in the new regions of the Far West than in the venerable commonwealths of Massachusetts and Virginia. The most significant fact about the practice in America is that one seldom hears it there commented on as a defect of the political system. Fierce as is the light of criticism which beats upon every part of that system, this point, which at once strikes the European as specially weak, remains uncensured, because assumed to be part of the order of nature.

Its results are unfortunate. So far as the restriction to residents in a State is concerned it is intelligible. The senator was—to some extent is still—a sort of ambassador from his State. He is chosen by the legislature or collective authority of his State. He cannot well be a citizen of one State and represent another. Even a representative in the House from one State who lived in another might be perplexed by a divided allegiance, though there are groups of States, such as those of the north-west, whose great industrial interests are substantially the same. But what reason can there be for preventing a man resident in one part of a State from representing another part, a Philadelphian, for instance, from being returned for Pittsburg, or a Bostonian for Lenox in the west of Massachusetts ? In England it is not found that a member is less active or successful in urging the local interests of his constituency because he does not live there. He is often more successful, because more personally influential or persuasive than any resident whom the constituency could supply ; and in case of a conflict of interests he always feels his efforts to be owing first to his constituents, and not to the place in which he happens to reside.

The mischief is twofold. Inferior men are returned, because there are many parts of the country which do not grow statesmen, where nobody, or at any rate nobody desiring to enter Congress, is to be found above a moderate level of political capacity. And men of marked ability and zeal are prevented from forcing their way in. Such men are produced chiefly in the great cities of the older States. There is not room enough there for nearly all of them, but no other doors to Congress are open. Boston, New York, Philadelphia, Baltimore, could furnish six or eight times as many good members as there are seats in these cities. As such men cannot enter from their place of residence, they do not enter at all, and the nation is deprived of the benefit of their services. Careers are moreover interrupted. A promising politician may lose his seat in his own district through some fluctuation of opinion, or perhaps because he has offended the local wire-pullers by too much independence. Since he cannot find a seat elsewhere, as would happen in England, he is stranded ; his political life is closed, while other young men inclined to independence take warning from his fate. Changes in the State laws would not remove the evil, for the habit of choosing none but local men is rooted so deeply that it would probably long survive the abolition of a restrictive law, and it is just as strong in States where no such law exists.

II. Every senator and representative receives a salary at present fixed at $5000 (£1000) per annum, besides an allowance (called mileage) of 20 cents (10d.) per mile for travelling expenses to and from Washington, and $125 (£25) for stationery. The salary is looked upon as a matter of course. It was not introduced for the sake of enabling working men to be returned as members, but on the general theory that all public work ought to be paid for. The reasons for it are stronger than in England or France, because the distance to Washington from most parts of the United States is so great, and the attendance required there so continuous, that a man cannot attend to his profession or business while sitting in Congress. If he loses his livelihood in serving the community, the community ought to compensate him, not to add that the class of persons whose private means put them above the need of a lucrative calling, or of compensation for interrupting it, is comparatively small even now, and hardly existed when the Constitution was framed. Cynics defend the payment of congressmen on another ground, viz. that "they would steal worse if they didn't get it," and would make politics, as Napoleon made war, support itself. Be the thing bad or good, it is at any rate necessary, so that no one talks of abolishing it. For that reason its existence furnishes no argument for its introduction into a small country with a large leisured and wealthy class. In fact, the conditions of European countries are so different from those of America that one must not cite American experience either for or against the remuneration of legislative work. I do not believe that the practice works ill by preventing good men from entering politics, for they feel no more delicacy in accepting their $5000 than an English duke does in drawing his salary as a secretary of state. It may strengthen the tendency of members to regard themselves as mere delegates, but that tendency has other and deeper roots. It contributes to keep up a class of professional politicians, for the salary, though small in comparison with the incomes earned by successful merchants or lawyers, is a prize to men of the class whence professional politicians mostly come. But those English writers who describe it as the formative cause of that class are mistaken. That class would have existed had members not been paid, would continue to exist if payment were withdrawn. On the other hand, the benefit which the English advocates of paid legislators dilate on, viz. the introduction of a large number of representative working men, has hitherto been little desired and nowise secured. Few such persons appear as candidates in America, and until recently the working class has not deemed itself, nor acted as, a distinct body with special interests.

In 1873 Congress passed an act increasing many official salaries, and among others those of senators and representatives, which it raised from $5000 to $7500 (£1500). All the increases were to take effect for the future only, except that of congressional salaries, which was made retroactive. This unblushing appropriation by Congress of nearly $200,000 to themselves roused so much indignation that the act, save as to the salaries of the President and Federal judges, was repealed by the next Congress. It is known as the "back-pay grab."

III. A congressman's tenure of his place is usually short. Senators are sometimes returned for two, three, or even four successive terms by the legislatures of their States, although it may befall even the best of them to be thrown out by a change in the balance of parties, or by the intrigues of an opponent. But a member of the House can seldom feel safe in the saddle. If he is so eminent as to be necessary to his party, or if he maintains intimate relations with the leading local wire-pullers of his district, he may in the eastern, middle, and southern States hold his ground for three or four Congresses, *i.e.* for six or eight years. Very few do more than this. In the West a member is extremely lucky if he does even this. Out there a seat is regarded as a good thing which ought to go round. It has a salary. It sends a man, free of expense, for two winters and springs to Washington and lets him see something of the fine world there, where he rubs shoulders with ambassadors from Europe. Local leaders cast sheep's eyes at the seat, and make more or less open bargains between themselves as to the order in which they shall enjoy it. So far from its being, as in England, a reason for re-electing a man that he has been a member already, it is a reason for passing him by, and giving somebody else a turn. Rotation in office, dear to the Democrats of Jefferson's school a century ago, still charms the less educated, who see in it a recognition of equality, and have no sense of the value of special knowledge or training. They like it for the same reason that the democrats of Athens liked the choice of magistrates by lot. It is a recognition and application of equality. An ambitious congressman is therefore forced to think day and night of his re-nomination, and to secure it not only by procuring, if he can, grants from the Federal treasury for local purposes, and places for the relatives and friends of the local wire-pullers who control the nominating conventions, but also by sedulously "nursing" the constituency during the vacations. No habit could more effectually discourage noble ambition or check the growth of a class of accomplished statesmen. There are few walks of life in which experience counts for more than it does in parliamentary politics. It is an education in itself, an education in which the quick-witted western American would make rapid progress were he suffered to remain long enough at Washington. At present he is not suffered, for, as observed above, nearly one half of each successive house consists of new men, while the old members are too much harassed by the trouble of procuring their re-election to have time or motive for the serious study of political problems. This is what comes of the doctrine that a member ought to be absolutely dependent on his constituents, and of the notion that politics is neither a science, nor an art, nor even an occupation, like farming or store-keeping, in which one learns by experience, but a thing which comes by nature, and for which one man of common sense is as fit as another.

IV. The last-mentioned evil is aggravated by the short duration of a Congress. Short as it seems, the two years term was warmly opposed, when the Constitution was framed, as being too long. The constitutions of the several States, framed when they shook off the supremacy of the British Crown, all fixed one year, except the ultra-democratic Connecticut and Rhode Island, where under the colonial charters a legislature met every six months, and South Carolina, which had fixed two years. So essential to republicanism was this principle deemed, that the maxim "where annual elections end tyranny begins" had passed into a proverb; and the authors of the *Federalist* were obliged to argue that the limited authority of Congress, watched by the executive on one side, and the State legislatures on the other, would prevent so long a period as two years from proving dangerous to liberty, while it was needed in order to enable the members to master the laws and understand the conditions of different parts of the Union. At present the two years term is justified on the ground that it furnishes a proper check on the President. The Congress elected in the autumn of 1884 at the same time as the President, meets in December 1885, while another, elected in 1886, meets in 1887, and thus covers the later part of his four years term. Thus the people can, if they please, express disapproval of the policy which he has so far followed. One is also told that these frequent elections are necessary to keep up popular interest in current politics, nor do some fail to hint that the temptations to jobbing would overcome the virtue of members who had a longer term before them. Where American opinion is unanimous, it would be presumptuous for a stranger to dissent. Yet the remark may be permitted that the dangers originally feared have proved chimerical. There is no country whose representatives are more dependent on popular opinion, more ready to trim their sails to the least breath of it. The public acts, the votes, and speeches of a member from Oregon or Texas can be more closely watched by his constituents than those of a Virginian member could be watched in 1789. And as the frequency of elections involves inexperienced members, the efficiency of Congress suffers.

V. The numbers of the two American houses seem small to a European when compared on the one hand with the population of the country, on the other with the practice of European States. The Senate has 84 members against the British House of Lords with about 560, and the French Senate with 300. The House has 330 against the British House of Commons with 670, and the French and Italian Chambers with 584 and 508 respectively.

The Americans, however, doubt whether both their Houses have not already become too large. They began with 26 in the Senate, 65 in the House, numbers then censured as too small, but which worked well, and gave less encouragement to idle talk and vain display than the crowded halls of to-day. The proportion of representatives to inhabitants, originally 1 to 30,000, is now 1 to 154,000, having constantly fallen as the population increased. The inclination of wise men is to stop further increase when the number of 400 has been reached, for they perceive that the House already suffers from disorganization, and fear that a much larger one would prove unmanageable. So much depends on the particular circumstances of each country that no general rule can be laid down as to the size of representative assemblies, and the experience of one nation is of no great value for another. So far as general principles go, a student of politics will be disposed to think that as the American Chamber ought not to be raised much further, so the British House of Commons ought to be rather reduced than increased.

VI. American congressmen are more assiduous in their attendance than the members of most European legislatures.

The great majority not only remain steadily at Washington through the session, but are usually to be found in the Capitol, often in their Chamber itself, while a sitting lasts. There is therefore comparatively little trouble in making a quorum, though the quorum consists of one half in each House, whereas in England the House of Lords, whose quorum is three, has usually less than thirty peers present, and the House of Commons finds a difficulty, through many private members' days and on government days from eight till tèn o'clock p.m., in making up its modest quorum of forty. This requirement of a high quorum, which is prescribed in the Constitution, has doubtless helped to secure a good attendance. Other causes are the distance from Washington of the residences of most members, so that it is not worth while to take the journey home for a short sojourn, and the fact that very few attempt to carry on any regular business or profession while the session lasts. Those who are lawyers, or merchants, or manufacturers, leave their work to partners; but many are politicians and nothing else. In Washington, a city without commerce or manufactures, political or semi-political intrigue is the only gainful occupation possible; for the Supreme Court practice employs only a few leading barristers. The more democratic a country is, so much the more regular is the attendance, so much closer the attention to the requests of constituents which a member is expected to render. Every extension of the suffrage in England has been followed not only by a change in the character of the House of Commons, but by an increase in the numbers usually present, and in the eagerness of members to defer to every wish of those who have returned them. Apart from that painful duty of finding places for constituents which consumes so much of a congressman's time, his duties are not heavier than those of a member of the English Parliament who desires to keep abreast of current questions. The sittings are neither so long nor so late as those of the House of Commons; the questions that come up not so multifarious, the blue books to be read less numerous, the correspondence (except about places) less troublesome. The position of senator is more onerous than that of a member of the House, not only because his whole State, and not merely a district, has a direct claim upon him, but also because, as one of a smaller body, he incurs a larger individual responsibility, and sits upon two or more committees instead of on one only.

VII. One of the reasons which make a political career unattractive to most Americans is the want of opportunities for distinction in Congress. It takes a new member at least a session to learn the procedure of the House. Full dress debates are rare, newspaper reports of speeches delivered are curt and little read. The most serious work is done in committees ; it is not known to the world, and much of it results in nothing, because many bills which a committee has considered are perhaps never even voted on by the House. A place on a good House committee is to be obtained by favour, and a high-spirited man may shrink from applying for it to the Speaker. Ability, tact, and industry make their way in the long run in Congress, as they do everywhere else. But in Congress there is, for most men, no long run. Only very strong local influence, or some remarkable party service rendered, will enable a member to keep his seat through two or three successive congresses. Nowhere therefore does the zeal of a young politician sooner wax cold than in the House of Representatives. Unfruitful toil, the toil of turning a crank which does nothing but register its own turnings, or of writing contributions which an editor steadily rejects, is of all things the most disheartening. It is more disheartening than the non-requital of merit; for that at least spares the self-respect of the sufferer. Now toil for the public is usually unfruitful in the House of Representatives, indeed in all Houses. But toil for the pecuniary interests of one's constituents and friends is fruitful, for it obliges people, it wins the reputation of energy and smartness, it has the promise not only of a re-nomination, but of a possible seat in the Senate. Now a seat in the Senate is the highest ambition of the congressman. Power, fame, perhaps even riches, sit upon that pinnacle. But the thin spun life is usually slit before the fair guerdon has been found. When I first went to America, I used to ask the ablest and most ambitious of the friends I made among young men whether they looked forward to entering Congress. Out of many scarcely one seemed drawn towards the career which those who have won success at the universities of England naturally look forward to. Presently I came to undertand their attitude, and to feel that the probable disappointments and vexations of a life in Congress so far outweighed its attractions that nothing but a strong sense of public duty would induce a man of fine tastes and high talents to adopt it. Law, education, literature, the higher walks of commerce, finance, or railway work, offer a better prospect of usefulness, enjoyment, or distinction.

Inside Washington, the representative is dwarfed by the senator and the Federal judges. Outside Washington he enjoys no great social consideration. His opinion is not quoted with respect. He seems to move about under a *prima facie* suspicion of being a jobber, and to feel that the burden of proof lies on him to show that the current jests on this topic do not apply to him. Rich men therefore do not seek, as in England, to enter the legislature in order that they may enter society. They will get no *entrée* which they could not have secured otherwise. Nor is there any opportunity for the exercise of those social influences which tell upon members, and still more upon members' wives and daughters, in European legislatures. It may of course be worth while to "capture" a particular senator, and for that purpose to begin by capturing his wife. But the *salon* plays no conspicuous part in American public life.

The country does not go to Congress to look for its presidential candidates as England looks to Parliament for its prime ministers. The opportunities by which a man can win distinction there are few. He does not make himself familiar to the eye and ear of the people. Congress, in short, is not a focus of political life as are the legislatures of France, Italy, and England. This has always been so, and is no less so now than formerly. Although Congress has become more powerful against the several States than it was formerly, though it has extended its arms in every direction, and encroached upon the executive, it has not become more interesting to the people, it has not strengthened its hold on their respect and affection.

VIII. Neither in the Senate nor in the House are there any recognized leaders. There is no ministry, no ex-ministry leading an opposition, no chieftains at the head of definite groups who follow their lead, as the Irish Nationalist members in the British Parliament follow Mr. Parnell, and a large section of the Left in the French chamber follow M. Clemenceau. In other words, no regular means exist for securing either that members shall be apprised of the approach of an important division, or that they shall vote in that division in a particular way.

To any one familiar with the methods of the English parliament this seems incomprehensible. How, he asks, can business go on at all, how can the party make itself felt as a party with neither leader nor Whips?

I have mentioned the Whips. Let me say a word on this vital, yet even in England little appreciated, part of the machinery of constitutional government. Each party in the House of Commons has, besides its leaders, a member of the House nominated by the chief leader as his aide-de-camp, and called the whipper-in, or, for shortness, the whip. The whip's duties are (1) to inform every member belonging to the party when an important division may be expected, and if he sees the member in or about the House, to keep him there until the division is called; (2) to direct the members of his own party how to vote; (3) to obtain pairs for them if they cannot be present to vote; (4) to "tell," *i.e.* count the members in every party division; (5) to "keep touch" of opinion within the party, and convey to the leader a faithful impression of that opinion, from which the latter can judge how far he may count on the support of his whole party in any course he proposes to take. A member in doubt how he shall vote on a question with regard to which he has no opinion of his own, goes to the whip for counsel. A member who without grave cause stays away unpaired from an important division to which the whip has duly summoned him is guilty of a misdemeanour only less flagrant than that of voting against his party. A ministerial whip is further bound to "keep a house," *i.e.* to secure that when government business is being considered there shall always be a quorum of members present, and of course also to keep a majority, *i.e.* to have within reach a number of supporters sufficient to give the ministry a majority on any ministerial division. Without the constant presence and activity of the ministerial whip the wheels of government could not go on for a day, because the ministry would be exposed to the risk of casual defeats which would destroy their credit and might involve their resignation. Similarly the Opposition, and any third or fourth party, find it necessary to have a whip, because it is only thus that they can act as a party, guide their supporters, and bring their full strength to bear on a division. Hence when a new party is formed, its first act, that by which it realizes and proclaims its existence, is to name a whip, to whom its adherents may go for counsel, and who may in turn receive their suggestions as to the proper strategy for the party to adopt. So essential are these officers to the discipline of

English parliamentary armies that an English politician's first question when he sees Congress is, "Where are the whips?" his next, "How in the world do you get on without them?"

The answer to this question is threefold. Whips are not so necessary at Washington as at Westminster. A sort of substitute for them has been devised. Congress does suffer from the want of them, that is, it suffers from the inadequacy of the substituted device.

A division in Congress has not the importance it has in the House of Commons. There it may throw out the ministry. In Congress it never does more than affirm or negative some particular bill or resolution. Even a division in the Senate which involves the rejection of a treaty or of an appointment to some great office, does not disturb the tenure of the executive. Hence it is not essential to the majority that its full strength should be always at hand, nor has a minority party any great prize set before it as the result of a successful vote.

Questions, however, arise in which some large party interest is involved. There may be a bill by which the party means to carry out its main views of policy or perhaps to curry favour with the people, or a resolution whereby it hopes to damage a hostile executive. In such cases it is important to bring up every vote. Accordingly a meeting of the party is convened, called a senatorial caucus or congressional (*i.e.* House) caucus (as the case may be).[1] The attitude to be assumed by the party is debated with closed doors, and a vote taken as to the course to be adopted. By this vote every member of the party is deemed bound, just as he would be in England by the request of the leader conveyed through the whip. Disobedience cannot be punished in Congress itself, except of course by social penalties; but it endangers the seat of the too independent member, for the party managers at Washington will communicate with the party managers in his district, and the latter will probably refuse to re-nominate him at the next election. The most important caucus of a Congress is that held at the opening to select the party candidate for the speakership, selection by the majority being of course equivalent to election. As the views and tendencies of the Speaker determine the composition of the committees, and thereby the course of legislation, his selection is a matter of supreme importance, and is preceded by weeks of intrigue and canvassing.

This process of "going into caucus" is the regular American substitute for recognized leadership, and has the advantage of seeming more consistent with democratic equality, because every member of the party has in theory equal weight in the party meeting. It is used whenever a line of policy has to be settled, or the whole party to be rallied for a particular party division. But of course it cannot be employed every day or for every bill. Hence when no party meeting has issued its orders, a member is free to vote as he pleases, or rather as he thinks his constituents please. If he knows nothing of the matter, he may take a friend's advice, or vote as he hears some prominent man on his own side vote. Anyhow, his vote is doubtful, unpredictable; and consequently divisions on minor questions are uncertain. This is a further reason, added to the power of the standing committees, why there is a want of consistent policy in the action of Congress. As its leading men have comparatively little authority, and there are no means whereby a leader could keep his party together on ordinary questions, so no definite ideas run through its conduct and express themselves in its votes. It moves in zig-zags.

The freedom thus enjoyed by members on minor questions has the interesting result of preventing dissensions and splits in the parties. There are substances which cohere best when their contact is loose. Fresh fallen snow keeps a smooth surface even on a steep slope, but when by melting and regelation it has become ice, cracks and rifts begin to appear. A loose hung carriage will hold together over a road whose roughness would strain and break a more solid one. Hence serious differences of opinion may exist in a congressional party without breaking its party unity, for nothing more is needed than that a solid front should be presented on the occasions, few in each session, when a momentous division arrives. The appearance of agreement is all the more readily preserved because there is little serious debating, so that the advocates of one view seldom provoke the other section of their party to rise and contradict them; while a member who dissents from the bulk of his party on an important issue is slow to vote against it, because he has little chance of defining and defending his position by an explanatory speech.

The congressional caucus is more or less called into action according to the number and gravity of the party issues that come before Congress. In troublous times it has to be supplemented by something like obedience to regular leaders. Mr.

Thaddeus Stevens, for instance, led with recognized authority the majority of the House in its struggle with President Andrew Johnson. The Senate is rather more jealous of the equality of all its members. No senator can be said to have any authority beyond that of exceptional talent and experience ; and of course a senatorial caucus, since it rarely consists of more than forty persons, is a better working body than a House caucus, which may reach two hundred.

The European reader may be perplexed by the apparent contradictions in what has been said regarding the party organization of Congress. "Is the American House after all," he will ask, "more or less a party body than the British House of Commons ? Is the spirit of party more or less strong in Congress than in the American people generally ?"

I answer firstly that the House of Representatives is for the purpose of serious party issues fully as much a party body as the House of Commons. A member voting against his party on such an issue is more certain to forfeit his party reputation and his seat than is an English member. This is true of both the Senate and the House. But for the purpose of ordinary questions, of issues not involving party fortunes, a representative is less bound by party ties than an English member, because he has neither leaders to guide him by their speeches nor whips by their private instructions. The apparent gain is that a wider field is left for independent judgment on non-partisan questions. The real loss is that legislation becomes weak and inconsistent. This conclusion is not encouraging to those who expect us to get rid of party in our legislatures. A deliberative assembly is, after all, only a crowd of men ; and the more intelligent a crowd is, so much the more numerous are its volitions ; so much greater the difficulty of agreement. Like other crowds, a legislature must be led and ruled. Its merit lies not in the independence of its members, but in the reflex action of its opinion upon the leaders, in its willingness to defer to them in minor matters, reserving disobedience for the issues in which some great principle overrides both the obligation of deference to established authority and the respect due to special knowledge.

The above remarks answer the second question also. The spirit of party may seem to be weaker in Congress than in the people at large. But this is only because the questions which the people decide at the polls are always questions of choice between candidates for office. These are definite questions, questions eminently of a party character, because candidates represent in the America of to-day not principles but parties. Whenever a vote upon persons occurs in Congress, Congress gives a strict party vote. Were the people to vote at the polls on matters not explicitly comprised within a party platform, there would be the same uncertainty as Congress displays. The habit of joint action which makes the life of a party is equally intense in every part of the American system. But in England the existence of a Ministry and Opposition in Parliament sweeps within the circle of party action many topics which in America are left outside, and therefore Congress seems, but is not, less permeated than Parliament by party spirit.

CHAPTER 5

The Courts and the Constitution

No feature in the government of the United States has awakened
so much curiosity in the European mind, caused so much discussion, received so much admiration, and been more frequently
misunderstood, than the duties assigned to the Supreme Court
and the functions which it discharges in guarding the ark of the
Constitution. Yet there is really no mystery about the matter.
It is not a novel device. It is not a complicated device. It is
the simplest thing in the world if approached from the right side.

In England and many other modern States there is no difference in authority between one statute and another. All are
made by the legislature : all can be changed by the legislature.
What are called in England constitutional statutes, such as Magna
Charta, the Bill of Rights, the Act of Settlement, the Acts of
Union with Scotland and Ireland, are merely ordinary laws,
which could be repealed by Parliament at any moment in exactly
the same way as it can repeal a highway act or lower the duty
on tobacco. The habit has grown up of talking of the British
Constitution as if it were a fixed and definite thing. But there
is in England no such thing as a Constitution apart from the rest
of the law : there is merely a mass of law, consisting partly of
statutes and partly of decided cases and accepted usages, in con-
formity with which the government of the country is carried on
from day to day, but which is being constantly modified by fresh
statutes and cases. The same thing existed in ancient Rome,
and everywhere in Europe a century ago. It is, so to speak, the
"natural," and used to be the normal, condition of things in all
countries, free or despotic.

The condition of America is wholly different. There the
name Constitution designates a particular instrument adopted in
1788, amended in some points since, which is the foundation of

the national government.   This Constitution was ratified and
made binding, not by Congress, but by the people acting through
conventions assembled in the thirteen States which then composed the Confederation.   It created a legislature of two houses ;
but that legislature, which we call Congress, has no power to
alter it in the smallest particular.   That which the people have
enacted, the people only can alter or repeal.

Here therefore we observe two capital differences between
England and the United States.   The former has left the outlines as well as the details of her system of government to be
gathered from a multitude of statutes and cases.   The latter has
drawn them out in one comprehensive fundamental enactment.
The former has placed these so-called constitutional laws at the
mercy of her legislature, which can abolish when it pleases any
institution of the country, the Crown, the House of Lords, the
Established Church, the House of Commons, Parliament itself.
The latter has placed her Constitution altogether out of the
reach of Congress, providing a method of amendment whose
difficulty is shown by the fact that it has been very sparingly used.

In England Parliament is omnipotent.   In America Congress
is doubly restricted.   It can make laws only for certain purposes
specified in the Constitution, and in legislating for these purposes
it must not transgress any provision of the Constitution itself.
The stream cannot rise above its source.

Suppose, however, that Congress does so transgress, or does
overpass the specified purposes.   It may do so intentionally : it
is likely to do so inadvertently.   What happens ?   If the Constitution is to be respected, there must be some means of securing it against Congress.   If a usurpation of power is attempted,
how is it to be checked ?   If a mistake is committed, who sets it
right ?

The point may be elucidated by referring it to a wider
category, familiar to lawyers and easily comprehensible by lay-
men, that of acts done by an agent for a principal.   If a land-
owner directs his bailiff to collect rents for him, or to pay debts
due to tradesmen, the bailiff has evidently no authority to bind
his employer by any act beyond the instructions given him, as,
for instance, by contracting to buy a field.   If a manufacturer
directs his foreman to make rules for the hours of work and
meals in the factory, and the foreman makes rules not only for
those purposes, but also prescribing what clothes the workmen

shall wear and what church they shall attend, the latter rules have not the force of the employer's will behind them, and the workmen are not to be blamed for neglecting them.

The same principle applies to public agents. In every country it happens that acts are directed to be done and rules to be made by bodies which are in the position of agents, *i.e.* which have received from some superior authority a limited power of acting and of rule-making, a power to be used only for certain purposes or under certain conditions. Where this power is duly exercised, the act or rule of the subordinate body has all the force of an act done or rule made by the superior authority, and is deemed to be made by it. And if the latter be a law-making body, the rule of the subordinate body is therefore also a law. But if the subordinate body attempts to transcend the power committed to it, and makes rules for other purposes or under other conditions than those specified by the superior authority, these rules are not law, but are null and void. Their validity depends on their being within the scope of the law-making power conferred by the superior authority, and as they have passed outside that scope they are invalid. They do not justify any act done under them forbidden by the ordinary law. They ought not to be obeyed or in any way regarded by the citizens, because they are not law.

The same principle applies to acts done by an executive officer beyond the scope of his legal authority. In free countries an individual citizen is justified in disobeying the orders of a magistrate if he correctly thinks these orders to be in excess of the magistrate's legal power, because in that case they are not really the orders of a magistrate, but of a private person affecting to act as a magistrate. In England, for instance, if a secretary of state, or a police constable, does any act which the citizen affected by it rightly deems unwarranted, the citizen may resist, by force if necessary, relying on the ordinary courts of the land to sustain him. This is a consequence of the English doctrine that all executive power is strictly limited by the law, and is indeed a corner-stone of English liberty. It is applied even as against the dominant branch of the legislature. If the House of Commons should act in excess of the power which the law and custom of Parliament has secured to it, a private individual may resist the officers of the House and the courts will protect him by directing him to be acquitted if he is prosecuted, or, if he is plaintiff in a civil action, by giving judgment in his favour.

An obvious instance of the way in which rules or laws made by subordinate bodies are treated is afforded by the bye-laws made by an English railway company or municipal corporation under powers conferred by an Act of Parliament. So long as these bye-laws are within the scope of the authority which the Act of Parliament has given, they are good, *i.e.* they are laws, just as much as if enacted in the Act. If they go beyond it, they are bad, that is to say, they bind nobody and cannot be enforced. If a railway company which has received power to make bye-laws imposing fines up to the amount of forty shillings, makes a bye-law punishing any person who enters or quits a train in motion with a fine of fifty shillings or a week's imprisonment, that bye-law is invalid, that is to say, it is not law at all, and no magistrate can either imprison or impose a fine of fifty shillings on a person accused of contravening it. If a municipal corporation has been by statute empowered to enter into contracts for the letting of lands vested in it, and directed to make bye-laws, for the purpose of letting, which shall provide, among other things, for the advertising of all lands intended to be let, and if it makes a bye-law in which no provision is made for advertising, and under that bye-law contracts for the letting of a piece of land, the letting made in pursuance of this bye-law is void, and conveys no title to the purchaser. All this is obvious to a lay as well as to a legal mind ; and it is no less obvious that the question of the validity of the bye-law, and of what has been done under it, is one to be decided not by the municipal corporation or company, but by the courts of justice of the land.

Now, in the United States the position of Congress may for this purpose be compared to that of an English municipal corporation or railway company. The supreme law-making power is the People, that is, the qualified voters, acting in a prescribed way. The people have by their supreme law, the Constitution, given to Congress a delegated and limited power of legislation. Every statute passed under that power conformably to the Constitution has all the authority of the Constitution behind it. Any statute passed which goes beyond that power is invalid, and incapable of enforcement. It is in fact not a statute at all, because Congress in passing it was not really a law-making body, but a mere group of private persons.

There is of course this enormous difference between Congress and any subordinate law-making authority in England, that Congress is supreme within its proper sphere, the people having no higher permanent organ to override or repeal such statutes as Congress may pass within that sphere; whereas in England there exists in Parliament a constantly present supervising authority, which may at any moment cancel or modify what any subordinate body may have enacted, whether within or without the scope of its delegated powers. This is a momentous distinction. But it does not affect the special point which I desire to illustrate, viz. that a statute passed by Congress beyond the scope of its powers is of no more effect than a bye-law made *ultra vires* by an English municipality. There is no mystery so far : there is merely an application of the ordinary principles of the law of agency. But the question remains, How and by whom, in case of dispute, is the validity or invalidity of a statute to be determined ?

Such determination is to be effected by setting the statute side by side with the Constitution, and considering whether there is any discrepancy between them. Is the purpose of the statute one of the purposes mentioned or implied in the Constitution ? Does it in pursuing that purpose contain anything which violates any clause of the Constitution ? Sometimes this is a simple question, which an intelligent layman may answer. More frequently it is a difficult one, which needs not only the subtlety of the trained lawyer, but a knowledge of former cases which have thrown light on the same or a similar point. In any event it is an important question, whose solution ought to proceed from a weighty authority. It is a question of interpretation, that is, of determining the true meaning both of the superior law and of the inferior law, so as to discover whether they are inconsistent.

Now the interpretation of laws belongs to courts of justice. A law implies a tribunal, not only in order to direct its enforcement against individuals, but to adjust it to the facts, *i.e.* to determine its precise meaning and apply that meaning to the circumstances of the particular case. The legislature, which can only speak generally, makes every law in reliance on this power of interpretation. It is therefore obvious that the question, whether a congressional statute offends against the Constitution, must be determined by the courts, not merely because it is a question of legal construction, but because there is nobody else to determine it. Congress cannot do so, because Congress is a party interested. If such a body as Congress were permitted to decide whether the acts it had passed were constitutional, it would of course decide in its own favour, and to allow it to decide would be to put the Constitution at its mercy. The President cannot, because he is not a lawyer, and he also may be personally interested. There remain only the courts, and these must be the National or Federal courts, because no other courts can be relied on in such cases. So far again there is no mystery about the matter.

Now, however, we arrive at a feature which complicates the facts, though it introduces no new principle. The United States is a federation of commonwealths, each of which has its own constitution and laws. The Federal Constitution not only gives certain powers to Congress, as the national legislature, but recognizes certain powers in the States, in virtue whereof their respective peoples have enacted fundamental State laws (the State constitutions) and have enabled their respective legislatures to pass State statutes. However, as the nation takes precedence of the States, the Federal Constitution, which is the supreme law of the land everywhere, and the statutes duly made by Congress under it, are preferred to all State constitutions and statutes; and if any conflict arise between them, the latter must give way. The same phenomenon therefore occurs as in the case of an inconsistency between the Constitution and a congressional statute. Where it is shown that a State constitution or statute infringes either the Federal Constitution or a Federal (*i.e.* congressional) statute, the State constitution or statute must be held and declared invalid. And this declaration must, of course, proceed from the courts, nor solely from the Federal courts; because when a State court decides against its own statutes or constitution in favour of a Federal law, its decision is final.

It will be observed that in all this there is no conflict between the law courts and any legislative body. The conflict is between different kinds of laws. The duty of the judges is as strictly confined to the interpretation of the laws cited to them as it is in England or France; and the only difference is that in America there are laws of four different degrees of authority, whereas in England all laws (excluding mere bye-laws, Privy Council ordinances, etc.) are equal because all proceed from Parliament. These four kinds of American laws are :—

I. The Federal Constitution.
II. Federal statutes.
III. State constitutions.
IV. State statutes.

The American law court therefore does not itself enter on any conflict with the legislature. It merely secures to each kind of law its due authority. It does not even preside over a conflict and decide it, for the relative strength of each kind of law has been settled already. All the court does is to point out that a conflict exists between two laws of different degrees of authority. Then the question is at an end, for the weaker law is extinct.

This is the abstract statement of the matter ; but there is also an historical one. Many of the American colonies received charters from the British Crown, which created or recognized colonial assemblies, and endowed these with certain powers of making laws for the colony. Such powers were of course limited, partly by the charter, partly by usage, and were subject to the superior authority of the Crown or of the British Parliament. Questions sometimes arose in colonial days whether the statutes made by these assemblies were in excess of the powers conferred by the charter ; and if the statutes were found to be in excess, they were held invalid by the courts, that is to say, in the first instance, by the colonial courts, or, if the matter was carried to England, by the Privy Council.

When the thirteen American colonies asserted their independence in 1776, they replaced these old charters by new constitutions, and by these constitutions entrusted their respective legislative assemblies with certain specified and limited legislative powers. The same question was then liable to recur with regard to a statute passed by one of these assemblies. If such a statute was in excess of the power which the State constitution conferred on the State legislature, or in any way transgressed the provisions of that constitution, it was invalid, and acts done under it were void. The question, like any other question of law, came for decision before the courts of the State. Thus, in 1786, the supreme court of Rhode Island held a statute of the legislature void, on the ground that it made a penalty collectible on summary conviction, without trial by jury ; the colonial charter,

which was then still in force as the constitution of the State,
having secured the right of trial by jury in all cases.   When
the Constitution of the United States came into operation in
1789, and was declared to be paramount to all State constitutions
and State statutes, no new principle was introduced ; there was
merely a new application, as between the nation and the States,
of the old doctrine that a subordinate and limited legislature
cannot pass beyond the limits fixed for it.   It was clear, on
general principles, that a State law incompatible with a Federal
law must give way ; the only question was : What courts are to
pronounce upon the question whether such incompatibility exists ?
Who is to decide whether or no the authority given to Congress
has been exceeded, and whether or no the State law contravenes
the Federal Constitution or a Federal statute ?

In 1789 the only pre-existing courts were the State courts.
If a case coming before them raised the point whether a State
constitution or statute was inconsistent with the Federal Constitution or a statute of Congress, it was their duty to decide it, like
any other point of law.   But their decision could not safely be
accepted as final, because, being themselves the offspring of, and
amenable to the State governments, they would naturally tend
to uphold State laws against the Federal Constitution or statutes.
Hence it became necessary to call in courts created by the central
Federal authority and co-extensive with it—that is to say, those
Federal courts which have been already described.   The. matter
seems complicated, because we have to consider not only the
superiority of the Federal Constitution to the Federal Congress,
but also the superiority of both the Federal Constitution and
Federal statutes to all State laws.   But the principle is the
same and equally simple in both sets of cases.   Both are merely
instances of the doctrine, that a law-making body must not
exceed its powers, and that when it has attempted to exceed its
powers, its so-called statutes are not laws at all, and cannot be
enforced.

In America the supreme law-making power resides in the
people.   Whatever they enact binds all courts whatsoever.   All
other law-making bodies are subordinate, and the enactments of
such bodies must conform to the supreme law, else they will
perish at its touch, as a fishing smack goes down before an ocean
steamer.   And these subordinate enactments, if at variance with
the supreme law, are invalid from the first, although their in-

validity may remain for years unnoticed or unproved. It can be proved only by the decision of a court in a case which raises the point for determination. The phenomenon cannot arise in a country whose legislature is omnipotent, but naturally arises wherever we find a legislature limited by a superior authority, such as a constitution which the legislature cannot alter.

In England the judges interpret Acts of Parliament exactly as American judges interpret statutes coming before them. If they find an Act conflicting with a decided case, they prefer the Act to the case, as being of higher authority. As between two conflicting Acts, they prefer the latter, because it is the last expression of the mind of Parliament. If they misinterpret the mind of Parliament, *i.e.* if they construe an Act in a sense which Parliament did not really intend, their decision is nevertheless valid, and will be followed by other courts until Parliament speaks its mind again by another Act. The only difference between their position and that of their American brethren is that they have never to distinguish between the authority of one enactment and of another, otherwise than by looking to the date, and that they have therefore never to inquire whether an Act of Parliament was invalid when first passed. Invalid it could not have been, because Parliament is omnipotent, and Parliament is omnipotent because Parliament is deemed to be the people. Parliament is not a body with delegated or limited authority. The whole fulness of popular power dwells in it. The whole nation is supposed to be present within its walls. Its will is law ; or, as Dante says in a famous line, "its will is power."

There is a story told of an intelligent Englishman who, having heard that the Supreme Federal Court was created to protect the Constitution, and had authority given it to annul bad laws, spent two days in hunting up and down the Federal Constitution for the provisions he had been told to admire. No wonder he did not find them, for there is not a word in the Constitution on the subject. The powers of the Federal courts are the same as those of all other courts in civilized countries, or rather they differ from those of other courts by defect and not by excess, being limited to certain classes of cases. The so-called "power of annulling an unconstitutional statute" is a duty rather than a power, and a duty incumbent on the humblest State court when a case raising the point comes before it no less than on the Supreme Federal Court at Washington. When therefore people talk, as they sometimes do, even in the United States, of the Supreme court as "the guardian of the Constitution," they mean nothing more than that it is the final court of appeal, before which suits involving constitutional questions may be brought up by the parties for decision. In so far the phrase is legitimate. But the functions of the Supreme court are the same in kind as those of all other courts, State as well as Federal. Its duty and theirs is simply to declare and apply the law; and where any court, be it a State court of first instance, or the Federal court of last instance, finds a law of lower authority clashing with a law of higher authority, it must reject the former, as being really no law, and enforce the latter.

It is therefore no mere technicality to point out that the American judges do not, as Europeans are apt to say, "control the legislature," but simply interpret the law. The word "control" is misleading, because it implies that the person or body of whom it is used possesses and exerts discretionary personal Will. Now the American judges have no will in the matter any more than has an English court when it interprets an Act of Parliament. The will that prevails is the will of the people, expressed in the Constitution which they have enacted. All that the judges have to do is to discover from the enactments before them what the will of the people is, and apply that will to the facts of a given case. The more general or ambiguous the language which the people have used, so much the more difficult is the task of interpretation, so much greater the need for ability and integrity in the judges. But the task is always the same in its nature. The judges have no concern with the motives or the results of an enactment, otherwise than as these may throw light on the sense in which the enacting authority intended it. It would be a breach of duty for them to express, I might almost say a breach of duty to entertain, an opinion on its policy except so far as its policy explains its meaning. They may think a statute excellent in purpose and working, but if they cannot find in the Constitution a power for Congress to pass it, they must brush it aside as invalid. They may deem another statute pernicious, but if it is within the powers of Congress, they must enforce it. To construe the law, that is, to elucidate the will of the people as supreme lawgiver, is the beginning and end of their duty.

To press this point is not to minimize the importance of the functions exercised by the judiciary of the United States, but to indicate their true nature. The importance of those functions can hardly be exaggerated. It arises from two facts. One is that as the Constitution cannot easily be changed, a bad decision on its meaning, *i.e.* a decision which the general opinion of the profession condemns, may go uncorrected. In England, if a court has construed a statute in a way unintended or unexpected, Parliament sets things right next session by amending the statute, and so prevents future decisions to the same effect. But American history shows only one instance in which an unwelcome decision on the meaning of the Constitution has been thus dealt with, viz. the decision, that a State could be sued by a private citizen, which led to the eleventh amendment, whereby it was declared that the Constitution should not cover a case which the court had held it did cover.

The other fact which makes the function of an American judge so momentous is the brevity, the laudable brevity, of the Constitution. The words of that instrument are general, laying down a few large principles. The cases which will arise as to the construction of these general words cannot be foreseen till they arise. When they do arise the generality of the words leaves open to the interpreting judges a far wider field than is afforded by ordinary statutes which, since they treat of one particular subject, contain enactments comparatively minute and precise. Hence, although the duty of a court is only to interpret, the considerations affecting interpretation are more numerous than in the case of ordinary statutes, more delicate, larger in their reach and scope. They sometimes need the exercise not merely of legal acumen and judicial fairness, but of a comprehension of the nature and methods of government which one does not demand from the European judge who walks in the narrow path traced for him by ordinary statutes. It is therefore hardly an exaggeration to say that the American Constitution as it now stands, with the mass of fringing decisions which explain it, is a far more complete and finished instrument than it was when it came fire-new from the hands of the Convention. It is not merely their work but the work of the judges, and most of all of one man, the great Chief-Justice Marshall.

The march of democracy in England has disposed English writers and politicians of the very school which thirty or twenty years ago pointed to America as a terrible example, now to discover that her republic possesses elements of stability wanting in the monarchy of the mother country. They lament that England should have no supreme court. Some have even suggested that England should create one. They do not seem to perceive that the dangers they discern arise not from the want of a court but from the omnipotence of the British Parliament. They ask for a court to guard the British Constitution, forgetting that Britain has no constitution, in the American sense, and never had one, except for a short space under Oliver Cromwell. The strongest court that might be set up in England could effect nothing so long as Parliament retains its power to change every part of the law, including all the rules and doctrines that are called constitutional. If Parliament were to lose that power there would be no need to create a supreme court, because the existing judges of the land would necessarily discharge the very functions which American judges now discharge. If Parliament were to be split up into four parliaments for England, Scotland, Ireland, and Wales, and a new Federal Assembly were to be established with limited legislative powers, powers defined by an instrument which neither the Federal Assembly nor any of the four parliaments could alter, questions would forthwith arise as to the compatibility both of acts passed by the Assembly with the provisions of the instrument, and of acts passed by any of the four parliaments with those passed by the Assembly. These questions would come before the courts and be determined by them like any other question of law. The same thing would happen if Britain were to enter into a federal pact with her colonies, creating an imperial Council, and giving it powers which, though restricted by the pact to certain purposes, transcended those of the British Parliament. The interpretation of the pact would belong to the courts, and both Parliament and the supposed Council would be bound by that interpretation. If a new supreme court were created by Britain, it would be created not because there do not already exist courts capable of entertaining all the questions that could arise, but because the parties to the new constitution enacted for the United Kingdom, or the British Empire (as the case might be), might insist that a tribunal composed of persons chosen by some Federal authority would be more certainly impartial. The preliminary therefore to any such "judicial safeguard" as has been suggested is the extinction of the present British Parliament and the erection of a wholly different body or bodies in its room.

These observations may suffice to show that there is nothing strange or mysterious about the relation of the Federal courts to the Constitution. The plan which the Convention of 1787 adopted is simple, useful, and conformable to general legal principles. It is, in the original sense of the word, an elegant plan. But it is not novel. It was at work in the States before the Convention of 1787 met. It was at work in the thirteen colonies before they revolted from England. It is an application of old and familiar legal doctrines. Such novelty as there is belongs to the scheme of a Supreme or Rigid constitution, reserving the ultimate power to the people, and limiting in the same measure the power of a legislature.

It is nevertheless true that there is no part of the American system which reflects more credit on its authors or has worked better in practice. It has had the advantage of relegating questions not only intricate and delicate, but peculiarly liable to excite political passions, to the cool, dry atmosphere of judicial determination. The relations of the central Federal power to the States, and the amount of authority which Congress and the President are respectively entitled to exercise, have been the most permanently grave questions in American history, with which nearly every other political problem has become entangled. If they had been left to be settled by Congress, itself an interested party, or by any dealings between Congress and the State legislatures, the dangers of a conflict would have been extreme, and instead of one civil war there might have been several. But the universal respect felt for the Constitution, a respect which grows the longer it stands, has disposed men to defer to any decision which seems honestly and logically to unfold the meaning of its terms. In obeying such a decision they are obeying, not the judges, but the people who enacted the Constitution. To have foreseen that the power of interpreting the Federal Constitution and statutes, and of determining whether or no State constitutions and statutes transgress Federal provisions, would be sufficient to prevent struggles between the National government and the State governments, required great insight and great faith in the soundness and power of a principle. While the Constitution was being framed the suggestion was made, and for a time seemed likely to be adopted, that a veto on the acts of State legislatures should be conferred upon the Federal Congress. Discussion revealed the objections to such a plan. Its introduction would have offended the sentiment of the States, always jealous of their autonomy; its exercise would have provoked collisions with them. The disallowance of a State statute, even if it did really offend against the Federal Constitution, would have seemed a political move, to be resented by a political counter-move. And the veto would often have been pronounced before it could have been ascertained exactly how the State statute would work, sometimes, perhaps, pronounced in cases where the statute was neither pernicious in itself nor opposed to the Federal Constitution. But by the action of the courts the self-love of the States is not wounded, and the decision annulling their laws is nothing but a tribute to the superior authority of that supreme enactment to which they were themselves parties, and which they may themselves desire to see enforced against another State on some not remote occasion. However, the idea of a veto by Congress was most effectively demolished in the Convention by Roger Sherman, who acutely remarked that a veto would seem to recognize as valid the State statute objected to, whereas if inconsistent with the Constitution it was really invalid already and needed no veto.

By leaving constitutional questions to be settled by the courts of law another advantage was incidentally secured. The court does not go to meet the question; it waits for the question to come to it. When the court acts it acts at the instance of a party. Sometimes the plaintiff or the defendant may be the National government or a State government, but far more frequently both are private persons, seeking to enforce or defend their private rights. For instance, in the famous case which established the doctrine that a statute passed by a State repealing a grant of land to an individual made on certain terms by a previous statute is a law "impairing the obligation of a contract," and therefore invalid, under Art. i. § 10 of the Federal Constitution; the question came before the court on an action by one Fletcher against one Peck on a covenant contained in a deed made by the latter; and to do justice between plaintiff and defendant it was necessary to examine the validity of a statute passed by the legislature of Georgia. This method has the merit of not hurrying a question on, but leaving it to arise of itself. Full legal argument on both sides is secured by the private interests which the parties have in setting forth their contentions ; and the decision when pronounced, since it appears to be, as in fact it is, primarily a decision upon private rights, obtains that respect and moral support which a private plaintiff or defendant establishing his legal right is entitled to from law-abiding citizens. A State might be provoked to resistance if it saw, as soon as it had passed a statute, the Federal government inviting the Supreme court to declare that statute invalid. But when the Federal authority stands silent, and a year after in an ordinary action between Smith and Jones the court decides in favour of Jones, who argued that the statute on which the plaintiff relied was invalid because it transgressed some provision of the Constitution, everybody feels that Jones was justified in so arguing, and that since judgment was given in his favour he must be allowed to retain the money which the court has found to be his, and the statute which violated his private right must fall to the ground.

This feature has particularly excited the admiration of Continental critics. To an Englishman it seems perfectly natural, because it is exactly in this way that much of English constitutional law has been built up. The English courts had indeed no rigid documentary constitution by which to test the ordinances or the executive acts of the Crown, and their decisions on constitutional points have often been pronounced in proceedings to which the Crown or its ministers were parties. But they have repeatedly established principles of the greatest moment by judgments delivered in cases where a private interest was involved, grounding themselves either on a statute which they interpreted or on some earlier decision. Lord Mansfield's famous declaration that slavery was legally impossible in England was pronounced in such a private case. *Stockdale* v. *Hansard*, in which the law regarding the publishing of debates in Parliament was settled, was an action by a private person against printers. The American method of settling constitutional questions, like all other legal questions, in actions between private parties, is therefore no new device, but a part of that priceless heritage of the English Common Law which the colonists carried with them across the sea, and which they have preserved and developed in a manner worthy of its own free spirit and lofty traditions.

Europeans commonly suppose that the functions above described as pertaining to the American courts are peculiar to and essential to a Federal government. This is a mistake. They are not peculiar to a federation, because the distinction of fundamental laws and inferior laws may exist equally well in a unified government, did exist in each of the thirteen colonies up till 1776, did exist in each of the thirteen States from 1776 till 1789, does exist in every one of the thirty-eight States now. Nor are they essential, because a federation may be imagined in which the central or national legislature should be theoretically sovereign in the same sense and to the same full extent as is the British Parliament. The component pai.. of any confederacy will no doubt be generally disposed to place their respective State rights under the protection of a compact unchangeable by the national legislature. But they need not do so, for they may rely on the command which as electors they have over that legislature, and may prefer the greater energy which a sovereign legislature promises to the greater security for State rights which a limited legislature implies. In the particular case of America it is abundantly clear that if there had been in 1787 no States jealous of their powers, but an united nation creating for itself an improved frame of government, the organs of that government would have been limited by a fundamental law just as they are now, because the nation, fearing and distrusting the agents it was creating, was resolved to fetter them by reserving to itself the ultimate and over-riding sovereignty.

The case of Switzerland shows that the American plan is not the only one possible to a federation. The Swiss Federal Court, while instituted in imitation of the American, is not the only authority competent to determine whether a Cantonal law is void because inconsistent with the Federal Constitution, for in some cases recourse must be had not to the Court but to the Federal Council, which is a sort of executive cabinet of the Confederation. And the Federal Court is bound to enforce every law passed by the Federal legislature, even if it violate the Constitution. In other words, the Swiss Constitution has reserved some points of Cantonal law for an authority not judicial but political, and has made the Federal legislature the sole judge of its own powers, the authorized interpreter of the Constitution, and an interpreter not likely to proceed on purely legal grounds. To an English or American lawyer the Swiss copy seems neither so consistent with sound theory nor so safe in practice as the American original. But the statesmen of Switzerland felt that a method fit for America might be ill-fitted for their own country, where the latitude given to the executive is greater; and the Swiss habit of constantly recurring to popular vote makes it less necessary to restrain the legislature by a permanently enacted instrument. The political traditions of the European continent differ widely from those of England and America; and the Federal Judicature is not the only Anglo-American institution which might fail to thrive anywhere but in its native soil.

CHAPTER 6

Working Relations of the National and the State Governments

THE characteristic feature and special interest of the American Union is that it shows us two governments covering the same ground, yet distinct and separate in their action. It is like a great factory wherein two sets of machinery are at work, their revolving wheels apparently intermixed, their bands crossing one another, yet each set doing its own work without touching or hampering the other. To keep the National government and the State governments each in the allotted sphere, preventing collision and friction between them, was the primary aim of those who formed the Constitution, a task the more needful and the more delicate because the States had been until then almost independent and therefore jealous of their privileges, and because, if friction should arise, the National government could not remove it by correcting defects in the machinery. For the National government had not been made supreme and omnipotent. It was itself the creature of the Constitution. It was not permitted to amend the Constitution, but could only refer it back for amendment to the people of the States or to their legislatures. Hence the men of 1787, feeling the cardinal importance of anticipating and avoiding occasions of collision, sought to accomplish their object by the concurrent application of two devices. One was to restrict the functions of the National government to the irreducible minimum of functions absolutely needed for the national welfare, so that everything else should be left to the States. The other was to give that government, so far as those functions extended, a direct and immediate relation to the citizens, so that it should act on them not through the States but of its own authority and by its own officers. These are fundamental principles whose soundness experience has approved, and which will deserve to be considered by those who in time to come may have in other countries to frame federal or quasi-federal constitutions. They were studied, and to a large extent, though in no slavish spirit, adopted by the founders of the present constitution of the Swiss Confederation, a constitution whose success bears further witness to the soundness of the American doctrines.

The working relations of the National government to the States may be considered under two heads, viz. its relations to the States as corporate bodies, and its relations to the citizens of the States as individuals, they being also citizens of the Union.

The National government touches the States as corporate commonwealths in three points. One is their function in helping to form the National government; another is the control exercised over them by the Federal Constitution through the Federal courts; the third is the control exercised over them by the Federal Legislature and Executive in the discharge of the governing functions which these latter authorities possess.

I. The States serve to form the National government by choosing presidential electors, by choosing senators, and by fixing the franchise which qualifies citizens to vote for members of the House of Representatives. No difficulty has ever arisen (except during the Civil War) from any unwillingness of the States to discharge these duties, for each State is eager to exercise as much influence as it can on the national executive and Congress. But note how much latitude has been left to the States. A State may appoint its presidential electors in any way it pleases. All States now do appoint them by popular vote. But during the first thirty years of the Union many States left the choice of electors to their respective legislatures. So a State may, by its power of prescribing the franchise for its State elections, prescribe whatever franchise it pleases for the election of its members of the Federal House of Representatives, and may thus admit persons who would in other States be excluded from the suffrage, or exclude persons who would in other States be admitted. For instance, thirteen States now allow aliens (*i.e.* foreigners not yet naturalized) to vote; and any State which should admit women to vote at its own State elections would thereby admit them also to vote at congressional elections.[1] The

---

[1] So in some States tribal Indians are permitted to vote. It is odd that the votes of persons who are not citizens of the United States might, in a State where parties are nearly equal, turn the choice of presidential electors in that State, and thereby perhaps turn the presidential election in the Union.

only restriction imposed on State discretion in this respect is that of the fifteenth amendment, which forbids any person to be deprived of suffrage, on "account of race, colour, or previous condition of servitude." [1]

II. The Federal Constitution deprives the States of certain powers they would otherwise enjoy. Some of these, such as that of making treaties, are obviously unpermissible, and such as the State need not regret. Others, however, seriously restrain their daily action. They are liable to be sued in the Federal courts by another State or by a foreign Power. They cannot, except with the consent of Congress, tax exports or imports, or in any case pass a law impairing the obligation of a contract. They must surrender fugitives from the justice of any other State. Whether they have transgressed any of these restrictions is a question for the courts of law, and, if not in the first instance, yet always in the last resort a question for the Federal Supreme court. If it is decided that they have transgressed, their act, be it legislative or executive, is null and void.

The President as national executive, and Congress as national legislature, have also received from the Constitution the right of interfering in certain specified matters with the governments of the States. Congress of course does this by way of legislation, and when an Act of Congress, made within the powers conferred by the Constitution, conflicts with a State statute, the former prevails against the latter. It prevails by making the latter null and void, so that if a State statute has been duly passed upon a matter not forbidden to a State by the Constitution, and subsequently Congress passes an act on the same matter, being one whereon Congress has received the right to legislate, the State statute, which was previously valid, now becomes invalid to the extent to which it conflicts with the Act of Congress. For instance, Congress has power to establish a uniform law of bankruptcy over the whole Union. It has formerly, in the exercise of this power, passed bankruptcy laws; but these have been repealed, and at present the subject is left to the State laws, which are accordingly in full force in the several States. Were Congress again to legislate on the subject, these State laws would lose their force; and if the law passed by Congress were again repealed, they would again spring into life.

1 The Constitutions of some States retain the old exclusion of negroes from the suffrage, and two exclude natives of China; but these provisions are overridden by the fifteenth constitutional amendment.

The field of this so-called concurrent legislation is large, for Congress has not yet exercised all the powers vested in it of superseding State action.

In determining the powers of Congress on the one hand and of a State government on the other, opposite methods have to be followed. The presumption is always in favour of the State; and in order to show that it cannot legislate on a subject, there must be pointed out within the four corners of the Constitution some express prohibition of the right which it *prima facie* possesses, or some implied prohibition arising from the fact that legislation by it would conflict with legitimate federal authority. On the other hand, the presumption is always against Congress, and to show that it can legislate, some positive grant of power to Congress in the Constitution must be pointed out. When the grant is shown, then the Act of Congress has, so long as it remains on the statute book, all the force of the Constitution itself. In some instances the grant of power to Congress to legislate is auxiliary to a prohibition imposed on the States. This is notably the case as regards the amendments to the Constitution, passed for the protection of the lately liberated negroes. They interdict the States from either recognizing slavery, or discriminating in any way against any class of citizens; they go even beyond citizens in their care, and declare that "no State shall deny to any person within its jurisdiction the equal protection of the laws." Now, by each of these amendments, Congress is also empowered, which practically means enjoined, to "enforce by appropriate legislation" the prohibitions laid upon the States. Congress has done so, but some of its efforts have been held to go beyond the directions of the amendments, and to be therefore void. The grant of power has not covered them.

Where the President interferes with a State, he does so either under his duty to give effect to the legislation of Congress, or under the discretionary executive functions which the Constitution has entrusted to him. So if any State were to depart from a republican form of government, it would be his duty to bring the fact to the notice of Congress in order that the guarantee of that form contained in the Constitution might be made effective. If an insurrection broke out against the authority of the Union, he would (as in 1861) send Federal troops to suppress it. If there should be rival State governments, each claiming to be legitimate, the President might, especially if Congress were not sitting, recognize and support the one which he deemed regular and constitutional.

Are these, it may be asked, the only cases in which Federal authority can interfere within the limits of a State to maintain order? Are law and order, *i.e.* the punishment of crimes and the enforcement of civil rights, left entirely to State authorities? The answer is :—

Offences against Federal statutes are justiciable in Federal courts, and punishable under Federal authority. There is no Federal common law of crimes.

Resistance offered to the enforcement of a Federal statute may be suppressed by Federal authority.

Attacks on the property of the Federal government may be repelled, and disturbances thence arising may be quelled by Federal authority.

The judgments pronounced in civil causes by Federal courts are executed by the officers of these courts.

All other offences and disorders whatsoever are left to be dealt with by the duly constituted authorities of the State, who are, however, entitled in one case to summon the power of the Union to their aid.

This case is that of the breaking out in a State of serious disturbances. The President is bound on the application of the State legislature or executive to quell such disturbances by the armed forces of the Union, or by directing the militia of another State to enter. Thus in 1794 Washington suppressed the so-called Whisky Insurrection in Pennsylvania by the militia of Pennsylvania, New Jersey, Virginia, and Maryland. President Grant was obliged to use military force during the troubles which disturbed several of the Southern States after the Civil War; as was President Hayes, during the tumults in Pennsylvania caused by the great railway strikes of 1877. There have, however, been cases, such as the Dorr rebellion in Rhode Island in 1842. in which a State has itself suppressed an insurrection against its legitimate government. It is the duty of a State to do so if it can, and to seek Federal aid only in extreme cases, when resistance is formidable.

So far we have been considering the relations of the National government to the States as political communities. Let us now see what are its relations to the individual citizens of these

States. They are citizens of the Union as well as of the States, and owe allegiance to both powers. Each power has a right to command their obedience. To which then, in case of conflict, is obedience due?

The right of the State to obedience is wider in the area of matters which it covers. *Prima facie*, every State law, every order of a competent State authority, binds the citizen, whereas the National government has but a limited power: it can legislate or command only for certain purposes or on certain subjects. But within the limits of its power, its authority is higher than that of the State, and must be obeyed even at the risk of disobeying the State. A recent instance in which a State official suffered for obeying his State where its directions clashed with a provision of the Federal Constitution may set the point in a clear light. A statute of California had committed to the city and county authority of San Francisco the power of making regulations for the management of gaols. This authority had in 1876 passed an ordinance directing that every male imprisoned in the county gaol should "immediately on his arrival have his hair clipped to a uniform length of one inch from the scalp." The sheriff having, under this ordinance, cut off the queue of a Chinese prisoner, Ho Ah Kow, was sued for damages by the prisoner, and the court, holding that the ordinance had been passed with a special view to the injury of the Chinese, who consider the preservation of their queue a matter of religion as well as of honour, and that it operated unequally and oppressively upon them, in contravention of the fourteenth amendment to the Constitution of the United States, declared the ordinance invalid, and gave judgment against the sheriff. Similar subsequent attempts against the Chinese, made under cover of the constitution of California of 1879 and divers statutes passed thereunder, have been defeated by the courts.

The safe rule for the private citizen may be thus expressed: "Ascertain whether the Federal law is constitutional (*i.e.* such as Congress has power to pass). If it is, conform your conduct to it at all hazards. If it is not, disregard it, and obey the law of your State." This may seem hard on the private citizen. How shall he settle for himself such a delicate point of law as whether Congress had power to pass a particular statute, seeing that the question may be doubtful and not have come before the courts? But in practice little inconvenience arises, for Congress and the State legislatures have learnt to keep within their respective spheres, and the questions that arise between them are seldom such as need disturb an ordinary man.

The same remarks apply to conflicts between the commands of executive officers of the National government on the one hand, and those of State officials on the other. If the national officer is acting within his constitutional powers, he is entitled to be obeyed in preference to a State official, and conversely, if the State official is within his powers, and the national officer acting in excess of those which the Federal Constitution confers, the State official is to be obeyed.

The limits of judicial power are more difficult of definition. Every citizen can sue and be sued or indicted both in the courts of his State and in the Federal courts, but in some classes of cases the former, in others the latter, is the proper tribunal, while in many it is left to the choice of the parties before which tribunal they will proceed. Sometimes a plaintiff who has brought his action in a State court finds when the case has gone a certain length that a point of Federal law turns up which entitles either himself or the defendant to transfer it to a Federal court, or to appeal to such a court should the decision have gone against the applicability of the Federal law. Suits are thus constantly transferred from State courts to Federal courts, but you can never reverse the process and carry a suit from a Federal court to a State court. Within its proper sphere of pure State law, and of course the great bulk of the cases turn on pure State law, there is no appeal from a State court to a Federal court; and though the point of law on which the case turns may be one which has arisen and been decided in the Supreme court of the Union, a State judge, in a State case, is not bound to regard that decision. It has only a moral weight, such as might be given to the decision of an English court, and where the question is one of State law, whether common law or statute law, in which State courts have decided one way and a Federal court the other way, the State judge ought to follow his own courts. So far does this go, that a Federal court in administering State law, ought to reverse its own previous decision rather than depart from the view which the highest State court has taken. All this seems extremely complex. I can only say that it is less troublesome in practice than could have been expected, because American lawyers are accustomed to the intricacies of their system.

When a plaintiff has the choice of proceeding in a State court or in a Federal court, he is sometimes, especially if he has a strong case, inclined to select the latter, because the Federal judges are more independent than those of most of the States, and less likely to be influenced by any bias. So, too, if he thinks that local prejudice may tell against him, he will prefer a Federal court, because the jurors are summoned from a wider area, and because the judges are accustomed to exert a larger authority in guiding and controlling the jury. But it is usually more convenient to sue in a State court, seeing that there is such a court in every county, whereas Federal courts are comparatively few; in many States there is but one.

How does the Federal authority, be it executive or judicial, act upon the citizens of a State? It acts on them directly by means of its own officers, who are quite distinct from and independent of the State officials. Federal indirect taxes, for instance, are levied all along the coast and over the country by Federal custom-house collectors and excisemen, acting under the orders of the treasury department at Washington. The judgments of Federal courts are carried out by United States marshals, likewise dispersed over the country and supplied with a staff of assistants. This is a provision of the utmost importance, for it enables the central national government to keep its finger upon the people everywhere, and make its laws and the commands of its duly constituted authorities respected whether the State within whose territory it acts be heartily loyal or not, and whether the law which is being enforced be popular or obnoxious. The machinery of the National government ramifies over the whole Union as the nerves do over the human body, placing every point in direct connection with the central executive. The same is, of course, true of the army : but the army is so small and stationed in so few spots, mostly in the Far West where Indian raids are feared, that it scarcely comes into a view of the ordinary working of the system.

What happens if the authority of the National government is opposed, if, for instance, an execution levied in pursuance of a judgment of a Federal court is resisted, or Federal excisemen are impeded in the seizure of an illicit distillery ?

Supposing the United States marshal or other Federal officer to be unable to overcome the physical force opposed to him, he may summon all good citizens to assist him, just as the sheriff may summon the *posse comitatus*. If this appeal proves insufficient, he must call upon the President, who may either order national troops to his aid or may require the militia of the State in which resistance is offered to overcome that resistance. Inferior Federal officers are not entitled to make requisitions for State force. The common law principle that all citizens are bound to assist the ministers of the law holds good in America as in England, but it is as true in the one country as in the other, that what is everybody's business is nobody's business. Practically, the Federal authorities are not resisted in the more orderly States and more civilized districts. In such regions, however, as the mountains of Tennessee and North Carolina the inland revenue officials find it very hard to enforce the excise laws, because the country is wild, concealment is easy among the woods and rocks, and the population sides with the smugglers. And in some of the western States an injunction granted by a court, whether a Federal or a State court, is occasionally disregarded. Things were, of course, much worse before the War of Secession had established the authority of the central government on an immovable basis. Federal law did not prove an unquestioned protection either to persons who became in some districts unpopular from preaching Abolitionism, or who, like the Southern slave-catchers, endeavoured, under the Fugitive Slave laws, to recapture in the northern States slaves who had escaped from their masters. Passion ran high, and great as is the respect for law, passion in America, as everywhere else in the world, will have its way.

If the duly constituted authorities of a State resist the laws and orders of the National government, a more difficult question arises. This has several times happened.

In 1798 the legislatures of Kentucky and Virginia adopted resolutions whereby they declared that the Constitution was not a submission of the States to a general government, but a mere compact between the States vesting in such a government certain strictly specified powers, that the general government had not been made the final and exclusive judge of the extent of its own powers, and that when it went beyond the powers actually granted, its assumptions were unauthoritative and its acts invalid. They then went on to declare that certain statutes recently passed by Congress were void, and asked the other States to join in this pronouncement and to co-operate in securing the repeal of the statutes.

In 1808 the legislatures of some of the New England States passed resolutions condemning the embargo which the National government had laid upon shipping by an Act of that year. The State judges, emboldened by these resolutions, "took an attitude consistently hostile to the embargo," holding it to be unconstitutional; and the Federal courts in New England "seldom succeeded in finding juries which would convict even for the most flagrant violation of its provisions." In 1812 the governors of Massachusetts and Connecticut refused to allow the State militia to leave their State in pursuance to a requisition made by the President under the authority of an Act of Congress, alleging the requisition to be unconstitutional. In 1828-30 Georgia refused to obey an Act of Congress regarding the Cherokee Indians, and to respect the treaties which the United States had made with this tribe and the Creeks. The Georgian legislature passed and enforced Acts in contempt of Federal authority, and disregarded the orders of the Supreme court, President Jackson, who had an old frontiersman's hatred to the Indians, declining to interfere.

Finally, in 1832, South Carolina, first in a State convention and then by her legislature, amplified while professing to repeat the claim of the Kentucky resolutions of 1798, declared the tariff imposed by Congress to be null and void as regarded herself, and proceeded to prepare for secession and war. In none of these cases was the dispute fought out either in the courts or in the field; and the questions as to the right of a State to resist Federal authority, and as to the means whereby she could be coerced, were left over for future settlement. Settled they finally were by the Civil War of 1861-65, since which time the following doctrines may be deemed established:—

No State has a right to declare an act of the Federal government invalid.

No State has a right to secede from the Union.

The only authority competent to decide finally on the constitutionality of an act of Congress or of the national executive is the Federal judiciary.

Any act of a State legislature or State executive conflicting with the Constitution, or with an act of the National government done under the Constitution, is really an act not of the State government, which cannot legally act against the Constitution, but of persons falsely assuming to act as such government, and is therefore *ipso jure* void. Those who disobey Federal authority on the ground of the commands of a State authority are therefore insurgents against the Union who must be coerced by its power. The coercion of such insurgents is directed not against the State but against them as individual though combined wrongdoers. A State cannot secede and cannot rebel. Similarly, it cannot be coerced.

This view of the matter, which seems on the whole to be that taken by the Supreme court in the cases that arose after the Civil War, disposes of the difficulty which President Buchanan felt (see his message of 3d December 1860) as to the coercion of a State by the Union. He argued that because the Constitution did not provide for such coercion, a proposal in the Convention of 1787 to authorize it having been ultimately dropped, it was legally impossible. The best answer to this contention is that such a provision would have been superfluous, because a State cannot legally act against the Constitution. All that is needed is the power, unquestionably contained in the Constitution (Art. iii. § 3), to subdue and punish individuals guilty of treason against the Union.

Except in the cases which have been already specified, the National government has no right whatever of interfering either with a State as a commonwealth or with the individual citizens thereof, and may be lawfully resisted should it attempt to do so.

"What then?" the European reader may ask. "Is the National government without the power and the duty of correcting the social and political evils which it may find to exist in a particular State, and which a vast majority of the nation may condemn. Suppose widespread brigandage to exist in one of the States, endangering life and property. Suppose contracts to be habitually broken, and no redress to be obtainable in the State courts. Suppose the police to be in league with the assassins. Suppose the most mischievous laws to be enacted, laws, for instance, which recognize polygamy, leave homicide unpunished, drive away capital by imposing upon it an intolerable load of taxation. Is the nation obliged to stand by with folded arms while it sees a meritorious minority oppressed, the prosperity of the State ruined, a pernicious example set to other States? Is it to be debarred from using its supreme authority to rectify these mischiefs?"

The answer is, Yes. Unless the legislation or administration of such a State transgresses some provision of the Federal Constitution (such as that forbidding *ex post facto* laws, or laws impairing the obligation of a contract), the National government not only ought not to interfere but cannot interfere. The State must go its own way, with whatever injury to private rights and common interests its folly or perversity may cause.

Such a case is not imaginary. In the Slave States before the war, although the negroes were not generally ill treated, many shocking laws were passed, and society was going from bad to worse. In parts of a few of the western, and especially of the south-western States at this moment, the roads and even the railways are infested by robbers, justice is uncertain and may be unattainable when popular sentiment does not support the law. Homicide often goes unpunished by the courts, though sometimes punished by Judge Lynch. So, too, in a few of these States statutes opposed to sound principles of legislation have been passed, and have brought manifold evils in their train. But the Federal government looks on unperturbed, with no remorse for neglected duty.

The obvious explanation of this phenomenon is that the large measure of independence left to the States under the Federal system makes it necessary to tolerate their misdoings in some directions. As a distinguished authority observes, "The Federal Constitution provided for the protection of contracts, and against those oppressions most likely to result from popular passion and demoralization ; and if it had been proposed to go further and give to the Federal authority a power to intervene in still more extreme cases, the answer would probably have been that such cases were far less likely to arise than was the Federal power to intervene improperly under the pressure of party passion or policy, if its intervention were permitted. To have authorized such intervention would have been to run counter to the whole spirit of the Constitution, which kept steadily in view as the wisest policy local government for local affairs, general government for general affairs only. Evils would unquestionably arise. But the Philadelphia Convention believed that they would be kept at a minimum and most quickly cured by strict adherence to this policy. The scope for Federal interference was considerably enlarged after the Civil War, but the general division of authority between the States and the nation was not disturbed."

So far from lamenting as a fault, though an unavoidable fault, of their Federal system, the State independence I have

described, the Americans are inclined to praise it as a merit.
They argue, not merely that the best way on the whole is to
leave a State to itself, but that this is the only way in which a
permanent cure of its diseases will be effected. They are consistent not only in their Federal principles but in their democratic principles. " As *laissez aller*," they say, " is the necessary
course in a Federal government, so it is the right course in all
free governments. Law will never be strong or respected unless
it has the sentiment of the people behind it. If the people of a
State make bad laws, they will suffer for it. They will be the
first to suffer. Let them suffer. Suffering, and nothing else,
will implant that sense of responsibility which is the first step to
reform. Therefore let them stew in their own juice : let them
make their bed and lie upon it. If they drive capital away,
there will be less work for the artisans : if they do not enforce
contracts, trade will decline, and the evil will work out its
remedy sooner or later. Perhaps it will be later rather than
sooner : if so, the experience will be all the more conclusive. Is
it said that the minority of wise and peaceable citizens may
suffer ? Let them exert themselves to bring their fellows round
to a better mind. Reason and experience will be on their side.
We cannot be democrats by halves ; and where self-government
is given. the majority of the community must rule. Its rule will
in the end be better than that of any external power." No
doctrine more completely pervades the American people, the
instructed as well as the uninstructed. Philosophers will tell
you that it is the method by which Nature governs, in whose
economy error is followed by pain and suffering, whose laws
carry their own sanction with them. Divines will tell you that
it is the method by which God governs : God is a righteous
Judge and God is provoked every day, yet He makes His sun to
rise on the evil and the good, and sends His rain upon the just
and the unjust. He does not directly intervene to punish faults,
but leaves sin to bring its own appointed penalty. Statesmen
will point to the troubles which followed the attempt to govern
the reconquered seceding States, first by military force and then
by keeping a great part of their population disfranchised, and
will declare that such evils as still exist in the South are far less
grave than those which the denial of ordinary self-government
involved. " So," they pursue, " Texas and California will in
time unlearn their bad habits and come out right if we leave

them alone : Federal interference, even had we the machinery needed for prosecuting it, would check the natural process by which the better elements in these raw communities are purging away the maladies of youth, and reaching the settled health of manhood."

A European may say that there is a dangerous side to this application of democratic faith in local majorities and in *laissez aller*.   Doubtless there is : yet those who have learnt to know the Americans will answer that no nation so well understands its own business.

CHAPTER 7

Merits of the Federal System

I DO not propose to discuss in this chapter the advantages of Federalism in general, for to do this we should have to wander off to other times and countries, to talk of Achaia and the Hanseatic League and the Swiss Confederation. I shall comment on those merits only which the experience of the American Union illustrates.

There are two distinct lines of argument by which their Federal system was recommended to the framers of the Constitution, and upon which it is still held forth for imitation to other countries. These lines have been so generally confounded that it is well to present them in a precise form.

The first set of arguments point to Federalism proper, and are the following :—

1. That Federalism furnishes the means of uniting commonwealths into one nation under one national government without extinguishing their separate administrations, legislatures, and local patriotisms. As the Americans of 1787 would probably have preferred complete State independence to the fusion of their States into a unified government, Federalism was the only resource. So when the new Germanic Empire, which is really a Federation, was established in 1870, Bavaria and Wurtemberg could not have been brought under a national government save by a Federal scheme. Similar suggestions, as every one knows, have been made for re-settling the relations of Ireland to Great Britain, and of the self-governing British colonies to the United Kingdom. There are causes and conditions which dispose nations living under a loosely compacted government, or under a number of almost independent governments, to form a closer union in a Federal form. There are other causes and conditions which dispose the subjects of one government, or sections of these subjects,

to desire to make their governmental union less close by substituting a system of a Federal character. In both sets of cases, the centripetal or centrifugal forces spring from the local position, the history, the sentiments, the economic needs of those among whom the problem arises ; and that which is good for one people or political body is not necessarily good for another. Federalism may be an equally legitimate resource where it is adopted for the sake of tightening or of loosening a pre-existing bond.

2. That Federalism supplies the best means of developing a new and vast country. It permits an expansion whose extent, and whose rate and manner of progress, cannot be foreseen to proceed with more variety of methods, more adaptation of laws and administration to the circumstances of each part of the territory, and altogether in a more truly natural and spontaneous way, than can be expected under a centralized government, which is disposed to apply its settled system through all its dominions. Thus the special needs of a new region are met by the inhabitants in the way they find best : its special evils are cured by special remedies, perhaps more drastic than an old country demands, perhaps more lax than an old country would tolerate ; while at the same time the spirit of self-reliance among those who build up these new communities is stimulated and respected.

3. That it prevents the rise of a despotic central government, absorbing other powers, and menacing the private liberties of the citizen. This may now seem to have been an idle fear, so far as America was concerned. It was, however, a very real fear among the great-grandfathers of the present Americans, and nearly led to the rejection even of so undespotic an instrument as the Federal Constitution of 1789. Congress (or the President, as the case may be) is still sometimes described as a tyrant by the party which does not control it, simply because it is a central government : and the States are represented as bulwarks against its encroachments.

The second set of arguments relate to and recommend not so much Federalism as local self-government. I state them briefly because they are familiar.

4. Self-government stimulates the interest of people in the affairs of their neighbourhood, sustains local political life, educates the citizen in his daily round of civic duty, teaches him that perpetual vigilance and the sacrifice of his own time and labour are

to desire to make their governmental union less close by substituting a system of a Federal character.   In both sets of cases,
the centripetal or centrifugal forces spring from the local position, the history, the sentiments, the economic needs of those
among whom the problem arises ; and that which is good for one
people or political body is not necessarily good for another.
Federalism may be an equally legitimate resource where it is
adopted for the sake of tightening or of loosening a pre-existing
bond.

2. That Federalism supplies the best means of developing a
new and vast country.   It permits an expansion whose extent,
and whose rate and manner of progress, cannot be foreseen to
proceed with more variety of methods, more adaptation of laws
and administration to the circumstances of each part of the territory, and altogether in a more truly natural and spontaneous way,
than can be expected under a centralized government, which is
disposed to apply its settled system through all its dominions.
Thus the special needs of a new region are met by the inhabitants in the way they find best : its special evils are cured by
special remedies, perhaps more drastic than an old country
demands, perhaps more lax than an old country would tolerate ;
while at the same time the spirit of self-reliance among those who
build up these new communities is stimulated and respected.

3. That it prevents the rise of a despotic central government,
absorbing other powers, and menacing the private liberties of the
citizen.   This may now seem to have been an idle fear, so far as
America was concerned.   It was, however, a very real fear among
the great-grandfathers of the present Americans, and nearly led
to the rejection even of so undespotic an instrument as the
Federal Constitution of 1789.   Congress (or the President, as
the case may be) is still sometimes described as a tyrant by the
party which does not control it, simply because it is a central
government : and the States are represented as bulwarks against
its encroachments.

The second set of arguments relate to and recommend not so
much Federalism as local self-government.   I state them briefly
because they are familiar.

4. Self-government stimulates the interest of people in the
affairs of their neighbourhood, sustains local political life, educates
the citizen in his daily round of civic duty, teaches him that perpetual vigilance and the sacrifice of his own time and labour are

tion and administration which could not be safely tried in a large centralized country. A comparatively small commonwealth like an American State easily makes and unmakes its laws; mistakes are not serious, for they are soon corrected; other States profit by the experience of a law or a method which has worked well or ill in the State that has tried it.

7. Federalism, if it diminishes the collective force of a nation, diminishes also the risks to which its size and the diversities of its parts expose it. A nation so divided is like a ship built with water-tight compartments. When a leak is sprung in one compartment, the cargo stowed there may be damaged, but the other compartments remain dry and keep the ship afloat. So if social discord or an economic crisis has produced disorders or foolish legislation in one member of the Federal body, the mischief may stop at the State frontier instead of spreading through and tainting the nation at large.

8. Federalism, by creating many local legislatures with wide powers, relieves the national legislature of a part of that large mass of functions which might otherwise prove too heavy for it. Thus business is more promptly despatched, and the great central council of the nation has time to deliberate on those questions which most nearly touch the whole country.

All of these arguments recommending Federalism have proved valid in American experience.

To create a nation while preserving the States was the main reason for the grant of powers which the National government received; an all-sufficient reason, and one which holds good to day. The several States have changed greatly since 1789, but they are still commonwealths whose wide authority and jurisdiction practical men are agreed in desiring to maintain.

Not much was said in the Convention of 1787 regarding the best methods of extending government over the unsettled territories lying beyond the Alleghany mountains. It was, however, assumed that they would develop as the older colonies had developed, and in point of fact each district, when it became sufficiently populous, was formed into a self-governing State, the less populous divisions still remaining in the status of semi-self-governing Territories. Although many blunders have been committed in the process of development, especially in the reckless contraction of debt and the wasteful disposal of the public lands, greater evils might have resulted had the creation of local institutions and the control of new communities been left to the Central government. Congress would have been not less improvident than the State governments, for it would have been even less closely watched. The opportunities for jobbery would have been irresistible, the growth of order and civilization probably slower. It deserves to be noticed that, in granting self-government to all those of her colonies whose population is of English race, England has practically adopted the same plan as the United States have done with their western territory. The results have been generally satisfactory, although England, like America, has found that her colonists are disposed to treat the aboriginal inhabitants, whose lands they covet and whose persons they hate, with a harshness and injustice which the mother country would gladly check.

The arguments which set forth the advantages of local self-government were far more applicable to the States of 1787 than to those of 1887. Virginia, then the largest State, had only half a million free inhabitants, less than the present population of Chicago or Liverpool. Massachusetts had 450,000, Pennsylvania 400,000, New York 300,000 ; while Georgia, Rhode Island, and Delaware had (even counting slaves) less than 200,000 between them. These were communities to which the expression "local self-government" might be applied, for, although the population was scattered, the numbers were small enough for the citizens to have a personal knowledge of their leading men, and a personal interest (especially as a large proportion were landowners) in the economy and prudence with which common affairs were managed. Now, however, when of the forty-two States twenty-two have more than a million inhabitants, and four have more than three millions, the newer States, being, moreover, larger in area than most of the older ones, the stake of each citizen is relatively smaller, and generally too small to sustain his activity in politics, and the party chiefs of the State are known to him only by the newspapers or by their occasional visits on a stumping tour.

All that can be claimed for the Federal system under this head of the argument is that it provides the machinery for a better control of the taxes raised and expended in a given region of the country, and a better oversight of the public works undertaken there than would be possible were everything left to the Central government. As regards the educative effect of numerous and frequent elections, a European observer is apt to think that elections in America are too many and come too frequently. Overtaxing the attention of the citizen and frittering away his interest, they leave him at the mercy of knots of selfish adventurers.

The utility of the State system in localizing disorders or discontents, and the opportunities it affords for trying easily and safely experiments which ought to be tried in legislation and administration, constitute benefits to be set off against the risk that evils may continue in a district, may work injustice to a minority and invite imitation by other States, which the wholesome stringency of the Central government might have suppressed. Europeans are startled by the audacity with which Americans apply the doctrine of *laissez aller;* Americans declare that their method is not only the most consistent but in the end the most curative.

A more unqualified approval may be given to the division of legislative powers. The existence of the State legislatures relieves Congress of a burden too heavy for its shoulders ; for although it has far less foreign policy to discuss than the Parliaments of England, France, or Italy, and although the separation of the executive from the legislative department gives it less responsibility for the ordinary conduct of the administration than devolves on those Chambers, it could not possibly, were its competence as large as theirs, deal with the multiform and increasing demands of the different parts of the Union. There is great diversity in the material conditions of different parts of the country, and at present the people, particularly in the West, are eager to have their difficulties handled, their economic and social needs satisfied, by the State and the law. Having only a limited field of legislation left to it, Congress may be thought to enjoy better opportunities than the overtasked English Parliament of cultivating that field well. Nevertheless its public legislation is scanty, and its private legislation careless and wasteful.

These merits of the Federal system of government which I have enumerated are the counterpart and consequences of limitation of the central authority. They are, if one may reverse the French phrase, the qualities of Federalism's defects. The problem which all federalized nations have to solve is how to secure an efficient central government and preserve national unity, while allowing free scope for the diversities, and free play to the authorities, of the members of the federation. It is, to adopt that favourite astronomical metaphor which no American panegyrist of the Constitution omits, to keep the centrifugal and centripetal forces in equilibrium, so that neither the planet States shall fly off into space, nor the sun of the Central government draw them into its consuming fires. The characteristic merit of the American Constitution lies in the method by which it has solved this problem. It has given the National government a direct authority over all citizens, irrespective of the State governments, and has therefore been able safely to leave wide powers in the hands of those governments. And by placing the Constitution above both the National and the State governments, it has referred the arbitrament of disputes between them to an independent body, charged with the interpretation of the Constitution, a body which is to be deemed not so much a third authority in the government as the living voice of the Constitution, the unfolder of the mind of the people whose will stands expressed in that supreme instrument.

The application of these two principles, unknown to, or at any rate little used by, any previous federation, has contributed more than anything else to the stability of the American system, and to the reverence which its citizens feel for it, a reverence which is the best security for its permanence. Yet even these devices would not have succeeded but for the presence of a mass of moral and material influences stronger than any political devices, which have maintained the equilibrium of centrifugal and centripetal forces. On the one hand there has been the love of local independence and self-government; on the other, the sense of community in blood, in language, in habits and ideas, a common pride in the national history and the national flag.

Quid leges sine moribus? The student of institutions, as well as the lawyer, is apt to overrate the effect of mechanical contrivances in politics. I admit that in America they have had one excellent result; they have formed a legal habit in the mind of the nation. But the true value of a political contrivance resides not in its ingenuity but in its adaptation to the temper and circumstances of the people for whom it is designed, in its power of using, fostering, and giving a legal form to those forces of sentiment and interest which it finds in being. So it has been with the American system. Just as the passions which the question of slavery evoked strained the Federal fabric, disclosing unforeseen weaknesses, so the love of the Union, the sense of the material and social benefits involved in its preservation, appeared in unexpected strength, and manned with zealous defenders the ramparts of the sovereign Constitution. It is this need of determining the suitability of the machinery for the workmen and its probable influence upon them, as well as the capacity of the workmen for using and their willingness to use the machinery, which makes it so difficult to predict the operation of a political contrivance, or, when it has succeeded in one country, to advise its imitation in another. The growing strength of the national government in the United States is largely due to sentimental forces that were weak a century ago, and to a development of internal communications which was then undreamt of. And the devices which we admire in the Constitution might prove unworkable among a people less patriotic and self-reliant, less law-loving and law-abiding, than are the English of America.

Part 2

THE STATE GOVERNMENTS

CHAPTER 1

Nature of the American State

FROM the study of the National Government, we may go on to examine that of the several States which make up the Union. This is the part of the American political system which has received least attention both from foreign and from native writers. Finding in the Federal president, cabinet, and Congress a government superficially resembling those of their own countries, and seeing the Federal authority alone active in international relations, Europeans have forgotten and practically ignored the State Governments to which their own experience supplies few parallels, and on whose workings the intelligence published on their side of the ocean seldom throws light. Even the European traveller who makes the six or seven days' run across the American continent, from New York *via* Philadelphia and Chicago to San Francisco, though he passes in this journey of 2100 miles over the territories of eleven self-governing commonwealths, hardly notices the fact. He uses one coinage and one post-office; he is stopped by no custom-houses; he sees no officials in a state livery; he thinks no more of the difference of jurisdictions than the passenger from London to Liverpool does of the counties traversed by the line of the North-Western Railway. So, too, our best informed English writers on the science of politics, while discussing copiously the relation of the American States to the central authority, have failed to draw on the fund of instruction which lies in the study of State Governments themselves. Mill in his *Representative Government* scarcely refers to them. Mr. Freeman in his learned essays, Sir H. Maine in his ingenious book on Popular Government, pass by phenomena which would have admirably illustrated some of their reasonings.

American publicists, on the other hand, have been too much absorbed in the study of the Federal system to bestow much thought on the State governments. The latter seem to them the most simple and obvious things in the world, while the former, which has been the battle-ground of their political parties for a century, excites the keenest interest, and is indeed regarded as a sort of mystery, on which all the resources of their metaphysical subtlety and legal knowledge may well be expended. Thus while the dogmas of State sovereignty and State rights, made practical by the great struggle over slavery, have been discussed with extraordinary zeal and acumen by three generations of men, the character power and working of the States as separate self-governing bodies have received little attention or illustration. Yet they are full of interest; and he who would understand the changes that have passed on the American democracy will find far more instruction in a study of the State governments than of the Federal Constitution. The materials for this study are unfortunately, at least to a European, either inaccessible or unmanageable. They consist of constitutions, statutes, the records of the debates and proceedings of constitutional conventions and legislatures, the reports of officials and commissioners, together with that continuous transcript and picture of current public opinion which the files of newspapers supply. Of these sources only one, the constitutions, is practically available to a person writing on this side the Atlantic. To be able to use the rest one must go to the State and devote one's self there to these original authorities, correcting them, where possible, by the recollections of living men. It might have been expected that in most of the States, or at least of the older States, persons would have been found to write political, and not merely antiquarian or genealogical, State histories, describing the political career of their respective communities, and discussing the questions on which political contests have turned. But this has been done in comparatively few instances, so that the European inquirer finds a scanty measure of the assistance which he would naturally have expected from previous labourers in this field. I call it a field: it is rather a primeval forest, where the vegetation is rank, and through which scarcely a trail has yet been cut. The new historical school which is growing up at the leading American universities, and has already done excellent work on the earlier history of the Eastern States, will doubtless ultimately grapple with this task; in the meantime, the difficulties I have stated must be my excuse for treating this branch of my subject with a brevity out of proportion to its real interest and importance. It is better to endeavour to bring into relief a few leading features, little understood in Europe, than to attempt a detailed account which would run to inordinate length.

The American State is a peculiar organism, unlike anything in modern Europe, or in the ancient world. The only parallel is to be found in the cantons of Switzerland, the Switzerland of our own day, for until 1815, if one ought not rather to say until 1848, Switzerland was not so much a nation or a state as a league of neighbour commonwealths. But Europe, and particularly England, so persistently ignores the history of Switzerland, that most instructive patent museum of politics, apparently only because she is a small country, and because people go there to see lakes and to climb mountains, that I should perplex instead of enlightening the reader by attempting to illustrate American from Swiss phenomena.

Let me attempt to sketch the American States as separate political entities, forgetting for the moment that they are also parts of a Federation.

There are forty-two States in the American Union, varying in size from Texas, with an area of 265,780 square miles, to Rhode Island, with an area of 1250 square miles; and in population from New York, with 5,082,871 inhabitants, to Nevada, with 62,266. That is to say, the largest State is much larger than either France or the Germanic Empire; the most populous much more populous than Sweden, or Portugal, or Denmark, while the smallest is smaller than Warwickshire or Corsica, and the least populous less populous than the parish of Clerkenwell in London (69,076), or the town of Greenock in Scotland (65,-884). Considering not only these differences of size, but the differences in the density of population (which in Nevada is .6, and in Oregon 1.8 to the square mile, while in Rhode Island it is 254.9 and in Massachusetts 221.8 to the square mile); in its character (in South Carolina the blacks are 604,332 against 391,105 whites, in Mississippi 650,291 against 479,398 whites); in its birthplace (in North Carolina the foreign-born persons are less than $\frac{1}{360}$ of the population, in California more than $\frac{1}{3}$); in the occupations of the people, in the amount of accumulated wealth, in the proportion of educated persons to the rest of the community,—it is plain that immense differences might be looked for between the aspects of politics and conduct of government in one State and in another.

Be it also remembered that the older colonies had different historical origins. Virginia and North Carolina were unlike Massachusetts and Connecticut; New York, Pennsylvania, and Maryland different from both; while in recent times the stream of European immigration has filled some States with Irishmen, others with Germans, others with Scandinavians, and has left most of the Southern States wholly untouched.

Nevertheless, the form of government is in its main outlines, and to a large extent even in its actual working, the same in all these forty-two republics, and the differences, instructive as they are, relate to points of secondary consequence.

The States fall naturally into five groups :—

The New England States—Massachusetts, Connecticut, Rhode Island, New Hampshire, Vermont, Maine.

The Middle States—New York, New Jersey, Pennsylvania, Delaware, Maryland, Ohio, Indiana.

The Southern, or old Slave States—Virginia, West Virginia (separated from Virginia during the war), North Carolina, South Carolina, Georgia, Alabama, Florida, Kentucky, Tennessee, Mississippi, Louisiana, Arkansas, Missouri, Texas.

The North-Western States—Michigan, Illinois, Wisconsin, Minnesota, Iowa, Nebraska, Kansas, Colorado, N. Dakota, S. Dakota, Montana.

The Pacific States—California, Nevada, Oregon, Washington.

Each of these groups has something distinctive in the character of its inhabitants, which is reflected, though more faintly now than formerly, in the character of its government and politics.

New England is the old home of Puritanism, the traces whereof, though waning under the influence of Irish and French Canadian immigration, are by no means yet extinct. The Southern States will long retain the imprint of slavery, not merely in the presence of a host of negroes, but in the degradation of the poor white population, and in certain attributes, laudable as well as regrettable, of the ruling class. The North-West is the land of hopefulness, and consequently of bold experiments in legislation : its rural inhabitants have the honesty and the narrow-mindedness of agriculturists. The Pacific West, or rather California and Nevada, for Oregon belongs in political character to the Upper Mississippi or North-western group, tinges the energy and sanguine good nature of the Westerns with a speculative recklessness natural to mining communities, where great fortunes have rapidly grown and vanished, and into which elements have been suddenly swept together from every part of the world, as a Rocky Mountain rainstorm fills the bottom of a valley with sand and pebbles from all the surrounding heights.

As the dissimilarity of population and of external conditions seems to make for a diversity of constitutional and political arrangements between the States, so also does the large measure of legal independence which each of them enjoys under the Federal Constitution. No State can, as a commonwealth, politically deal with or act upon any other State. No diplomatic relations can exist nor treaties be made between States, no coercion can be exercised by one upon another. And although the government of the Union can act on a State, it rarely does act, and then only in certain strictly limited directions, which do not touch the inner political life of the commonwealth.

Let us pass on to consider the circumstances which work for uniformity among the States, and work more powerfully as time goes on.

He who looks at a map of the Union will be struck by the fact that so many of the boundary lines of the States are straight lines. Those lines tell the same tale as the geometrical plans of cities like St. Petersburg or Washington, where every street runs at the same angle to every other. The States are not natural growths. Their boundaries are for the most part not natural boundaries fixed by mountain ranges, nor even historical boundaries due to a series of events, but purely artificial boundaries, determined by an authority which carved the national territory into strips of convenient size, as a building company lays out its suburban lots. Of the States subsequent to the original thirteen, California is the only one with a genuine natural boundary, finding it in the chain of the Sierra Nevada on the east and the Pacific ocean on the west. No one of these later States can be regarded as a naturally developed political organism. They are trees planted by the forester, not self-sown with the help of the seed-scattering wind. This absence of physical lines of demarcation has tended and must tend to prevent the growth of local distinctions. Nature herself seems to have designed the Mississippi basin, as she has designed the unbroken levels of Russia, to be the dwelling-place of one people.

Each State makes its own Constitution; that is, the people agree on their form of government for themselves, with no interference from the other States or from the Union. This form is subject to one condition only: it must be republican. But in each State the people who make the constitution have lately come from other States, where they have lived under and worked constitutions which are to their eyes the natural and almost necessary model for their new State to follow; and in the absence of an inventive spirit among the citizens, it was the obvious course for the newer States to copy the organizations of the older States, especially as these agreed with certain familiar features of the Federal Constitution. Hence the outlines, and even the phrases of the elder constitutions reappear in those of the more recently formed States. The precedents set by Virginia, for instance, had much influence on Tennessee, Alabama, Mississippi, and Florida, when they were engaged in making or amending their constitutions during the early part of this century.

Nowhere is population in such constant movement as in America. In some of the newer States only one-fourth or one-fifth of the inhabitants are natives of the United States. Many of the townsfolk, not a few even of the farmers, have been till lately citizens of some other State, and will, perhaps, soon move on farther west. These Western States are like a chain of lakes through which there flows a stream which mingles the waters of the higher with those of the lower. In such a constant flux of population local peculiarities are not readily developed, or if they have grown up when the district was still isolated, they disappear as the country becomes filled. Each State takes from its neighbours and gives to its neighbours, so that the process of assimilation is always going on over the whole wide area.

Still more important is the influence of railway communication, of newspapers, of the telegraph. A Greek city like Samos or Mitylene, holding her own island, preserved a distinctive character in spite of commercial intercourse and the sway of Athens. A Swiss canton like Uri or Appenzell, entrenched behind its mountain ramparts, remains, even now under the strengthened central government of the Swiss nation, unlike its neighbours of the lower country. But an American State traversed by great trunk lines of railway, and depending on the markets of the Atlantic cities and of Europe for the sale of its grain, cattle, bacon, and minerals, is attached by a hundred always tightening ties to other States, and touched by their weal or woe as nearly as by what befalls within its own limits. The leading newspapers are read over a vast area. The inhabitants of each State know every morning the events of yesterday over the whole Union.

Finally the political parties are the same in all the States. The tenets (if any) of each party are the same everywhere, their methods the same, their leaders the same, although of course a prominent man enjoys especial influence in his own State. Hence, State politics are largely swayed by forces and motives external to the particular State, and common to the whole country, or to great sections of it; and the growth of local parties, the emergence of local issues and development of local political schemes, are correspondingly restrained.

These considerations explain why the States, notwithstanding the original diversities between some of them, and the wide scope for political divergence which they all enjoy under the Federal Constitution, are so much less dissimilar and less peculiar than might have been expected. European statesmen have of late years been accustomed to think of federalism and local autonomy as convenient methods either for recognizing and giving free scope to the sentiment of nationality which may exist in any part of an empire, or for meeting the need for local institutions and distinct legislation which may arise from differences between such a part and the rest of the empire. It is one or other or both of these reasons that have moved statesmen in such cases as those of Finland in her relations to Russia, Hungary in her relations to German-Austria, Iceland in her relations to Denmark, Bulgaria in her relations to the Turkish Sultan, Ireland in her relations to the United Kingdom. But the final causes, so to speak, of the recognition of the States of the American Union as autonomous commonwealths, have been different. Their self-government is not the consequence of differences which can be made harmless to the whole body politic only by being allowed free course. It has been due primarily to the historical fact that they existed as commonwealths before the Union came into being; secondarily, to the belief that localized government is the best guarantee for civic freedom, and to a sense of the difficulty of administering a vast territory and population from one centre and by one government.

I return to indicate the points in which the legal independence and right of self-government of the several States appears. Each of the thirty-eight has its own—

Constitution (whereof more anon).

Executive, consisting of a governor, and various other officials.

Legislature of two Houses.

System of local government in counties, cities, townships, and school districts.

System of State and local taxation.

Debts, which it may (and sometimes does) repudiate at its own pleasure.

Body of private law, including the whole law of real and personal property, of contracts, of torts, and of family relations.

Courts, from which no appeal lies (except in cases touching Federal legislation or the Federal constitution) to any Federal court.

System of procedure, civil and criminal.

Citizenship, which may admit persons (*e.g.* recent immigrants) to be citizens at times, or on conditions, wholly different from those prescribed by other States.

Three points deserve to be noted as illustrating what these attributes include.

I. A man gains active citizenship of the United States (*i.e.* a share in the government of the Union) only by becoming a citizen of some particular State. Being such citizen, he is forthwith entitled to the national franchise. That is to say, voting power in the State carries voting power in Federal elections, and however lax a State may be in its grant of such power, *e.g.* to foreigners just landed or to persons convicted of crime, these State voters will have the right of voting in congressional and presidential elections.[1] The only restriction on the States in this matter is that of the fourteenth and fifteenth

---

[1] Congress has power to pass a uniform rule of naturalization (Const. Art. i. § 8).

Under the present naturalization laws a foreigner must have resided in the United States for five years, and for one year in the State or Territory where he seeks admission to United States citizenship, and must declare two years before he is admitted that he renounces allegiance to any foreign prince or state. Naturalization makes him a citizen not only of the United States, but of the State or Territory where he is admitted, but does not necessarily confer the electoral franchise, for that depends on State laws.

In more than a third of the States the electoral franchise is now enjoyed by persons not naturalized as United States citizens.

Constitutional amendments, which have already been discussed. They were intended to secure equal treatment to the negroes, and incidentally they declare the protection given to all citizens of the United States. Whether they really enlarge it, that is to say, whether it did not exist by implication before, is a legal question, which I need not discuss.

II. The power of a State over all communities within its limits is absolute. It may grant or refuse local government as it pleases. The population of the city of Providence is more than one-third of that of the State of Rhode Island, the population of New York city more than one-fifth that of the State of New York. But the State might in either case extinguish the municipality, and govern the city by a single State commissioner appointed for the purpose, or leave it without any government whatever. The city would have no right of complaint to the Federal President or Congress against such a measure. Massachusetts has lately remodelled the city government of Boston just as the British Parliament might remodel that of Birmingham. Let an Englishman imagine a county council for Warwickshire suppressing the municipality of Birmingham, or a Frenchman imagine the department of the Rhone extinguishing the municipality of Lyons, with no possibility of intervention by the central authority, and he will measure the difference between the American States and the local governments of Western Europe.

III. A State commands the allegiance of its citizens, and may punish them for treason against it. The power has rarely been exercised, but its undoubted legal existence had much to do with inducing the citizens of the Southern States to follow their governments into secession in 1861. They conceived themselves to owe allegiance to the State as well as to the Union, and when it became impossible to preserve both, because the State had declared its secession from the Union, they might hold the earlier and nearer authority to be paramount. Allegiance to the State must now, since the war, be taken to be subordinate to allegiance to the Union. But allegiance to the State still exists; treason against the State is still possible. One cannot think of treason against Warwickshire or the department of the Rhone.

These are illustrations of the doctrine which Europeans often fail to grasp, that the American States were originally in a certain sense, and still for certain purposes remain, sovereign States. Each of the original thirteen became sovereign when it revolted from the mother country in 1776. By entering the Confederation of 1781-88 it parted with one or two of the attributes of sovereignty, by accepting the Federal Constitution in 1788 it subjected itself for certain specified purposes to a central government, but claimed to retain its sovereignty for all other purposes. That is to say, the authority of a State is an inherent, not a delegated, authority. It has all the powers which any independent government can have, except such as it can be affirmatively shown to have stripped itself of, while the Federal Government has only such powers as it can be affirmatively shown to have received. To use the legal expression, the presumption is always for a State, and the burden of proof lies upon any one who denies its authority in a particular matter.

What State sovereignty means and includes is a question which incessantly engaged the most active legal and political minds of the nation, from 1789 down to 1870. Some thought it paramount to the rights of the Union. Some considered it as held in suspense by the Constitution, but capable of reviving as soon as a State should desire to separate from the Union. Some maintained that each State had in accepting the Constitution finally renounced its sovereignty, which thereafter existed only in the sense of such an undefined domestic legislative and administrative authority as had not been conferred upon Congress. The conflict of these views, which became acute in 1830 when South Carolina claimed the right of nullification, produced Secession and the war of 1861-65. Since the defeat of the Secessionists, the last of these views may be deemed to have been established, and the term "State sovereignty" is now but seldom heard. Even "States rights" have a different meaning from that which they had thirty years ago.

A European who now looks calmly back on this tremendous controversy of tongue, pen, and sword, will be apt to express his ideas of it in the following way. He will remark that much of the obscurity and perplexity arose from confounding the sovereignty of the American nation with the sovereignty of the Federal Government. The Federal Government clearly was sovereign only for certain purposes, *i.e.* only in so far as it had received specified powers from the Constitution. These powers did not, and in a strict legal construction do not now, abrogate the supremacy of the States. A State still possesses one important attribute of sovereignty—immunity from being sued except by another State. But the American nation which had made the Constitution, had done so in respect of its own sovereignty, and might well be deemed to retain that sovereignty as paramount to any rights of the States. The feeling of this ultimate supremacy of the nation was what swayed the minds of those who resisted Secession, just as the equally well-grounded persuasion of the limited character of the central Federal Government satisfied the conscience of the seceding South.

The Constitution of 1789 was a compromise, and a compromise arrived at by allowing contradictory propositions to be represented as both true. It has been compared to the declarations made with so much energy and precision of language in the ancient hymn *Quicunque Vult*, where, however, the apparent contradiction has always been held to seem a contradiction only because the human intellect is unequal to the comprehension of such profound mysteries. To every one who urged that there were thirteen States, and therefore thirteen governments, it was answered, and truly, that there was one government, because the people were one. To every one who declared that there was one government, it was answered with no less truth that there were thirteen. Thus counsel was darkened by words without knowledge ; the question went off into metaphysics, and found no end, in wandering mazes lost.

There was, in fact, a divergence between the technical and the practical aspects of the question. Technically, the seceding States had an arguable case ; and if the point had been one to be decided on the construction of the Constitution as a court decides on the construction of a commercial contract, they were possibly entitled to judgment. Practically, the defenders of the Union stood on firmer ground, because circumstances had changed since 1789 so as to make the nation more completely one nation than it then was, and had so involved the fortunes of the majority which held to the Union with those of the minority seeking to depart that the majority might feel justified in forbidding their departure. Stripped of legal technicalities, the dispute resolved itself into the problem often proposed but capable of no general solution : When is a majority entitled to use force for the sake of retaining a minority in the same political body with itself ? To this question, when it appears in a concrete shape, as to the similar question when an insurrection is justifiable, an answer can seldom be given beforehand. The result decides. When treason prospers, none dare call it treason.

The Constitution, which had rendered many services to the American people, did them an inevitable dis-service when it fixed their minds on the legal aspects of the question. Law was meant to be the servant of politics, and must not be suffered to become the master. A case had arisen which its formulæ were unfit to deal with, a case which had to be settled on large moral and historical grounds. It was not merely the superior physical force of the North that prevailed ; it was the moral forces which rule the world, forces which had long worked against slavery, and were ordained to save North America from the curse of hostile nations established side by side.

The word "sovereignty," which has in many ways clouded the domain of public law and jurisprudence, confused men's minds by making them assume that there must in every country exist, and be discoverable by legal inquiry, either one body invested legally with supreme power over all minor bodies, or several bodies which, though they had consented to form part of a larger body, were each in the last resort independent of it, and responsible to none but themselves. They forgot that a Constitution may not have determined where legal supremacy shall dwell. Where the Constitution of the United States placed it was at any rate doubtful, so doubtful that it would have been better to drop technicalities, and recognize the broad fact that the legal claims of the States had become incompatible with the historical as well as legal claims of the nation. In the uncertainty as to where legal right resided, it would have been prudent to consider where physical force resided. The South however thought herself able to resist any physical force which the rest of the nation might bring against her. Thus encouraged, she took her stand on the doctrine of States Rights : and then followed a pouring out of blood and treasure such as was never spent on determining a point of law before, not even when Edward III. and his successors waged war for a hundred years to establish the claim of females to inherit the crown of France.

What, then, do the rights of a State now include ? Every right or power of a Government except :—

The right of secession (not abrogated in terms, but admitted since the war to be no longer claimable. It is expressly negatived in the recent Constitutions of several Southern States).

Powers which the Constitution withholds from the States (including that of intercourse with foreign governments).

Powers which the Constitution expressly confers on the Federal Government.

As respects some powers of the last class, however, the States may act concurrently with, or in default of action by, the Federal Government. It is only from contravention of its action that they must abstain. And where contravention is alleged to exist, whether legislative or executive, it is by a court of law, and, in case the decision is in the first instance favourable to the pretensions of the State, ultimately by a Federal court, that the question falls to be decided.

A reference to the preceding list of what each State may create in the way of distinct institutions will show that these rights practically cover nearly all the ordinary relations of citizens to one another and to their Government.   An American may, through a long life, never be reminded of the Federal Government, except when he votes at presidential and congressional elections, lodges a complaint against the post-office, and opens his trunks for a custom-house officer on the pier at New York when he returns from a tour in Europe.   His direct taxes are paid to officials acting under State laws.   The State, or a local authority constituted by State statutes, registers his birth, appoints his guardian, pays for his schooling, gives him a share in the estate of his father deceased, licenses him when he enters a trade (if it be one needing a licence), marries him, divorces him, entertains civil actions against him, declares him a bankrupt, hangs him for murder.   The police that guard his house, the local boards which look after the poor, control highways, impose water rates, manage schools—all these derive their legal powers from his State alone. Looking at this immense compass of State functions, Jefferson would seem to have been not far wrong when he said that the Federal government was nothing more than the American department of foreign affairs.   But although the National government touches the direct interests of the citizen less than does the State government, it touches his sentiment more.   Hence the strength of his attachment to the former and his interest in it must not be measured by the frequency of his dealings with it.

In the partitionment of governmental functions between nation and State, the State gets the most but the nation the highest, so the balance between the two is preserved.

Thus every American citizen lives in a duality of which Europeans, always excepting the Swiss, and to some extent the Germans, have no experience. He lives under two governments and two sets of laws; he is animated by two patriotisms and owes two allegiances. That these should both be strong and rarely be in conflict is must fortunate. It is the result of skilful adjustment and long habit, of the fact that those whose votes control the two sets of governments are the same persons, but above all of that harmony of each set of institutions with the other set, a harmony due to the identity of the principles whereon both are founded, which makes each appear necessary to the stability of the other, the States to the nation as its basis, the National Government to the States as their protector.

Chapter 2

State Constitutions

THE government of each of the thirty-eight States is determined by and set forth in its Constitution, a comprehensive fundamental law, or rather group of laws included in one instrument, which has been directly enacted by the people of the State, and is capable of being repealed or altered, not by their representatives, but by themselves alone. As the Constitution of the United States stands above Congress and out of its reach, so the Constitution of each State stands above the legislature of that State, cannot be varied in any particular by Acts of the State legislature, and involves the invalidity of any statute passed by the legislature which a court of law may find to be inconsistent with it.

The State Constitutions are the oldest things in the political history of America, for they are the continuations and representatives of the royal colonial charters, whereby the earliest English settlements in America were created, and under which their several local governments were established, subject to the authority of the English Crown and ultimately of the British Parliament. But, like most of the institutions under which English-speaking peoples now live, they have a pedigree which goes back to a time anterior to the discovery of America itself. It begins with the English Trade Guild of the middle ages, itself the child of still more ancient corporations, dating back to the days of imperial Rome, and formed under her imperishable law. Charters were granted to merchant guilds in England as far back as the days of King Henry I. Edward IV. gave an elaborate one to the Merchant Adventurers trading with Flanders in 1463. In it we may already discern the arrangements which are more fully set forth in two later charters of greater historical interest, the charter of Queen Elizabeth to the East India Company in 1599, and the charter of Charles I. to the "Governor and Company of the Mattachusetts Bay in Newe-England" in 1628. Both these instruments establish and incorporate trading companies, with power to implead and be impleaded, to use a common seal, to possess and acquire lands tenements and hereditaments, with provisions for the making of ordinances for the welfare of the company. The Massachusetts Charter creates a frame of government consisting of a governor, deputy-governor, and eighteen assistants (the term still in use in many of the London city guilds), and directs them to hold four times a year a general meeting of the company, to be called the "greate and generall Court," in which general court "the Governor or deputie Governor, and such of the assistants and Freemen of the Company as shall be present, shall have full power and authority to choose other persons to be free of the Company, and to elect and constitute such officers as they shall thinke fitt for managing the affaires of the saide Governor and Company, and to make Lawes and Ordinances for the Good and Welfare of the saide Company, and for the Government and Ordering of the saide Landes and Plantasion, and the People inhabiting and to inhabite the same, soe as such Lawes and Ordinances be not contrary or repugnant to the Lawes and Statuts of this our realme of England." In 1691, the charter of 1628 having been declared forfeited in 1684, a new one was granted by King William and Queen Mary, and this instrument, while it retains much of the language and some of the character of the trade guild charter, is really a political frame of government for a colony. The assistants receive the additional title of councillors; their number is raised to twenty-eight; they are to be chosen by the general court, and the general court itself is to consist, together with the governor and assistants, of freeholders elected by towns or places within the colony, the electors being persons with a forty shilling freehold or other property worth £40. The governor is directed to appoint judges, commissioners of oyer and terminer, etc.; the general court receives power to establish judicatories and courts of record, to pass laws (being not repugnant to the laws of England), and to provide for all necessary civil offices. An appeal from the courts shall always be to the King in his privy council. This is a true political Constitution. Under it the colony was governed, and in the main well and wisely governed, till 1780. Much of it, not merely its terms, such as the name General Court, but its solid framework, was transferred bodily to the Massachusetts Constitution of 1780, which is now in force, and which profoundly influenced the Convention that prepared the Federal Constitution in 1787. Yet the charter of 1691 is nothing but an extension and development of the trading charter of 1628, in which there already appears, as there had appeared in Edward IV.'s charter of 1463, and in the East India Company's charter of 1599, the provision that the power of law-giving, otherwise unlimited, should be restricted by the terms of the charter itself, which required that every law for the colony should be agreeable to the laws of England. We have therefore in the three charters which I have named, those of 1463, 1599, and 1628, as well as in that of 1691, the essential and capital characteristic of a rigid or supreme Constitution—viz. a frame of government established by a superior authority, creating a subordinate law-making body, which can do everything except violate the terms and transcend the powers of the instrument to which it owes its own existence. So long as the colony remained under the British Crown, the superior authority, which could amend or remake the frame of government, was the British Crown or Parliament. When the connection with Britain was severed, that authority passed over, not to the State legislature, which remained limited, as it always had been, but to the people of the now independent commonwealth, whose will speaks through what is now the State Constitution, just as the will of the Crown or of Parliament had spoken through the charters of 1628 and 1691.

I have taken the case of Massachusetts as the best example of the way in which the trading Company grows into a colony, and the colony into a State. But some of the other colonies furnish illustrations scarcely less apposite. The oldest of them all, the acorn whence the oak of English dominion in America has sprung, the colony of Virginia, was, by the second charter, of 1609, established under the title of " The Treasurer and Company of Adventurers and Planters of the City of London for the first colony in Virginia." [1]

---

[1] The phrase First colony distinguishes what afterwards became the State of Virginia from the more northerly parts of Virginia, afterwards called New England. The Second colony was to be Plymouth, one of the two settlements which became Massachusetts.

Within the period of ten years, under the last of the Tudors and the first of the Stuarts, two trading charters were issued to two Companies of English adventurers. One of these charters is the root of English title to the East and the other to the West. One of these Companies has grown into the Empire of India; the other into the United States of North America. If England had done nothing else in history, she might trust for her fame to the work which these charters began. And the foundations of both dominions were laid in the age which was adorned by the greatest of all her creative minds, and gave birth to the men who set on a solid basis a frame of representative government which all the free nations of the modern world have copied.

When, in 1776, the thirteen colonies threw off their allegiance to King George III., and declared themselves independent States, the colonial charter naturally became the State Constitution. In most cases it was remodelled, with large alterations, by the revolting colony. But in three States it was maintained unchanged, except, of course, so far as Crown authority was concerned, viz. in Massachusetts till 1780, in Connecticut till 1818, and in Rhode Island till 1842. The other twenty-nine States admitted to the Union in addition to the original thirteen, have all entered it as organized self-governing communities, with their Constitutions already made by their respective peoples. Each Act of Congress which admits a new State admits it as a subsisting commonwealth, recognizing rather than affecting to sanction its Constitution. Congress may impose conditions which the State Constitution must fulfil. But the authority of the State Constitutions does not flow from Congress, but from acceptance by the citizens of the States for which they are made. Of these instruments, therefore, no less than of the Constitutions of the thirteen original States, we may say that although subsequent in date to the Federal Constitution, they are, so far as each State is concerned, *de jure* prior to it. Their authority over their own citizens is nowise derived from it.[1] Nor is this a mere piece of technical law. The antiquity of the older States as separate commonwealths, running back into the heroic ages of the first colonization of America and the days of the Revolutionary War, is a potent source of the local patriotism of their inhabitants, and gives these States a sense of historic growth and indwelling corporate life which they could not have possessed had they been the mere creatures of the Federal Government.

The State Constitutions of America well deserve to be com-- pared with those of the self-governing British colonies. But one remarkable difference must be noted here. The constitutions of British colonies have all proceeded from the Imperial Parliament of the United Kingdom, which retains its full legal power of legislating for every part of the British dominions. In many cases a colonial constitution provides that it may be itself altered by the colonial legislature, of course with the assent of the Crown ; but inasmuch as in its origin it is a statutory constitu- tion, not self-grown, but planted as a shoot by the Imperial Parliament at home, Parliament may always alter or abolish it. Congress, on the other hand, has no power to alter a State con- stitution. And whatever power of alteration has been granted to a British colony is exercisable by the legislature of the colony, not, as in America, by the citizens at large.

The original Constitutions of the States, whether of the old thirteen or of the newer twenty-five, have been in nearly every case subsequently recast, in some instances five, six, or even seven times, as well as amended in particular points. Thus Con- stitutions of all dates are now in force in different States, from that of Massachusetts, enacted in 1780, but largely amended since, to that of Florida enacted in 1886.[1]

Every existing Constitution is the work of the people, not of the legislature of the State. The Constitutions of the revolutionary period were in a few instances enacted by the State legislature, acting as a body with plenary powers, but more usually by the people acting through a Convention, *i.e.* a body especially chosen by the voters at large for the purpose, and invested with full powers, not only of drafting, but of adopting the instrument of government. But since 1792, when Kentucky framed her Constitution, the invariable practice has been for the Convention, elected by the voters, to submit, in accordance with the pre- cedent set by Massachusetts in 1780, the draft Constitution framed by it to the citizens of the State at large, who vote upon it Yes or No. They usually vote on t as a whole, and adopt or reject it *en bloc*, but sometimes provision s made for voting separately on some particular point or points.

The people of a State retain for ever in their hands, alto- gether independent of the National government, the power of

---

[1] The four new States are now (1889) enacting their respective constitutions, but in what follows these are not, because they could not be, referred to.

altering their Constitution. When a new Constitution is to be prepared, or the existing one amended, the initiative usually comes from the legislature, which (either by a simple majority, or by a two-thirds majority, or by a majority in two successive legislatures, as the Constitution may in each instance provide) submits the matter to the voters in one of two ways. It may either propose to the people certain specific amendments, or it may ask the people to decide by a direct popular vote on the propriety of calling a constitutional Convention to revise the whole existing Constitution. In the former case the amendments suggested by the legislature are directly voted on by the citizens ; in the latter the legislature, so soon as the citizens have voted for the holding of a convention, provides for the election by the people of this convention. When elected, the Convention meets, sets to work, goes through the old Constitution, and prepares a new one, which is then presented to the people for ratification or rejection at the polls. Only in the little State of Delaware is the function of amending the Constitution still left to the legislature without the subsequent ratification of a popular vote, subject, however, to the provision that changes must be passed by two successive legislatures, and must have been put before the people at the election of members for the second. Some States provide for the submission to the people at fixed intervals, of seven, ten, sixteen, or twenty years, of the propriety of calling a convention to revise the Constitution, so as to secure that the attention of the people shall be drawn to the question whether their scheme of government ought or ought not to be changed. Be it observed, however, that whereas the Federal Constitution can be amended only by a vote of three-fourths of the States, a Constitution can in nearly every State be changed by a bare majority of the citizens voting at the polls. Hence we may expect, and shall find, that these instruments are altered more frequently and materially than the Federal Constitution has been.

A State Constitution is not only independent of the central national government (save in certain points already specified), it is also the fundamental organic law of the State itself. The State exists as a commonwealth by virtue of its Constitution, and all State authorities, legislative, executive, and judicial, are the creatures of, and subject to, the State Constitution. Just as the President and Congress are placed beneath the Federal Constitution, so the Governor and Houses of a State are subject to its Constitution, and any act of theirs done either in contravention of its provisions, or in excess of the powers it confers on them, is absolutely void. All that has been said in preceding chapters regarding the functions of the courts of law where an Act of Congress is alleged to be inconsistent with the Federal Constitution, applies equally where a statute passed by a State legislature is alleged to transgress the Constitution of the State, and of course such validity may be contested in any court, whether a State court or a Federal court, because the question is an ordinary question of law, and is to be solved by determining whether or no a law of inferior authority is inconsistent with a law of superior authority. Whenever in any legal proceeding before any tribunal, either party relies on a State statute, and the other party alleges that this statute is *ultra vires* of the State legislature, and therefore void, the tribunal must determine the question just as it would determine whether a bye-law made by a municipal council or a railway company was in excess of the law-making power which the municipality or the company had received from the higher authority which incorporated it and gave it such legislative power as it possesses. But although Federal courts are fully competent to entertain a question arising on the construction of a State Constitution, their practice is to follow the precedents set by any decision of a court of the State in question, just as they would follow the decision of an English court in determining a point of purely English law. They hold not only that each State must be assumed to know its own law better than a stranger can, but also that the supreme court of a State is the authorized exponent of the mind of the people who enacted its Constitution.

A State Constitution is really nothing but a law made directly by the people voting at the polls upon a draft submitted to them. The people of a State when they so vote act as a primary and constituent assembly, just as if they were all summoned to meet in one place like the folkmoots of our Teutonic forefathers. It is only their numbers that prevent them from so meeting in one place, and oblige the vote to be taken at a variety of polling places. Hence the enactment of a Constitution is an exercise of direct popular sovereignty to which we find few parallels in modern Europe, though it was familiar enough to the republics of antiquity, and has lasted till now in some of the cantons of Switzerland.

The importance of this character of a State Constitution as a popularly-enacted law, overriding every minor State law, becomes all the greater when the contents of these Constitutions are examined. Europeans conceive of a constitution as an instrument, usually a short instrument, which creates a frame of government, defines its departments and powers, and declares the "primordial rights" of the subject or citizen as against the rulers. An American State Constitution does this, but does more ; and in most cases, infinitely more. It deals with a variety of topics which in Europe would be left to the ordinary action of the legislature, or of administrative authorities ; and it pursues these topics into a minute detail hardly to be looked for in a fundamental instrument. Some of these details will be mentioned presently. Meantime I will sketch in outline the frame and contents of the more recent constitutions.

A normal Constitution consists of five parts :—

I. The definition of the boundaries of the State. (This does not occur in the case of the older States.)

II. The so-called Bill of Rights—an enumeration (whereof more anon) of the citizens' primordial rights to liberty of person and security of property. This usually stands at the beginning of the Constitution, but occasionally at the end.

III. The frame of government—*i.e.* the names functions and powers of the executive officers, the legislative bodies, and the courts of justice. This occupies several articles.

IV. Miscellaneous provisions relating to administration and law, including articles treating of schools, of the militia, of taxation and revenue, of the public debts, of local government, of State prisons and hospitals, of agriculture, of labour, of impeachment, and of the method of amending the Constitution, besides other matters, to be mentioned presently, still less political in their character. The order in which these occur differs in different instruments, and there are some in which some of the above topics are not mentioned at all. The more recent Constitutions and those of the newer States are much fuller on these points.

V. The Schedule, which contains provisions relating to the method of submitting the Constitution to the vote of the people, and arrangements for the transition from the previous Constitution to the new one which is to be enacted by that vote. Being of a temporary nature, the schedule is not strictly a part of the Constitution.

The Bill of Rights is historically the most interesting part of these Constitutions, for it is the legitimate child and representative of Magna Charta, and of those other declarations and enactments, down to the Bill of Rights of the Act of 1 William and Mary, session 2, by which the liberties of Englishmen have been secured. Most of the thirteen colonies when they asserted their independence and framed their Constitutions inserted a declaration of the fundamental rights of the people, and the example then set has been followed by the newer States, and, indeed, by the States generally in their most recent Constitutions. Considering that all danger from the exercise of despotic power upon the people of the States by the executive has long since vanished, their executive authorities being the creatures of popular vote and nowadays rather too weak than too strong, it may excite surprise that these assertions of the rights and immunities of the individual citizen as against the government should continue to be repeated in the instruments of to-day. A reason may be found in the remarkable constitutional conservatism of the Americans, and in their fondness for the enunciation of the general maxims of political freedom. But it is also argued that these declarations of principle have a practical value, as asserting the rights of individuals and of minorities against arbitrary conduct by a majority in the legislature, which might, in the absence of such provisions, be tempted at moments of excitement to suspend the ordinary law and arm the magistrates with excessive powers. They are therefore, it is held, still safeguards against tyranny; and they serve the purpose of solemnly reminding a State legislature and its officers of those fundamental principles which they ought never to overstep. Although such provisions certainly do restrain a State legislature in ways which the British Parliament would find inconvenient, few complaints of practical evils thence arising are heard.

A general notion of these Bills of Rights may be gathered from the Constitution of the State of California (1879). I may mention, in addition, a few curious provisions which occur in some of them.

All provide for full freedom of religious opinion and worship, and for the equality before the law of all religious denominations and their members; and many forbid the establishment of any particular church or sect, and declare that no public money ought to be applied in aid of any religious body or sectarian institution. But Delaware holds it to be "the duty of all men frequently to assemble for public worship;" and Vermont adds that "every sect or denomination of Christians ought to observe the Sabbath or Lord's Day." And thirteen States declare that the provisions for freedom of conscience are not to be taken to excuse acts of licentiousness, or justify practices inconsistent with the peace and safety of the State.[1]

Louisiana (Constitution of 1879) declares that "all government of right originates with the people, is founded on their will alone, and is instituted solely for the good of the whole, deriving its just powers from the consent of the governed. Its only legitimate end is to protect the citizen in the enjoyment of life, liberty, and property. When it assumes other functions, it is usurpation and oppression."

Twenty-six States declare that "all men have a natural, inherent, and inalienable right to enjoy and defend life and liberty;" and all of these, except the melancholy Missouri, add, the "natural right to pursue happiness."

Eighteen declare that all men have "a natural right to acquire, possess, and protect property."

Mississippi (Constitution of 1868) provides that "the right of all citizens to travel upon public conveyances shall not be infringed upon nor in any manner abridged." A similar provision occurs in the Constitution of Louisiana of 1868.[2]

Kentucky (Constitution of 1850, which is still in force) lays down "that absolute arbitrary power over the lives, liberty, and property of freemen exists nowhere in a republic, not even in the largest majority. The right of property is before and higher than any constitutional sanction; and the right of the owner of a slave to such slave and its increase is the same and as inviolable as the right of the owner of any property whatever.[3] All power is inherent in the people, and all free governments are founded on their authority, and instituted for their peace, safety, happiness, and security, and the protection of property."

[1] In Arkansas, Maryland, Mississippi, North Carolina, South Carolina, and Texas, a man is declared ineligible for office if he denies the existence of God; in Pennsylvania and Tennessee he is ineligible if he does not believe in God, and in the existence of future rewards and punishments. In Arkansas and Maryland such a person is also incompetent as a witness or juror.

[2] These provisions were inserted shortly after the Civil War in order to protect the negroes.

[3] This proposition has of course been annulled, in effect, by the latest amendments (xiii. xiv. xv.) to the Federal Constitution.

All in one form or another secure the freedom of writing and speaking opinions, and some add that the truth of a libel may be given in evidence.

Nearly all secure the freedom of public meeting and petition. Considering that these are the last rights likely to be infringed by a State government, it is odd to find Florida in her Constitution of 1886 providing that "the people shall have the right to assemble together to consult for the common good, to instruct their representatives, and to petition the legislature for redress of grievances."

Many provide that no *ex post facto* law, nor law impairing the obligation of a contract, shall be passed by the State legislature; and that private property shall not be taken by the State without just compensation.

Many forbid the creation of any title of nobility.

Many declare that the right of citizens to bear arms shall never be denied, a provision which might be expected to prove inconvenient where it was desired to check the habit of carrying revolvers. Tennessee therefore (Constitution of 1870) prudently adds that "the legislature shall have power to regulate the wearing of arms, with a view to prevent crime." So also Texas, where such a provision is certainly not superfluous. And five others[1] allow the legislature to forbid the carrying of concealed weapons.

Some declare that the estates of suicides shall descend in the ordinary course of law.

Most provide that conviction for treason shall not work corruption of blood nor forfeiture of estate.

Seven forbid white and coloured children to be taught in the same public schools.

Many declare the right of trial by jury to be inviolate, even while permitting the parties to waive it.

Some forbid imprisonment for debt, except in case of fraud, and secure the acceptance of reasonable bail, except for the gravest charges.

Several declare that "perpetuities and monopolies are contrary to the genius of a free State, and ought not to be allowed."

Some declare that aliens or foreigners shall have the same rights of holding property as citizens.

Many forbid the granting of any hereditary honours, privileges, or emoluments.

North Carolina declares that "as political rights and privileges are not dependent upon or modified by property, therefore no property qualification ought to affect the right to vote or hold office;" and also, "secret political societies are dangerous to the liberties of a free people, and should not be tolerated."

Massachusetts sets forth, as befits a Puritan State, high moral views : " A frequent recurrence to the fundamental principles of the Constitution, and a constant adherence to those of piety, justice, moderation, temperance, industry, and frugality, are absolutely necessary to preserve the advantages of liberty and to maintain a free government. The people ought consequently to have a particular attention to all those principles in the choice of their officers and representatives, and they have a right to require of their law-givers and magistrates an exact and constant observance of them."

New York (Constitution of 1846) provides : " All lands within this State are declared to be allodial, so that, subject only to the liability to escheat, the entire and absolute property is vested in the owners, according to the nature of their respective estates."

Maryland (Constitution of 1867) declares that "a long continuance in the executive departments of power or trust is dangerous to liberty ; a rotation, therefore, in those departments is one of the best securities of permanent freedom." She also pronounces all gifts for any religious purpose (except of a piece of land not exceeding five acres for a place of worship, parsonage, or burying-ground) to be void unless sanctioned by the legislature.

These instances, a few out of many, may suffice to show how remote from the common idea of a Bill of Rights, are some of the enactments which find a place under that heading. The constitution makers seem to have inserted here such doctrines or legal reforms as seemed to them matters of high import or of wide application, especially when they could find no suitable place for them elsewhere in the instrument.

To meet these difficulties some State Constitutions provide Provisions. These are of great interest as revealing the spirit and tendencies of popular government in America, the economic and social condition of the country, the mischiefs that have arisen, the remedies applied to these mischiefs, the ideas and beliefs of the people in matters of legislation.

Among such provisions we find a great deal of matter which is in no **distinctive** sense constitutional law, but general law, *e.g.* administrative law, the law of judicial procedure, the ordinary private law of family, inheritance, contract, and so forth ; matter therefore which seems out of place in a constitution because fit to be dealt with in ordinary statutes. We find minute provisions regarding the management and liabilities of banking companies, of railways, or of corporations generally ; regulations as to the salaries of officials, the quorum of courts sitting in banco, the length of time for appealing, the method of changing the venue, the publication of judicial reports ; detailed arrangements for school boards and school taxation (with rules regarding the separation of white and black children in schools), for a department of agriculture, a canal board, or a labour bureau ; we find a prohibition of lotteries, of bribery, of the granting of liquor licences, of usurious interest on money, an abolition of the distinction between sealed and unsealed instruments, a declaration of the extent of a mechanic's lien for work done. We even find the method prescribed in which stationery and coals for the use of the legislature shall be contracted for, and provisions for fixing the rates which may be charged for the storage of corn in warehouses. The framers of these more recent constitutions have in fact neither wished nor cared to draw a line of distinction between what is proper for a constitution and what ought to be left to be dealt with by the State legislature. And, in the case of three-fourths at least of the States, no such distinction now, in fact, exists.

How is this confusion to be explained ? Four reasons may be suggested.

The Americans, like the English, have no love for scientific arrangement. Although the Constitutions have been drafted by lawyers, and sometimes by the best lawyers of each State, logical classification and discrimination have not been sought after.

The people found the enactment of a new Constitution a convenient opportunity for enunciating doctrines they valued and carrying through reforms they desired. It was a simpler and quicker method than waiting for legislative action, so, when there was a popular demand for the establishment of an institution, or for some legal change, this was shovelled into the new Constitution and enacted accordingly.

The peoples of the States have come to distrust their respective legislatures. Hence they desire not only to do a thing forthwith and in their own way rather than leave it to the chance of legislative action, but to narrow as far as they conveniently can (and sometimes farther) the sphere of the legislature.

There is an unmistakable wish in the minds of the people to act directly rather than through their representatives in legislation. This sentiment is characteristic of democracies everywhere. The same conscious relish for power which leads some democracies to make their representatives mere delegates, finds a further development in passing by the representatives, and setting the people itself to make and repeal laws.

Those who have read the chapters describing the growth and expansion of the Federal Constitution, will naturally ask how far the remarks there made apply to the Constitutions of the several States.

These instruments have less capacity for development, whether by interpretation or by usage, than the Constitution of the United States : firstly, because they are more easily, and therefore more frequently, amended or recast ; secondly, because they are far longer, and go into much more minute detail. The Federal Constitution is so brief and general that custom must fill up what it has left untouched, and judicial construction evolve the application of its terms to cases they do not expressly deal with. But the later State Constitutions are so full and precise that they need little in the way of expansive construction, and leave comparatively little room for the action of custom.

The rules of interpretation are in the main the same as those applied to the Federal Constitution. One important difference must, however, be noted, springing from the different character of the two governments. The National Government is an artificial creation, with no powers except those conferred by the instrument which created it. A State Government is a natural growth, which *prima facie* possesses all the powers incident to any government whatever. Hence, if the question arises whether a State legislature can pass a law on a given subject, the presumption is that it can do so : and positive grounds must be adduced to prove that it cannot. It may be restrained by some inhibition either in the Federal Constitution, or in the Constitution of its own State. But such inhibition must be affirmatively shown to have been imposed, or, to put the same point in other words, a State Constitution is held to be, not a document conferring defined and specified powers on the legislature, but one regulating and limiting that general authority which the representatives of the people enjoy *ipso jure* by their organization into a legislative body.

"It has never been questioned that the American legislatures have the same unlimited power in regard to legislation which resides in the British Parliament, except where they are restrained by written Constitutions. That must be conceded to be a fundamental principle in the political organization of the American States. We cannot well comprehend how, upon principle, it could be otherwise. The people must, of course, possess all legislative power originally. They have committed this in the most general and unlimited manner to the several State legislatures, saving only such restrictions as are imposed by the Constitution of the United States or of the particular State in question."

"The people, in framing the Constitution, committed to the legislature the whole law-making powers of the State which they did not expressly or impliedly withhold. Plenary power in the legislature, for all purposes of civil government, is the rule. A prohibition to exercise a particular power is an exception."

It must not, however, be supposed from these dicta that even if the States were independent commonwealths, the Federal Government having disappeared, their legislatures would enjoy anything approaching the omnipotence of the British Parliament, "whose power and jurisdiction is," says Sir Edward Coke, "so transcendent and absolute that it cannot be confined, either for persons or causes, within any bounds." "All mischiefs and grievances," adds Blackstone, "operations and remedies that transcend the ordinary course of the laws are within the reach of this extraordinary tribunal." Parliament being absolutely sovereign, can command, or extinguish and swallow up the executive and the judiciary, appropriating to itself their functions. But in America, a legislature is a legislature and nothing more. The same instrument which creates it creates also the executive governor and the judges. They hold by a title as good as its own. If the legislature should pass a law depriving the governor of an executive function conferred by the Constitution, that law would be void. If the legislature attempted to interfere with the jurisdiction of the courts, their action would be even more palpably illegal and ineffectual.

The executive and legislative departments of a State government have of course the right and duty of acting in the first instance on their view of the meaning of the Constitution. But the ultimate expounder of that meaning is the judiciary; and when the courts of a State have solemnly declared the true construction of any provision of the Constitution, all persons are bound to regulate their conduct accordingly. As was observed in considering the functions of the Federal judiciary, this authority of the American courts is not in the nature of a political or discretionary power vested in them; it is a legitimate and necessary consequence of the existence of a fundamental law superior to any statute which the legislature may enact, or to any right which a governor may conceive himself to possess. To quote the words of an American decision:—

"In exercising this high authority the judges claim no judicial supremacy; they are only the administrators of the public will. If an Act of the legislature is held void, it is not because the judges have any control over the legislative power, but because the Act is forbidden by the Constitution, and because the will of the people, which is therein declared, is paramount to that of their representatives expressed in any law."

It is a well-established rule that the judges will always lean in favour of the validity of a legislative Act; that if there be a reasonable doubt as to the constitutionality of a statute they will solve that doubt in favour of the statute; that where the legislature has been left a discretion they will assume the discretion to have been wisely exercised; that where the construction of a statute is doubtful, they will adopt such construction as will harmonize with the Constitution, and enable it to take effect. So it has been well observed that a man might with perfect consistency argue as a member of a legislature against a bill on the ground that it is unconstitutional, and after having been appointed a judge, might in his judicial capacity sustain its constitutionality. Judges must not inquire into the motives of the legislature, nor refuse to apply an Act because they may suspect that it was obtained by fraud or corruption, still less because they hold it to be opposed to justice and sound policy. "But when a statute is adjudged to be unconstitutional, it is as if it had never been. Rights cannot be built up under it; contracts which depend upon it for their consideration are void; it constitutes a protection to no one who has acted under it; and no one can be punished for having refused obedience to it before the decision was made. And what is true of an Act void *in toto*, is true also as to any part of an Act which is found to be unconstitutional, and which consequently is to be regarded as having never at any time been possessed of legal force."

It may be thought, and the impression will be confirmed when we consider as well the minuteness of the State Constitutions as the profusion of State legislation and the inconsiderate haste with which it is passed, that as the risk of a conflict between the Constitution and statutes is great, so the inconveniences of a system under which the citizens cannot tell whether their obedience is or is not due to a statute must be serious. How is a man to know whether he has really acquired a right under a statute ? how is he to learn whether to conform his conduct to it or not ? How is an investor to judge if he may safely lend money which a statute has empowered a community to borrow, when the statute may be itself subsequently overthrown ?

To meet these difficulties some State Constitutions provide that the judges of the supreme court of the State may be called upon by the governor or either house of the legislature to deliver their opinions upon questions of law, without waiting for these questions to arise and be determined in an ordinary lawsuit between parties. This expedient seems a good one, for it procures a judicial and non-partisan interpretation, and procures it at once before rights or interests have been created. But it is open to the objection that the opinions so pronounced by judges are given before cases have arisen which show how in fact a statute is working, and what points it may raise ; and that in giving them the judges have not, as in contested lawsuits, the assistance of counsel arguing for their respective clients. And this is perhaps the reason why in most of the States where the provision exists, the judges have declared that they act under it in a purely advisory capacity, and that their deliverances are to be deemed merely expressions of opinion, not binding upon them should the point afterwards arise in a lawsuit involving the rights of parties.

The highest court of a State may depart from a view it has previously laid down, even in a legal proceeding, regarding the construction of the Constitution, that is to say, it has a legal right to do so if convinced that the former view was wrong. But it is reluctant to do so, because such a course unsettles the law and impairs the respect felt for the bench. And there is less occasion for it to do so than in the parallel case of the supreme Federal court, because as the process of amending a State Constitution is simpler and speedier than that of altering the Federal Constitution, a remedy can be more easily applied to any mistake which the State judiciary has committed. This unwillingness to unsettle the law goes so far that State courts have sometimes refused to disturb a practice long acquiesced in by the legislature, which they have nevertheless declared they would have pronounced unconstitutional had it come before them while still new.

CHAPTER 3

State Legislators

THE similarity of the frame of government in the thirty-eight republics which make up the United States, a similarity which appears the more remarkable when we remember that each of the republics is independent and self-determined as respects its frame of government, is due to the common source whence the governments flow. They are all copies, some immediate, some mediate, of ancient English institutions, viz. chartered self-governing corporations, which, under the influence of English habits, and with the precedent of the English parliamentary system before their eyes, developed into governments resembling that of England in the eighteenth century. Each of the thirteen colonies had up to 1776 been regulated by a charter from the British Crown, which, according to the best and oldest of all English traditions, allowed it the practical management of its own affairs. The charter contained a sort of skeleton constitution, which usage had clothed with nerves, muscles, and sinews, till it became a complete and symmetrical working system of free government. There was in each a governor, in two colonies chosen by the people,[1] in the rest nominated by the Crown; there was a legislature; there were executive officers acting under the governor's commission and judges nominated by him; there were local self-governing communities. In none, however, did there exist what we call cabinet government, *i.e.* the rule of the legislature through a committee of its own members, coupled with the irresponsibility of the permanent nominal head of the executive. This separation of the executive from the legislature, which naturally arose from the fact that the governor was an officer directly responsible to another power than the colonial legislature, viz. the British Crown, his own master to whom he stood or fell, distinguishes the old colonial governments of North America from those of the British colonies of the present day, in all of which cabinet government prevails. The latter are copies of the present Constitution of England; the former resembled it as it existed in the seventeenth and beginning of the eighteenth century before cabinet government had grown up.

When the thirteen colonies became sovereign States at the Revolution, they preserved this frame of government, substituting a governor chosen by the State for one appointed by the Crown. As the new States admitted to the Union after 1789 successively formed their constitutions prior to their admission to the Union, each adopted the same scheme, its people imitating, as was natural, the older commonwealths whence they came, and whose working they understood and admired. They were the more inclined to do so because they found in the older constitutions that sharp separation of the executive, legislative, and judicial powers which the political philosophy of those days taught them to regard as essential to a free government, and they all take this separation as their point of departure.

I have observed in an earlier chapter that the influence on the framers of the Federal Constitution of the examples of free government which they found in their several States, had been profound. We may sketch out a sort of genealogy of Governments as follows :—

First. The English incorporated Company, a self-governing body, with its governor, deputy-governor, and assistants chosen by the freemen of the company, and meeting in what is called the General Court or Assembly.

Next. The Colonial Government, which out of this Company evolves a governor or executive head and a legislature, consisting of representatives chosen by the citizens and meeting in one or two chambers.

Thirdly. The State Government, which is nothing but the colonial government developed and somewhat democratized, with a governor chosen originally by the legislature, now always by the people at large, and now in all cases with a legislature of two chambers. From the original thirteen States this form has spread over the Union and prevails in every State.

Lastly. The Federal Government, modelled after the State Governments, with its President chosen, through electors, by the people, its two-chambered legislature, its judges named by the President.

Out of such small beginnings have great things grown.

It would be endless to describe the minor differences in the systems of the thirty-eight States. I will sketch the outlines only, which, as already observed, are in the main the same everywhere.

Every State has—

An executive elective head, the governor.

A number of other administrative officers.

A legislature of two houses.

A system of courts of justice.

Various subordinate local self-governing communities, counties, cities, townships, villages, school districts.

The governor and the other chief officials are not now chosen by the legislature, as was the case under most of the older State Constitutions, but by the people. They are as far as possible disjoined from the legislature. Neither the governor nor any other State official can sit in a State legislature. He cannot lead it. It cannot, except of course by passing statutes, restrain him. There can therefore be no question of any government by ministers who link the executive to the legislature according to the system of the free countries of modern Europe and of the British colonies.

Of these several powers it is best to begin by describing the legislature, because it is by far the strongest and most prominent.

An American State legislature always consists of two houses, the smaller called the Senate, the larger usually called the House of Representatives, though in six States it is entitled "The Assembly," and in three "The House of Delegates." The origin of this very interesting feature is to be sought rather in history than in theory. It is due partly to the fact that in some colonies there had existed a small governor's council in addition to the popular representative body, partly to a natural disposition to imitate the mother country with its Lords and Commons, a disposition which manifested itself both in colonial days and when the revolting States were giving themselves new Constitutions, for up to 1776 some of the colonies had gone on with a legislature of one house only. Now, however, the need for two chambers has become an axiom of political science, being based on the belief that the innate tendency of an assembly to become hasty, tyrannical, and corrupt, needs to be checked by the coexistence of another house of equal authority. The Americans restrain their legislatures by dividing them, just as the Romans restrained their executive by substituting two consuls for one king. The only States that ever tried to do with a single house were Pennsylvania, Georgia, and Vermont, all of whom gave it up : the first after four years' experience, the second after twelve years, the last after fifty years. It is with these trifling exceptions the *quod semper, quod ubique, quod ab omnibus* of American constitutional doctrine.

Both houses are chosen by popular vote, generally in equal electoral districts, and by the same voters, although in a few States there are minor variations as to modes of choice.

The following differences between the rules governing the two Houses are general :—

1. The senatorial electoral districts are always larger, usually twice or thrice as large as the House districts, and the number of senators is, of course, in the same proportion smaller than that of representatives.

2. A senator is usually chosen for a longer term than a representative. In twenty-four States he sits for four years, in one (New Jersey) for three, in eleven for two, in two (Massachusetts and Rhode Island) for one year only.

3. In most cases the Senate, instead of being elected all at once like the House, is only partially renewed, half its members going out when their two or four years have been completed, and a new half coming in. This gives it a sense of continuity which the House wants.

4. In some States the age at which a man is eligible for the Senate is fixed higher than that for the House of Representatives ; and in one (Delaware) he must own freehold land of 200 acres or real or personal estate of the value of £1000. Other restrictions on eligibility, such as the exclusion of clergymen (which still exists in six States, and is of old standing), that of salaried public officials (which exists everywhere), that of United States officials and members of Congress, and that of persons not resident in the electoral district (frequent by law and practically universal by custom), apply to both Houses. In some States this last restriction goes so far that a member who ceases to reside in the district for which he was elected loses his seat *ipso facto*.

The strength of this local feeling regarding congressional elections and the results it produces must to a European eye seem most

unfortunate.   It is certainly no weaker in State elections.   Nobody
dreams of offering himself as a candidate for a place in which he
does not reside, even in new States, where it might be thought
that there had not been time for local feeling to spring up.
Hence the educated and leisured residents of the greater cities
have no chance of entering the State legislature except for the
city district wherein they dwell ; and as these city districts are
those most likely to be in the hands of some noxious and selfish
ring of professional politicians, the prospect for such an aspirant
is a dark one.   Some of these State legislatures sadly need reform in
their methods and their tone.   Nothing more contributes to make reform difficult than the inveterate habit of choosing residents only as
members.   Suppose an able and public-spirited man desiring to enter the Assembly or the Senate of his State and shame the offenders
who are degrading or plundering it. He may be wholly unable to find
a seat, because in his place of residence the party opposed to his
own may hold a permanent majority, and he will not be even
considered elsewhere.   Suppose a group of earnest men who,
knowing how little one man can effect, desire to enter the legislature at the same time and work together.   Such a group can
hardly arise except in or near a great city.   It cannot effect an
entrance, because the city has at best very few seats to be seized,
and the city men cannot offer themselves in any other part of the
State.   That the restriction often rests on custom, not on law,
makes the case more serious.   A law can be repealed, but custom
has to be unlearned ; the one may be done in a moment of happy
impulse, the other needs the teaching of long experience applied
to receptive minds.

The fact is, that the Americans have ignored in all their
legislative as in many of their administrative arrangements, the
differences of capacity between man and man.   They underrate
the difficulties of government and overrate the capacities of the
man of common sense.   Great are the blessings of equality ; but
what follies are committed in its name !

The unfortunate results of this local sentiment have been
aggravated by the tendency to narrow the election areas, allot-
ting one senator or representative to each district.   Under the
older Constitution of Connecticut, for instance, the twelve senators were elected out of the whole State by a popular vote.
Now (Amdts. of A.D. 1828) the twenty-four senators are chosen
by districts, and the Senate is to-day an inferior body, because

then the best men of the whole State might be chosen, now it is possible only to get the leading men of the districts. In Massachusetts, under the Constitution of 1780, the senators were chosen by districts, but a district might return as many as six senators: the Assembly men were chosen by towns, each corporate town having at least one representative, and more in proportion to its population, the proportion being at the rate of one additional member for every 275 ratable polls. In 1836 the scale of population to representatives was raised, and a plan prescribed (too complicated to be here set forth) under which towns below the population entitling them to one representative, should have a representative during a certain number of years out of every ten years, the census being taken decennially. Thus a small town might send a member to the Assembly for five years out of every ten, choosing alternate years, or the first five, or the last five, as it pleased. Now, however (Amdts. of A.D. 1857), the State has been divided into forty Senatorial districts, each of which returns one senator only, and into 175 Assembly districts, returning, one, two, or, in a few cases, three representatives each. The composition of the legislature has declined ever since this change was made. The area of choice being smaller, inferior men are chosen ; and in the case of the Assembly districts which return one member, but are composed of several small towns, the practice has grown up of giving each town its turn, so that not even the leading man of the district, but the leading man of the particular small community whose turn has come round, is chosen to sit in the Assembly.

Universal manhood suffrage, subject to certain disqualifications in respect of crime (including bribery) and of the receipt of poor law relief, which prevail in many States—in eight States no pauper can vote—is the rule in nearly all the States. A property qualification was formerly required in many, but now exists only in Rhode Island, where the possession of real estate valued at $134, or the payment of a tax of at least $1 is required from all citizens not natives of the United States. Four other States (Delaware, Massachusetts, Pennsylvania, and Tennessee) require the voter to have paid some State or county tax (Massachusetts and Tennessee call it a poll tax) ; but if he does not pay it, his party usually pay it for him, so the restriction is of little practical importance. Massachusetts also requires that he shall be able to read the State Constitution in English, and to write his name (Amdt. of 1857), Connecticut, that he shall be able to read any section of the Constitution or of the statutes, and shall sustain a good moral character (Amdts. of 1855 and 1845). So far as I have been able to ascertain, this educational test is of little practical consequence. In Massachusetts it does not seem to be generally enforced, perhaps because the party managers on both sides agree not to trouble voters about it. Of course certain terms of residence within the United States, in the particular State, and in the voting districts, are also prescribed : these vary greatly from State to State, but are usually short.

The suffrage is generally the same for other purposes as for that of elections to the legislature, and is in every State confined to male inhabitants. In a few States, however, women are permitted to vote at school district and in one at municipal elections, and in these no distinction is made between married and unmarried women ; nor has it been attempted, in the various constitutional amendments framed to give political suffrage to women, but hitherto always rejected by the people, to draw such a distinction, which would indeed be abhorrent to the genius of American law.

It is important to remember that, by the Constitution of the United States, the right of suffrage in Federal or national elections (*i. e.* for presidential electors and members of Congress) is in each State that which the State confers on those who vote at the election of its more numerous House. Thus there might exist great differences between one State and another in the free bestowal of the Federal franchise. That such differences are at present insignificant is due, partly to the prevalence of democratic theories of equality over the whole Union, partly to the provision of the fourteenth amendment to the Federal Constitution, which reduces the representation of a State in the Federal House of Representatives, and therewith also its weight in a presidential election, in proportion to the number of adult male citizens disqualified in that State. As a State desires to have its full weight in national politics, it has a strong motive for the widest possible enlargement of its Federal franchise, and this implies a corresponding width in its domestic franchise.

The number of members of the legislature varies greatly from State to State. Delaware, with nine senators, has the smallest Senate, Illinois, with fifty-one, the largest. Delaware has also the smallest House of Representatives, consisting of twenty-one members ; while New Hampshire, a very small State, has the largest with 321. The New York houses number 32 and 128 respectively, those of Pennsylvania 50 and 201, those of Massachusetts 40 and 240. In the Western and Southern States the number of representatives rarely exceeds 120.

As there is a reason for everything in the world, if one could but find it out, so for this difference between the old New England States and those newer States which in many other points have followed their precedents. In the New England States local feeling was and is intensely strong, and every little town wanted to have its member. In the West and South, local divisions have had less natural life; in fact, they are artificial divisions rather than genuine communities that arose spontaneously. Hence the same reason did not exist in the West and South for having a large Assembly; while the distrust of representatives, the desire to have as few of them as possible and pay them as little as possible, have been specially strong motives in the West and South, as also in New York and Pennsylvania, and have caused a restriction of numbers.

In all States the members of both Houses receive salaries, which in some cases are fixed at an annual sum of from $150 (Maine) to $1500 (New York), the average being $500 (£100). More frequently, however, they are calculated at so much for every day during which the session lasts, varying from $1 (in Rhode Island) to $8 (in California and Nevada) per day (4s. 2d. to £1:13:4), besides a small allowance, called mileage, for travelling expenses. These sums, although unremunerative to a man who leaves a prosperous profession or business to attend in the State capital, are an object of such desire to many of the representatives of the people, that the latter have thought it prudent to restrict the length of the legislative sessions, which now stand generally limited to a fixed number of days, varying from forty days in Georgia, Nebraska, and Oregon, to 150 days in Pennsylvania. The States which pay by the day are also those which limit the session. Some States secure themselves against prolonged sessions by providing that the daily pay shall diminish, or shall absolutely cease and determine, at the expiry of a certain number of days, hoping thereby to expedite business and check inordinate zeal for legislation.

It was formerly usual for the legislature to meet annually, but the experience of bad legislation and over legislation has led to fewer as well as shorter sittings; and sessions are now biennial in all States but six: viz. Massachusetts, Connecticut, Rhode Island, New York, New Jersey, South Carolina, all of them old States. In these the sessions are annual, save in that odd little nook Rhode Island, which still convokes her legislature every May at Newport, and afterwards holds an adjourned session at Providence, the other chief city of the commonwealth. There is, however, in nearly all States a power reserved to the governor to summon the Houses in extraordinary session should a pressing occasion arise, but the provisions for daily pay do not usually apply to these extra sessions.

Bills may originate in either House, save that in nineteen States money bills must originate in the House of Representatives, a rule for which, in the present condition of things, when both Houses are equally directly representative of the people and chosen by the same electors, no sufficient ground appears. It is a curious instance of the wish which animated the framers of the first Constitutions of the original thirteen States to reproduce the details of the English Constitution that had been deemed bulwarks of liberty. The newer States borrowed it from their elder sisters, and the existence of a similar provision in the Federal Constitution has no doubt helped to perpetuate it in all the States. But there is a reason for it in Congress, the Federal Senate not being directly representative of equal numbers of citizens, which is not found in the State legislatures: it is in these last a mere survival of no present functional value. Money bills may, however, be amended or rejected by the State Senates like any other bills, just as the Federal Senate amends money bills brought up from the House.

In one point a State Senate enjoys a special power, obviously modelled on that of the English House of Lords and the Federal Senate. It sits as a court under oath for the trial of State officials impeached by the House. Like the Federal Senate, it has in many States the power of confirming or rejecting appointments to office made by the governor. When it considers these it is said to "go into executive Session." The power is an important one in those States which allow the governor to nominate the higher judges. In other respects the powers and procedure of the two Houses of a State legislature are identical; except that, whereas the lieutenant-governor of a State is generally *ex officio* president of the Senate, with a casting vote therein, the House always chooses its own Speaker. The legal quorum is usually fixed, by the Constitution, at a majority of the whole number of members elected, though a smaller number may adjourn and compel the attendance of absent members. Both Houses do most of their work by committees, much after the fashion of Congress, and the committees are in both usually chosen by the Speaker (in the Senate by the President, though it is often provided that the House (or Senate) may on motion vary their composition. Both Houses sit with open doors, but in most States the Constitution empowers them to exclude strangers when the business requires secrecy.

The State governor has of course no right to dissolve the legislature, nor even to adjourn it unless the Houses, while agreeing to adjourn, disagree as to the date. Such control as the legislature can exercise over the State officers by way of inquiry into their conduct is generally exercised by committees, and it is in committees that the form of bills is usually settled and their fate decided, just as in the Federal Congress. The proceedings are rarely reported. Sometimes when a committee takes evidence on an important question reporters are present, and the proceedings more resemble a public meeting than a legislative session. It need scarcely be added that neither House separately, nor both Houses acting together, can control an executive officer otherwise than either by passing a statute prescribing a certain course of action for him, which if it be in excess of their powers will be held unconstitutional and void, or by withholding the appropriations necessary to enable him to carry out the course of action he proposes to adopt. The latter method, where applicable, is the more effective, because it can be used by a bare majority of either House, whereas a bill passed by both Houses may be vetoed by the governor, a point so important as to need a few words.

Four States, three of them original States, vest legislative authority in the legislature alone. These are Rhode Island, Delaware, North Carolina, and Ohio. All the rest require a bill to be submitted to the governor, and permit him to return it to the legislature with his objections. If he so returns it, it can only be again passed " over the veto " by something more than a bare majority. To so pass a bill over the veto there is required—

In two States a majority of three-fifths in each House.

In twenty-three States a majority of two-thirds in each House.

In nine States a majority in each House of all the members elected to that House.

Here, therefore, as in the Federal Constitution, we find a useful safeguard against the unwisdom or misconduct of a legislature, and a method provided for escaping, in extreme cases, from those deadlocks which the system of checks and balances tends to occasion.

I have adverted in a preceding chapter to the restrictions imposed on the legislatures of the States by their respective Constitutions. These restrictions, which are numerous, elaborate, and instructive, take two forms—

I. Exclusions of a subject from legislative competence, *i.e.* prohibitions to the legislature to pass any law on certain enumerated subjects. The most important classes of prohibited statutes are—

Statutes inconsistent with democratic principles, as, for example, granting titles of nobility, favouring one religious denomination, creating a property qualification for suffrage or office.

Statutes against public policy, *e.g.* tolerating lotteries, impairing the obligation of contracts, incorporating or permitting the incorporation of banks, or the holding by a State of bank stock.

Statutes special or local in their application, a very large and increasing category, the fulness and minuteness of which in many Constitutions show that the mischiefs arising from improvident or corrupt special legislation must have become alarming. The list of prohibited subjects in the Constitution of Missouri of 1875 is the most complete I have found.

Statutes increasing the State debt beyond a certain limited amount, or permitting a local authority to increase its debt beyond a prescribed amount, the amount being usually fixed in proportion to the valuation of taxable property within the area administered by the local authority.

II. Restrictions on the procedure of the legislature, *i.e.* directions as to the particular forms to be observed and times to be allowed in passing bills, sometimes all bills, sometimes bills of a certain specified nature. Among these restrictions will be found provisions—

As to the majorities necessary to pass certain bills. Sometimes a majority of the whole number of members elected to each House is required, or a majority exceeding a bare majority.

As to the method of taking the votes, *e.g.* by calling over the roll and recording the vote of each member.

As to allowing certain intervals to elapse between each reading of a measure, and for preventing the hurried passage of bills at the end of the session.

As to including in a bill only one subject, and expressing that subject in the title of the bill.

Against re-enacting, or amending, or incorporating, any former Act by reference to its title merely, without setting out its contents.[1]

The two latter classes of provisions might be found wholesome in England, where much of the difficulty complained of by the judges in construing the law arises from the modern habit of incorporating parts of former statutes, and dealing with them by reference.

Where statutes have been passed by a legislature upon a prohibited subject, or where the prescribed forms have been transgressed or omitted, the statute will be held void so far as inconsistent with the Constitution.

Even these multiform restrictions on the State legislatures have not been found sufficient. Bitted and bridled as they are by the Constitutions, they contrive, as will appear in a later chapter, to do plenty of mischief in the direction of private or special legislation.

Although State legislatures have of course no concern whatever with foreign affairs, this is not deemed a reason for abstaining from passing resolutions on that subject. The passion for resolutions is strong everywhere in America, and an expression of sympathy with an oppressed foreign nationality, or of displeasure at any unfriendly behaviour of a foreign power, is not only an obvious way of relieving the feelings of the legislators, but often an electioneering device, which appeals to some section of the State voters. Accordingly such resolutions are common, and, though of course quite irregular, quite innocuous.

Debates in these bodies are seldom well reported, and sometimes not reported at all. One result is that the conduct of members escapes the scrutiny of their constituents ; a better one that speeches are generally short and practical, the motive for rhetorical displays being absent. If a man does not make a reputation for oratory, he may for quick good sense and business habits. However, so much of the real work is done in committees that talent for intrigue or "management" usually counts for more than debating power.

Part 3

THE PARTY SYSTEM

CHAPTER 1

Political Parties and Their History

IN the preceding chapters I have endeavoured to describe the legal framework of American government as it exists both in the nation and in the States. Beginning from the Federal and State Constitutions we have seen what sort of a structure has been erected upon them as a foundation, what methods of legislation and administration have been developed, what results these methods have produced. It is only occasionally and incidentally that we have had to consider the influence upon political bodies and methods of those extra-legal groupings of men which we call political parties. But the spirit and force of party has in America been as essential to the action of the machinery of government as steam is to a locomotive engine; or, to vary the simile, party association and organization are to the organs of government almost what the motor nerves are to the muscles, sinews, and bones of the human body. They transmit the motive power, they determine the directions in which the organs act. A description of them is therefore a necessary complement to an account of the Constitution and government; for it is into the hands of the parties that the working of the government has fallen. Their ingenuity, stimulated by incessant rivalry, has turned many provisions of the Constitution to unforeseen uses, and given to the legal institutions of the country no small part of their present colour.

To describe the party system is, however, much harder than it has been to describe those legal institutions. Hitherto we have been on comparatively firm ground, for we have had definite data to rely upon, and the facts set forth have been mostly patent facts which can be established from books and documents. But now we come to phenomena for a knowledge of which one must trust to a variety of flying and floating sources, to newspaper paragraphs, to the conversation of American acquaintances, to impressions formed on the spot from seeing incidents and hearing stories and anecdotes, the authority for which, though it seemed sufficient at the time, cannot always be remembered. Nor have I the advantage of being able to cite any previous treatise on the subject; for though the books and articles dealing with the public life of the United States may be counted by hundreds, I know of no author who has set himself to describe impartially the actual daily working of that part of the vast and intricate political machine which lies outside the Constitution, nor, what are more important still, the influences which sway the men by whom this machine has been constructed and is daily manipulated. The task, however, cannot be declined; for it is that very part of my undertaking which, even though imperfectly performed, may be most serviceable to the student of modern politics. A philosopher in Germany, who had mastered all the treatises on the British Constitution, perused every statute of recent years, and even followed through the newspapers the debates in Parliament, would know far less about the government and politics of England than he might learn by spending a month there conversing with practical politicians, and watching the daily changes of sentiment during a parliamentary crisis or a general election.

So, too, in the United States, the actual working of party government is not only full of interest and instruction, but is so unlike what a student of the Federal Constitution could have expected or foreseen, that it is the thing of all others which any one writing about America ought to try to portray. In the knowledge of a stranger there must, of course, be serious gaps. I am sensible of the gaps in my own. But since no native American has yet essayed the task of describing the party system of his country, it is better that a stranger should address himself to it, than that the inquiring European should have no means of satisfying his curiosity. And a native American writer, even if he steered clear of partisanship, which I think he might, for in no country does one find a larger number of philosophically judicial observers of politics, would suffer from his own familiarity with many of those very things which a stranger finds perplexing. Describe English politics to an intelligent foreigner and you will find his questions directed to the points which you have passed over, because obvious to yourself, while they may probably suggest to you new aspects which it has never occurred to you to consider. Thus European and perhaps even American readers may find in the sort of perspective which a stranger gets of transatlantic phenomena some compensation for his necessarily inferior knowledge of details.

In America the great moving forces are the parties. The government counts for less than in Europe, the parties count for more ; and the fewer have become their principles and the fainter their interest in those principles, the more perfect has become their organization. The less of nature the more of art ; the less spontaneity the more mechanism. But before I attempt to describe this organization, something must be said of the doctrines which the parties respectively profess, and the explanation of the doctrines involves a few preliminary words upon the history of party in America.

Although the early colonists carried with them across the sea some of the habits of English political life, and others may have been subsequently imitated from the old country, the parties of the United States are pure home growths, developed by the circumstances of the nation. The English reader who attempts, as Englishmen are apt to do, to identify the great American parties with his own familiar Whigs and Tories, or even to discover a general similarity between them, had better give up the attempt, for it will lead him hopelessly astray. Here and there we find points of analogy rather than of resemblance, but the moment we try to follow out the analogy it breaks down, so different are the issues on which English and American politics have turned.

In the United States, the history of party begins with the Constitutional Convention of 1787 at Philadelphia. In its debates and discussions on the drafting of the Constitution there were revealed two opposite tendencies, which soon afterwards appeared on a larger scale in the State Conventions, to which the new instrument was submitted for acceptance. These were the centrifugal and centripetal tendencies—a tendency to maintain both the freedom of the individual citizen and the independence in legislation, in administration, in jurisdiction, indeed in everything except foreign policy and national defence, of the several States ; an opposite tendency to subordinate the States to the nation and vest large powers in the central Federal authority.

The charge against the Constitution that it endangered State rights evoked so much alarm that some States were induced to ratify only by the promise that certain amendments should be added, which were accordingly accepted in the course of the next three years. When the machinery had been set in motion by the choice of George Washington as president, and with him of a Senate and a House of Representatives, the tendencies which had opposed or supported the adoption of the Constitution reappeared not only in Congress but in the President's cabinet, where Alexander Hamilton, secretary of the treasury, counselled a line of action which assumed and required the exercise of large powers by the Federal government, while Jefferson, the secretary of state, desired to practically restrict its action to foreign affairs. The advocates of a central national authority had begun to receive the name of Federalists, and to act pretty constantly together, when an event happened which, while it tightened their union, finally consolidated their opponents also into a party. This was the creation of the French Republic and its declaration of war against England. The Federalists, who were shocked by the excesses of the Terror of 1793, counselled neutrality, and were more than ever inclined to value the principle of authority, and to allow the Federal power a wide sphere of action. The party of Jefferson, who had now retired from the administration, were pervaded by sympathy with French ideas, were hostile to England whose attitude continued to be discourteous, and sought to restrict the interference of the central government with the States, and to allow the fullest play to the sentiment of State independence, of local independence, of personal independence. This party took the name of Republicans or Democratic Republicans, and they are the predecessors of the present Democrats. Both parties were, of course, attached to republican government—that is to say, were alike hostile to a monarchy. But the Jeffersonians had more faith in the masses and in leaving things alone, together with less respect for authority, so that in a sort of general way one may say that while one party claimed to be the apostles of Liberty, the other represented the principle of Order.

These tendencies found occasions for combating one another, not only in foreign policy and in current legislation, but also in the construction and application of the Constitution. Like all documents, and especially documents which have been formed by a series of compromises between opposite views, it was and is susceptible of various interpretations, which the acuteness of both

sets of partisans was busy in discovering and expounding. While
the piercing intellect of Hamilton developed all those of its provisions which invested the Federal Congress and President with
far-reaching powers, and sought to build up a system of institutions which should give to these provisions their full effect,
Jefferson and his coadjutors appealed to the sentiment of indi-
vidualism, strong in the masses of the people, and, without
venturing to propose alterations in the text of the Constitution,
protested against all extensions of its letter, and against all the
assumptions of Federal authority which such extensions could be
made to justify. Thus two parties grew up with tenets, leaders,
impulses, sympathies, and hatreds, hatreds which soon became so
bitter as not to spare the noble and dignified figure of Washington
himself, whom the angry Republicans assailed with invectives the
more unbecoming because his official position forbade him to
reply.

At first the Federalists had the best of it, for the reaction
against the weakness of the old Confederation which the Union
had superseded disposed sensible men to tolerate a strong central
power. The President, though not a member of either party,
was, by force of circumstances, as well as owing to the influence
of Hamilton, practically with the Federalists. But during the
presidency of John Adams, who succeeded Washington, they
committed grave errors. When the presidential election of 1800
arrived, it was seen that the logical and oratorical force of
Hamilton's appeals to the reason of the nation told far less than
the skill and energy with which Jefferson played on their feelings
and prejudices. The Republicans triumphed in the choice of
their chief, who retained power for eight years (he was re-elected
in 1804), to be peaceably succeeded by his friend Madison for
another eight years (elected in 1808, re-elected in 1812), and
his disciple Monroe for eight years more (elected in 1816, re-
elected in 1820). Their long-continued tenure of office was due
not so much to their own merits, for neither Jefferson nor Madison conducted foreign affairs with success, as to the collapse of
their antagonists. The Federalists never recovered from the
blow given in the election of 1800. They lost Hamilton by
death in 1803. No other leader of equal gifts appeared, and
the party, which had shown little judgment in the critical years
1810-14, finally disappears from sight after the second peace with
England in 1815.

One cannot note the disappearance of this brilliant figure, to Europeans the most interesting in the earlier history of the Republic, without the remark that his countrymen seem to have never, either in his lifetime or afterwards, duly recognized his splendid gifts. Washington is, indeed, a far more perfect character. Washington stands alone and unapproachable, like a snow-peak rising above its fellows into the clear air of morning, with a dignity, constancy, and purity which have made him the ideal type of civic virtue to succeeding generations. No greater benefit could have befallen the republic than to have such a type set from the first before the eye and mind of the people. But Hamilton, of a virtue not so flawless, touches us more nearly, not only by the romance of his early life and his tragic death, but by a certain ardour and impulsiveness, and even tenderness of soul, joined to a courage equal to that of Washington himself. Equally apt for war and for civil government, with a profundity and amplitude of view rare in practical soldiers or statesmen, he stands in the front rank of a generation never surpassed in history, a generation which includes Burke and Fox and Pitt and Grattan, Stein and Hardenberg and William von Humboldt, Wellington and Napoleon. Talleyrand, who seems to have felt for him something as near affection as that cold heart could feel, said, after knowing all the famous men of the time, that only Fox and Napoleon were Hamilton's equals, and that he had divined Europe, having never seen it.

This period (1788-1824) may be said to constitute the first act in the drama of American party history. The people, accustomed hitherto to care only for their several commonwealths, learn to value and to work their new national institutions. They become familiar with the Constitution itself, as partners get to know, when disputes arise among them, the provisions of the partnership deed under which their business has to be carried on. It is found that the existence of a central Federal power does not annihilate the States, so the apprehensions on that score are allayed. It is also discovered that there are unforeseen directions, such for instance as banking and currency, through which the Federal power can strengthen its hold on the nation. Differences of view and feeling give rise to parties, yet parties are formed by no means solely on the basis of general principles, but owe much to the influence of prominent personalities, of transient issues, of local interests or prejudices. The small farmers and the Southern men generally follow the Republican standard borne aloft by the great State of Virginia, while the strength of the Federalists lies in New England and the middle States, led sometimes by Massachusetts, sometimes by Pennsylvania. The commercial interest was with the Federalists, and the staid solid Puritanism of all classes, headed by the clergy. Some one indeed has described the struggle from 1796 to 1808 as one between Jefferson, who was an avowed free-thinker, and the New England ministers, and no doubt the ministers of religion did in the Puritan States exert a political influence approaching that of the Presbyterian clergy in Scotland during the seventeenth century. Jefferson's importance lies in the fact that he became the representative not merely of democracy, but of local democracy, of the notion that government is hardly wanted at all, that the people are sure to go right if they are left alone, that he who resists authority is *prima facie* justified in doing so, because authority is *prima facie* tyrannical, that a country where each local body in its own local area looks after the objects of common concern, raising and administering any such funds as are needed, and is interfered with as little as possible by any external power, comes nearest to the ideal of a truly free people. Some intervention on the part of the State there must be, for the State makes the law and appoints the judges of appeal; but the less one has to do with the State, and *a fortiori* the less one has to do with the less popular and more encroaching Federal authority, so much the better. Jefferson impressed this view on his countrymen with so much force and such personal faith that he became a sort of patron saint of freedom in the eyes of the next generation, who used to name their children after him, and to give dinners and deliver high-flown speeches on his birthday, a festival only second in importance to the immortal Fourth of July. He had borrowed from the Revolutionists of France even their theatrical ostentation of simplicity. He rejected the ceremonial with which Washington had sustained the chief magistracy of the nation declaring that to him there was no majesty but that of the people.

As New England was, by its system of local self-government through the town meeting, as well as by the absence of slavery, in some respects the most democratic part of the United States, it may seem surprising that it should have been a stronghold of the Federalists. The reason is to be found partly in its Puritanism, which revolted at the deism or atheism of the French revolutionists, partly in the interests of its shipowners and merchants, who desired above all things a central government which, while strong enough to make and carry out treaties with England and so secure the development of American commerce, should be able also to reform the currency of the country and institute a national banking system. Industrial as well as territorial interests were already beginning to influence politics. That the mercantile and manufacturing classes, with all the advantages given them by their wealth, their intelligence, and their habits of co-operation, should have been vanquished by the agricultural masses, may be ascribed partly to the fact that the democratic impulse of the War of Independence was strong among the citizens who had grown to manhood between 1780 and 1800, partly to the tactical errors of the Federalist leaders, but largely also to the skill which Jefferson showed in organizing the hitherto undisciplined battalions of Republican voters. Thus early in American history was the secret revealed, which Europe is only now discovering, that in free countries with an extended suffrage, numbers without organization are helpless and with it omnipotent.

I have ventured to dwell on this first period, because being the first it shows the origin of tendencies which were to govern the subsequent course of party strife. But as I am not writing a history of the United States I pass by the particular issues over which the two parties wrangled, most of them long since extinct. One remark is however needed as to the view which each took of the Constitution. Although the Federalists were in general the advocates of a loose and liberal construction of the fundamental instrument, because such a construction opened a wider sphere to Federal power, they were ready, whenever their local interests stood in the way, to resist Congress and the executive, alleging that the latter were overstepping their jurisdiction. In 1814 several of the New England States, where the opposition to the war then being waged with England was strongest, sent delegates to a convention at Hartford, which, while discussing the best means for putting an end to the war and restricting the powers of Congress in commercial legislation, was suspected of meditating a secession of the trading States from the Union. On the other hand, the Republicans did not hesitate to stretch to their utmost, when they were themselves in power, all the authority which the Constitution could be construed to allow to the executive and the Federal government generally.

The boldest step which a president has ever taken, the purchase from Napoleon of the vast territories of France west of the Mississippi which went by the name of Louisiana, was taken by Jefferson without the authority of Congress. Congress subsequently gave its sanction. But Jefferson and many of his friends held that under the Constitution even Congress had not the power to acquire new territories to be formed into States. They were therefore in the dilemma of either violating the Constitution or losing a golden opportunity of securing the Republic against the growth on its western frontier of a powerful and possibly hostile foreign state. Some of them tried to refute their former arguments against a lax construction of the Constitution, but many others avowed the dangerous doctrine that if Louisiana could be brought in only by breaking down the walls of the Constitution, broken they must be.

The disappearance of the Federal party between 1815 and 1820 left the Republicans masters of the field. But in the United States if old parties vanish nature produces new ones. Sectional divisions soon arose among the men who joined in electing Monroe in 1820, and under the influence of the personal hostility of Henry Clay and Andrew Jackson (chosen President in 1828), two great parties were again formed (about 1830) which some few years later absorbed the minor groups. One of these two parties carried on, under the name of Democrats, the dogmas and traditions of the Jeffersonian Republicans. It was the defender of States' Rights and of a restrictive construction of the Constitution; it leant mainly on the South and the farming classes generally, and it was therefore inclined to free trade. The other section, which called itself at first the National Republican, ultimately the Whig party, represented many of the views of the former Federalists, such as their advocacy of a tariff for the protection of manufactures, and of the expenditure of public money on internal improvements. It was willing to increase the army and navy, and like the Federalists found its chief, though by no means its sole, support in the commercial and manufacturing parts of the country, that is to say, in New England and the middle States. Meantime a new question far more exciting, far more menacing, had arisen. In 1819, when Missouri applied to be admitted into the Union as a State, a sharp contest broke out in Congress as to whether slavery should be permitted within her limits, nearly all the Northern members voting against slavery, nearly all the Southern members for.

The struggle might have threatened the stability of the Union but for the compromise adopted next year, which, while admitting slavery in Missouri, forbade it for the future north of lat. 36° 30′. The danger seemed to have passed, but in its very suddenness there had been something terrible. Jefferson, then over seventy, said that it startled him "like a fire-bell in the night." After 1840 things grew more serious, for whereas up till that time new States had been admitted substantially in pairs, a slave State balancing a free State, it began to be clear that this must shortly cease, since the remaining territory out of which new States would be formed lay north of the line 36° 30′. As every State held two seats in the Senate, the then existing balance in that chamber between slave States and free States would evidently soon be overset by the admission of a larger number of the latter. The apprehension of this event, with its probable result of legislation unfriendly to slavery, stimulated the South to the annexation of Texas, and made them increasingly sensitive to the growth, slow as that growth was, of Abolitionist opinions at the North. The question of the extension of slavery west of the Missouri river had become by 1850 the vital and absorbing question for the people of the United States, and as in that year California, having organized herself without slavery, was knocking at the doors of Congress for admission as a State, it had become an urgent question which evoked the hottest passions, and the victors in which would be victors all along the line. But neither of the two great parties ventured to commit itself either way. The Southern Democrats hesitated to break with those Democrats of the Northern States who sought to restrict slavery. The Whigs of the North, fearing to alienate the South by any decided action against the growing pretensions of the slave-holders, temporized and suggested compromises which practically served the cause of slavery. They did not perceive that in trying to preserve their party they were losing hold of the people, alienating from themselves the men who cared for principle in politics, sinking into a mere organization without a faith worth fighting for. That this was so presently appeared. The Democratic party had by 1852 passed almost completely under the control of the slave-holders, and was adopting the dogma that Congress enjoyed under the Constitution no power to prohibit slavery in the territories. This dogma obviously overthrew as unconstitutional the Missouri compromise of 1820.

The Whig leaders discredited themselves by Henry Clay's compromise scheme of 1850, which, while admitting California as a free State, appeased the South by the Fugitive Slave Law. They received a crushing defeat at the presidential election of 1852; and what remained of their party finally broke in pieces in 1854 over the bill for organizing Kansas as a territory in which the question of slaves or no slaves should be left to the people, a bill which of course repealed the Missouri compromise. Singularly enough, the two great orators of the party, Henry Clay and Daniel Webster, both died in 1852, wearied with strife and disappointed in their ambition of reaching the presidential chair. Together with Calhoun, who passed away two years earlier, they are the ornaments of this generation, not indeed rising to the stature of Washington or Hamilton, but more remarkable than any, save one, among the statesmen who have followed them. With them ends the second period in the annals of American parties, which, extending from about 1820 to 1856, includes the rise and fall of the Whig party. Most of the controversies which filled it have become matter for history only. But three large results, besides the general democratization of politics, stand out. One is the detachment of the United States from the affairs of the Old World. Another is the growth of a sense of national life, especially in the Northern and Western States, along with the growth at the same time of a secessionist spirit among the slave-holders. And the third is the development of the complex machinery of party organization, with the adoption of the principle on which that machinery so largely rests, that public office is to be enjoyed only by the adherents of the President for the time being.

The Whig party having vanished, the Democrats seemed to be for the moment, as they had been once before, left in possession of the field. But this time a new antagonist was quick to appear. The growing boldness of the slave-owners had begun to alarm the Northern people when they were startled by the decision of the Supreme court, pronounced in the case of the slave Dred Scott, which laid down the doctrine that Congress had no power to forbid slavery anywhere, and that a slave-holder might carry his slaves with him where he pleased, seeing that they were mere objects of property, whose possession the Constitution guaranteed. This hastened the formation out of the wrecks of the Whigs of a new party, which took in 1856 the name of Republican, while at the same time it threw an apple of discord among the Democrats. In 1860 the latter could not agree upon a candidate for President. The Southern wing pledged themselves to one man, the Northern wing to another; a body of hesitating and semi-detached politicians put forward a third. Thus the Republicans through the divisions of their opponents triumphed in the election of Abraham Lincoln, presently followed by the secession of eleven slave States.

The Republican party, which had started by denouncing the Dred Scott decision and proclaiming the right of Congress to restrict slavery, was of course throughout the Civil War the defender of the Union and the assertor of Federal authority, stretched, as was unavoidable, to lengths previously unheard of. When the war was over, there came the difficult task of reconstructing the now reconquered slave States, and of securing the position in them of the lately liberated negroes. The outrages perpetrated on the latter, and on white settlers in some parts of the South, required further exertions of Federal authority, and made the question of the limit of that authority still a practical one, for the old Democratic party, almost silenced during the war, had now reappeared in full force as the advocate of State rights, and the watchful critic of any undue stretches of Federal authority. It was found necessary to negative the Dred Scott decision and set at rest all questions relating to slavery and to the political equality of the races by the adoption of three important amendments to the Constitution. The troubles of the South by degrees settled down as the whites regained possession of the State governments and the Northern troops were withdrawn. In the presidential election of 1876 the war question and negro question had become dead issues, for it was plain that a large and increasing number of the voters were no longer, despite the appeals of the Republican leaders, seriously concerned about them.

This election marks the close of the third period, which embraces the rise and overwhelming predominance of the Republican party. Formed to resist the extension of slavery, led on to destroy it, compelled by circumstances to expand the central authority in a way unthought of before, that party had now worked out its programme and fulfilled its original mission. The old aims were accomplished, but new ones had not yet been substituted, for though new problems had appeared, the party was not prepared with solutions. Similarly the Democratic party had discharged its mission in defending the rights of the reconstructed States, and criticizing excesses of executive power; similarly it too had refused to grapple either with the fresh questions which had begun to arise since the war, or with those older questions which had now reappeared above the subsiding flood of war days. The old parties still stood as organizations, and still claimed to be the exponents of principles. Their respective principles had, however, little direct application to the questions which confronted and divided the nation. A new era was opening which called either for the evolution of new parties, or for the transformation of the old ones by the adoption of tenets and the advocacy of views suited to the needs of the time. But this fourth period, which began with 1876, has not yet seen such a transformation, and we shall therefore find, when we come to examine the existing state of parties, that there is an unreality and lack of vital force in both Republicans and Democrats, powerful as their organizations are.

The foregoing sketch, given only for the sake of explaining the present condition of parties, suggests some observations on the foundations of party in America.

If we look over Europe we shall find that the grounds on which parties have been built and contests waged since the beginning of free governments have been in substance but few. In the hostility of rich and poor, or of capital and labour, in the fears of the Haves and the desires of the Have-nots, we perceive the most frequent ground, though it is often disguised as a dispute about the extension of the suffrage or some other civic right. Questions relating to the tenure of land have played a large part; so have questions of religion; so too have animosities or jealousies of race; and of course the form of government, whether it shall be a monarchy or a republic, has sometimes been in dispute. None of these grounds of quarrel substantially affected American parties during the three periods we have been examining. No one has ever advocated monarchy, or a restricted suffrage, or a unified instead of a Federal republic. Nor down to 1876 was there ever any party which could promise more to the poor than its opponents. In 1852 the Know-nothing party came forward as the organ of native American opinion against recent immigrants, then chiefly the Irish, for German immigration was comparatively small in those days. But as this party failed to face the problem of slavery, and roused jealousy by its secret organization, it soon passed away. The complete equality of all sects, with the complete neutrality of the government in religious matters, has fortunately kept religious passion outside the sphere of politics.

Have the American parties then been formed only upon narrow and local bases, have they contended for transient objects, and can no deeper historical meaning, no longer historical continuity, be claimed for them ?

Two permanent oppositions may, I think, be discerned running through the history of the parties, sometimes openly recognized, sometimes concealed by the urgency of a transitory question. One of this is the opposition between a centralized or unified and a federalized government. In every country there are centrifugal and centripetal forces at work, the one or the other of which is for the moment the stronger. There has seldom been a country in which something might not have been gained, in the way of good administration and defensive strength, by a greater concentration of power in the hands of the central government, enabling it to do things which local bodies, or a more restricted central government, could not do equally cheaply or well. Against this gain there is always to be set the danger that such concentration may weaken the vitality of local communities and authorities, and may enable the central power to stunt their development. Sometimes needs of the former kind are more urgent, or the sentiment of the people tends to magnify them ; sometimes again the centrifugal forces obtain the upper hand. English history shows several such alternations. But in America the Federal form of government has made this permanent and natural opposition specially conspicuous. The salient feature of the Constitution is the effort it makes to establish an equipoise between the force which would carry the planet States off into space and the force which would draw them into the sun of the National government. There have always therefore been minds inclined to take sides upon this fundamental question, and a party has always had something definite and weighty to appeal to when it claims to represent either the autonomy of communities on the one hand, or the majesty and beneficent activity of the National government on the other. The former has been the watchword of the Democratic party. The latter was seldom distinctly avowed, but was generally in fact represented by the Federalists of the first period, the Whigs of the second, the Republicans of the third.

The other opposition, though it goes deeper and is more pervasive, has been less clearly marked in America, and less consciously admitted by the Americans themselves. It is the opposition between the tendency which makes some men prize the freedom of the individual as the first of social goods, and that which disposes others to insist on checking and regulating his impulses. The opposition of these two tendencies, the love of liberty and the love of order, is permanent and necessary, because it springs from differences in the intellect and feelings of men which one finds in all countries and at all epochs. There are always persons who are struck by the weakness of mankind, by their folly, their passion, their selfishness : and these persons, distrusting the action of average mankind, will always wish to see them guided by wise heads and restrained by strong hands. Such guidance seems the best means of progress, such restraint the only means of security. Those on the other hand who think better of human nature, and have more hope in their own tempers, hold the impulses of the average man to be generally towards justice and peace. They have faith in the power of reason to conquer ignorance, and of generosity to overbear selfishness. They are therefore disposed to leave the individual alone, and to entrust the masses with power. Every sensible man feels in himself the struggle between these two tendencies, and is on his guard not to yield wholly to either, because the one degenerates into tyranny, the other into an anarchy out of which tyranny will eventually spring. The wisest statesman is he who best holds the balance between them.

Each of these tendencies found among the fathers of the American Republic a brilliant and characteristic representative. Hamilton, who had a low opinion of mankind, but a gift and a passion for large constructive statesmanship, went so far in his advocacy of a strong government as to be suspected of wishing to establish a monarchy after the British pattern. He has left on record his opinion that the free constitution of England, which he admired in spite of the faults he clearly saw, could not be worked without its corruptions. Jefferson carried further than any other person set in an equally responsible place has ever done, his faith that government is either needless or an evil, and that with enough liberty, everything will go well. An insurrection every few years, he said, must be looked for, and even desired, to keep government in order. The Jeffersonian tendency has always remained, like a leaven, in the Democratic party, though in applying Jeffersonian doctrines the slave-holders stopped when they came to a black skin. Among the Federalists, and their successors the Whigs, and the more recent Republicans, there has never been wanting a full faith in the power of freedom. The Republicans gave a remarkable proof of it when they bestowed the suffrage on the negroes. Neither they nor any American party has ever professed itself the champion of authority and order; that would be a damaging profession. Nevertheless it is rather towards what I may perhaps venture to call the Federalist-Whig-Republican party than towards the Democrats that those who have valued the principle of authority have been generally drawn. It is for that party that the Puritan spirit, not extinct in America, has felt the greater affinity, for this spirit, having realized the sinfulness of human nature, is inclined to train and control the natural man by laws and force.

The tendency that makes for a strong government being akin to that which makes for a central government, the Federalist-Whig-Republican party, which has, through its long history, and under its varying forms and names, been the advocate of the national principle, found itself for this reason also led, more frequently than the Democrats, to exalt the rights and powers of government. It might be thought that the same cause would have made the Republican party take sides in that profound opposition which we perceive to-day in all civilized peoples, between the tendency to enlarge the sphere of legislation and State action, and the doctrine of *laissez faire.* So far, however, this has not happened. There is more in the character and temper of the Republicans than of the Democrats that leans towards State interference. But neither party has thought out the question; neither has shown any more definiteness of policy regarding it than the Tories and the Liberals have done in England.

American students of history may think that I have pressed the antithesis of liberty and authority, as well as that of centrifugal and centripetal tendencies, somewhat too far in making one party a representative of each through the first century of the Republic. I do not deny that at particular moments the party which was usually disposed towards a strong government resisted and decried authority, while the party which specially professed itself the advocate of liberty sought to make authority more stringent.   Such deviations are however compatible with the general tendencies I have described.   And no one who has gained even a slight knowledge of the history of the United States will fall into the error of supposing that order and authority mean there what they have meant in the monarchies of Continental Europe.

Chapter 2

The Parties of Today

There are now two great and several minor parties in the United States. The great parties are the Republicans and the Democrats. What are their principles, their distinctive tenets, their tendencies? Which of them is for free trade, for civil service reform, for a spirited foreign policy, for the regulation of telegraphs by legislation, for a national bankrupt law, for changes in the currency, for any other of the twenty issues which one hears discussed in the country as seriously involving its welfare?

This is what a European is always asking of intelligent Republicans and intelligent Democrats. He is always asking because he never gets an answer. The replies leave him in deeper perplexity. After some months the truth begins to dawn upon him. Neither party has anything definite to say on these issues; neither party has any principles, any distinctive tenets. Both have traditions. Both claim to have tendencies. Both have certainly war cries, organizations, interests enlisted in their support. But those interests are in the main the interests of getting or keeping the patronage of the government. Tenets and policies, points of political doctrine and points of political practice, have all but vanished. They have not been thrown away but have been stripped away by Time and the progress of events, fulfilling some policies, blotting out others. All has been lost, except office or the hope of it.

The phenomenon may be illustrated from the case of England, where party government has existed longer and in a more fully developed form than in any other part of the Old World. The essence of the English parties has lain in the existence of two sets of views and tendencies which divide the nation into two sections, the party, let us say, though these general terms are not

151

very safe, of movement and the party of standing still, the party of liberty and the party of order. Each section believes in its own views, and is influenced by its peculiar tendencies, recollections, mental associations, to deal in its own peculiar way with every new question as it comes up. The particular dogmas may change : doctrines once held by Whigs alone may now be held by Tories also ; doctrines which Whigs would have rejected fifty years ago may now be part of the orthodox programme of the Liberal party. But the tendencies have been permanent and have always so worked upon the various fresh questions and problems which have presented themselves during the last two centuries, that each party has had not only a brilliant concrete life in its famous leaders and zealous members, but also an intellectual and moral life in its principles. These principles have meant something to those who held them, so that when a fresh question arose it was usually possible to predict how each party, how even the average members of each party, would regard and wish to deal with it. Thus even when the leaders have been least worthy and their aims least pure, an English party has felt itself ennobled and inspirited by the sense that it had great objects to fight for, a history and traditions which imposed on it the duty of battling for its distinctive principles. It is because issues have never been lacking which brought these respective principles into operation, forcing the one party to maintain the cause of order and existing institutions, the other that of freedom and what was deemed progress, that the two English parties have not degenerated into mere factions. Their struggles for office have been redeemed from selfishness by the feeling that office was a means of giving practical effect to their doctrines.

But suppose that in Britain all the questions which divide Tories from Liberals were to be suddenly settled and done with. Britain would be in a difficulty. Her free government has so long been worked by the action and reaction of the ministerialists and the opposition that there would probably continue to be two parties. But they would not be really, in the true old sense of the term, Tories and Liberals ; they would be merely Ins and Outs. Their combats would be waged hardly even in name for principles, but only for place. The government of the country, with the honour, power, and emoluments attached to it, would still remain as a prize to be contended for. The followers would still rally to the leaders; and friendship would still bind the members together into organized bodies; while dislike and suspicion would still rouse them against their former adversaries. Thus not only the leaders, who would have something tangible to gain, but even others who had only their feelings to gratify, would continue to form political clubs, register voters, deliver party harangues, contest elections, just as they do now. The difference would be that each faction would no longer have broad principles—I will not say to invoke, for such principles would probably continue to be invoked as heretofore—but to insist on applying as distinctively its principles to the actual needs of the state. Hence quiet or fastidious men would not join in party struggles; while those who did join would no longer be stimulated by the sense that they were contending for something ideal. Loyalty to a leader whom it was sought to make prime minister would be a poor substitute for loyalty to a faith. If there were no conspicuous leader, attachment to the party would degenerate either into mere hatred of antagonists or into a struggle over places and salaries. And almost the same phenomena would be seen if, although the old issues had not been really determined, both the parties should have so far abandoned their former position that these issues did not divide them, but each professed principles which were, at least in their application, practicably undistinguishable.

This is what has happened with the American parties. The chief practical issues which once divided them have been settled. Some others have not been settled, but as regards these, one or other party has so departed from its former attitude that we cannot now speak of any conflict of principles.

When life leaves an organic body it becomes useless, fetid, pestiferous: it is fit to be cast out or buried from sight. What life is to an organism, principles are to a party. When they which are its soul have vanished, its body ought to dissolve, and the elements that formed it be regrouped in some new organism:

> 'The times have been
> That when the brains were out the man would die."

But a party does not always thus die. It may hold together long after its moral life is extinct. Guelfs and Ghibelines warred in Italy for nearly two centuries after the Emperor had ceased to threaten the Pope, or the Pope to befriend the cities of Lombardy. Parties go on contending because their members have formed habits of joint action, and have contracted hatreds and prejudices, and also because the leaders find their advantage in using these habits and playing on these prejudices. The American parties now continue to exist, because they have existed. The mill has been constructed, and its machinery goes on turning, even when there is no grist to grind. But this is not wholly the fault of the men; for the system of government requires and implies parties, just as that of England does. These systems are made to be worked, and always have been worked, by a majority; a majority must be cohesive, gathered into a united and organized body: such a body is a party.

If you ask an ordinary Northern Democrat to characterize the two parties, he will tell you that the Republicans are corrupt and incapable, and will cite instances in which persons prominent in that party, or intimate friends of its leaders, have been concerned in frauds on the government or in disgraceful lobbying transactions in Congress. When you press him for some distinctive principles separating his own party from theirs, he will probably say that the Democrats are the protectors of States' rights and of local independence, and the Republicans hostile to both. If you go on to inquire what bearing this doctrine of States' rights has on any presently debated issue he will admit that, for the moment, it has none, but will insist that should any issue involving the rights of the States arise, his party will be, as always, the guardian of American freedom.

This is really all that can be predicated about the Democratic party. If a question involving the rights of a State against the Federal authority were to emerge, its instinct would lead it to array itself on the side of the State rather than of the central government, supposing that it had no direct motive to do the opposite. As it has at no point of time, from the outbreak of the war down to 1888, possessed a majority in both Houses of Congress as well as the President in power, its devotion to this principle has not been tested, and might not resist the temptation of any interest the other way. However, this is matter of speculation, for at present the States fear no infringement of their rights. So conversely of the Republicans. Their traditions ought to dispose them to support Federal power against the States, but their action in a concrete case would probably depend on whether their party was at the time in condition to use that power for its own purposes. If they were in a minority in

Congress, they would be little inclined to strengthen Congress against the States. The simplest way of proving or illustrating this will be to run quickly through the questions of present practical interest.

That which most keenly interests the people, though of course not all the people, is the regulation or extinction of the liquor traffic. On this neither party has committed or will commit itself. The traditional dogmas of neither cover it, though the Democrats have been rather more disposed to leave men to themselves than the Republicans, and rather less amenable to the influence of ethical sentiment. Practically for both parties the point of consequence is what they can gain or lose. Each has clearly something to lose. The drinking part of the population is chiefly foreign. Now the Irish are mainly Democrats, so the Democratic party dare not offend them. The Germans are mainly Republican, so the Republicans are equally bound over to caution. It is true that though the parties, as parties, are neutral, most Temperance men are, in the North and West, Republicans, most whisky-men and saloon-keepers Democrats. The Republicans therefore more frequently attempt to conciliate the anti-liquor party by flattering phrases. They suffer by the starting of a Prohibitionist candidate, since he draws more voting strength away from them than he does from the Democrats.

Free Trade *v.* Protection is another burning question, and has been so since the early days of the Union. The old controversy as to the constitutional right of Congress to impose a tariff for any object but that of raising revenue, has been laid to rest, for whether the people in 1788 meant or did not mean to confer such a power, it has been exerted for so many years, and on so superb a scale, that no one now doubts its legality. Before the war the Democrats were advocates of a tariff for revenue only *i.e.* of Free Trade. Most of them still clung to the doctrine, and have favoured a reduction of the present system of import duties. But the party trumpet has often given an uncertain sound, for Pennsylvania is Protectionist on account of its iron industries ; northern Georgia and southern Tennessee are tending that way for the same reason ; Louisiana is inclined to protection on account of its sugar. As it would never do to alienate the Democrats of three such districts, the party has generally sought to remain unpledged, or, at least, in winking with one eye to the Free Traders of the North-west and South-east, it has been tempted to wink with the other to the iron men of Pittsburg and the sugar planters of New Orleans. And though it has come to advocate more and more strongly a reduction of the present high tariff, it does this not so much on Free Trade principles, as on the ground that the present surplus must be got rid of. The Republicans are bolder, and pledge themselves, when they frame a platform, to maintain the protective tariff. But some of the keenest intellects in their ranks, including a few leading journalists, are strong for free trade and therefore sorely tempted to break with their party.

Civil service reform, whereof more hereafter, has for some time past received the lip service of both parties, a lip service expressed by both with equal warmth, and by the average professional politicians of both with equal insincerity. Such reforms as have been effected in the mode of filling up places, have been forced on the parties by public opinion, rather than carried through by either. None of the changes made—and they are perhaps the most beneficial of recent changes—has raised an issue between the parties, or given either of them a claim on the confidence of the country. The best men in both parties support the Civil Service Commission; the worst men in both would gladly get rid of it.

The advantages of regulating, by Federal legislation, railroads and telegraphic lines extending over a number of States, is a subject frequently discussed. Neither party has had anything distinctive to say upon it in the way either of advocacy or of condemnation. Both have asserted that it is the duty of railways to serve the people, and not to tyrannize over or defraud them, so the Inter-State Commerce Bill which has lately been passed with this view cannot be called a party measure. Finances have on the whole been well managed, and debt paid off with surprising speed. But there have been, and are still, serious problems raised by the condition of the currency. Both parties have made mistakes, and mistakes about equally culpable, for though the Republicans, having more frequently commanded a Congressional majority, have had superior opportunities for blundering, the Democrats have once or twice more definitely committed themselves to pernicious doctrines. Neither party now proposes a clear and definite policy.

It is the same as regards minor questions, such as women's suffrage or international copyright, or convict labour. Neither party has any distinctive attitude on these matters; neither is more likely, or less likely, than the other to pass a measure dealing with them. It is the same with regard to the doctrine of *laissez faire* as opposed to governmental interference. Neither Republicans nor Democrats can be said to be friends or foes of State interference: each will advocate it when there seems a practically useful object to be secured, or when the popular voice seems to call for it. It is the same with foreign policy. Both parties are practically agreed not only as to the general principles which ought to rule the conduct of the country, but as to the application of these principles. The party which opposes the President may at any given moment seek to damage him by defeating some particular proposal he has made, but this it will do as a piece of temporary strategy, not in pursuance of any settled doctrine.

Yet one cannot say that there is to-day no difference between the two great parties. There is a difference of spirit or sentiment perceptible even by a stranger when, after having mixed for some time with members of the one he begins to mix with those of the other, and doubtless much more patent to a native American. It resembles (though it is less marked than) the difference of tone and temper between Tories and Liberals in England. The intellectual view of a Democrat of the better sort is not quite the same as that of his Republican compeer, neither is his ethical standard. Each of course thinks meanly of the other; but while the Democrat thinks the Republican "dangerous" (*i.e.* likely to undermine the Constitution) the Republican is more apt to think the Democrat vicious and unscrupulous. So in England your Liberal fastens on stupidity as the characteristic fault of the Tory, while the Tory suspects the morals and religion more than he despises the intelligence of the Radical.

It cannot be charged on the American parties that they have drawn towards one another by forsaking their old principles. It is time that has changed the circumstances of the country, and made those old principles inapplicable. They would seem to have erred rather by clinging too long to outworn issues, and by neglecting to discover and work out new principles capable of solving the problems which now perplex the country. In a country so full of change and movement as America new questions are always coming up, and must be answered. New troubles surround a government, and a way must be found to escape from them; new diseases attack the nation, and have to be cured. The duty of a great party is to face these, to find answers and remedies, applying to the facts of the hour the doctrines it has lived by, so far as they are still applicable, and when they have ceased to be applicable, thinking out new doctrines conformable to the main principles and tendencies which it represents. This is a work to be accomplished by its ruling minds, while the habit of party loyalty to the leaders powerfully serves to diffuse through the mass of followers the conclusions of the leaders and the reasonings they have employed.

"But," the European reader may ask, "is it not the interest as well as the duty of a party thus to adapt itself to new conditions? Does it not, in failing to do so, condemn itself to sterility and impotence, ultimately, indeed, to supersession by some new party which the needs of the time have created?"

This is what happens in England and in Europe generally. Probably it will happen in the long run in America also, unless the parties adapt themselves to the new issues, just as the Whig party fell in 1852-57 because it failed to face the problem of slavery. That it happens more slowly may be ascribed partly to the completeness and strength of the party organizations, which make the enthusiasm generated by ideas less necessary, partly to the fact that the questions on which the two great parties still hesitate to take sides are not presently vital to the well-being of the country, partly also to the smaller influence in America than in Europe of individual leaders. English parties, which hesitate long over secondary questions, might hesitate longer than is now their practice over vital ones also, were they not accustomed to look for guidance to their chiefs, and to defer to the opinion which the chiefs deliver. And it is only by courage and the capacity for initiative that the chiefs themselves retain their position.

CHAPTER 3

The Politicians

INSTITUTIONS are said to form men, but it is no less true that men give to institutions their colour and tendency. It profits little to know the legal rules and methods and observances of government, unless one also knows something of the human beings who tend and direct this machinery, and who, by the spirit in which they work it, may render it the potent instrument of good or evil to the people. These men are the politicians.

What is one to include under this term? In England it usually denotes those who are actively occupied in administering or legislating, or discussing administration and legislation. That is to say, it includes ministers of the Crown, members of Parliament (though some in the House of Commons and the majority in the House of Lords care little about politics), a few leading journalists, and a small number of miscellaneous persons, writers, lecturers, organizers, agitators, who occupy themselves with trying to influence the public. Sometimes the term is given a wider sweep, being taken to include all who labour for their political party in the constituencies, as *e.g.* the chairmen and secretaries of local party associations, and the more active committee men of the same bodies. The former, whom we may call the Inner Circle men, are professional politicians in this sense, and in this sense only, that politics is the main though seldom the sole business of their lives. But at present extremely few of them make anything by it in the way of money. A handful hope to get some post; a somewhat larger number find that a seat in Parliament enables them to push their financial undertakings or gives them at least a better standing in the commercial world. But the making of a livelihood does not come into the view of the great majority at all. The other class, who may be called the Outer Circle, are not professionals in any

159

sense, being primarily occupied with their own avocations; and none of them, except here and there an organizing secretary, paid lecturer, or registration agent, makes any profit out of the work. The phenomena of France and Italy and Germany are generally similar, that is to say, those who devote their whole time to politics are a very small class, those who make a living by it an even smaller one. Of all the countries of Europe, Greece is that in which persons who spend their life in politics seem to bear the largest proportion to the whole population; and in Greece the pursuit of politics is usually the pursuit of place.

To see why things are different in the United States, why the Inner Circle is much larger both absolutely and relatively to the Outer Circle than in Europe, let us go back a little and ask what are the conditions which develop a political class. The point has so important a bearing on the characteristics of American politicians that I do not fear to dwell somewhat fully upon it.

In self-governing communities of the simpler kind—for one may leave absolute monarchies and feudal monarchies on one side—the common affairs are everybody's business and nobody's special business. Some few men by their personal qualities get a larger share of authority, and are repeatedly chosen to be archons, or generals, or consuls, or burgomasters, or landammans, but even these rarely give their whole time to the State, and make little or nothing in money out of it. This was the condition of the Greek republics, of early Rome, of the cities of mediæval Germany and Italy, of the cantons of Switzerland till very recent times.

When in a large country public affairs become more engrossing to those who are occupied in them, when the sphere of government widens, when administration is more complex and more closely interlaced with the industrial interests of the community and of the world at large, so that there is more to be known and to be considered, the business of a nation falls into the hands of the men eminent by rank, wealth, and ability, who form a sort of governing class, largely hereditary. The higher civil administration of the state is in their hands; they fill the chief council or legislative chamber and conduct its debates. They have residences in the capital, and though they receive salaries when actually filling an office, the majority possess independent means, and pursue politics for the sake of fame, power, or excitement. Those few who have not independent means can follow their business or profession in the capital, or can frequently visit the place where their business is carried on. This was the condition of Rome under the later republic, and of England and France till quite lately—indeed it is largely the case in England still—as well as of Prussia and Sweden.

Let us see what are the conditions of the United States.

There is a relatively small leisured class of persons engaged in no occupation and of wealth sufficient to leave them free for public affairs. So far as such persons are to be found in the country, for some are to be sought abroad, they are to be found in a few great cities.

There is no class with a hereditary prescription to public office, no great families whose names are known to the people, and who, bound together by class sympathy and ties of relationship, help one another by keeping offices in the hands of their own members.

The country is a very large one, and has its political capital in a city without trade, without manufactures, without professional careers. Even the seats of State governments are often placed in comparatively small towns. Hence a man cannot carry on his gainful occupation at the same time that he attends to "Inner Circle" politics.

Members of Congress and of State legislatures are invariably chosen from the places where they reside. Hence a person belonging to the leisured class of a great city cannot get into the House of Representatives or the legislature of his State except as member for a district of his own city.

The shortness of terms of office, and the large number of offices filled by election, make elections very frequent. All these elections, with trifling exceptions, are fought on party lines, and the result of a minor one for some petty local office, such as county treasurer, affects one for a more important post, *e.g.* that of member of Congress. Hence constant vigilance, constant exertions on the spot, are needed. The list of voters must be incessantly looked after, newly-admitted or newly-settled citizens enrolled, the active local men frequently consulted and kept in good humour, meetings arranged for, tickets (*i.e.* lists of candidates) for all vacant offices agreed upon. One election is no

sooner over than another approaches and has to be provided
for, as the English sporting man reckons his year by "events,"
and thinks of Newmarket after Ascot, and of Goodwood after
Newmarket.

Now what do these conditions amount to ? To this—A great
deal of hard and dull election and other local political work to
be done. Few men of leisure to do it, and still fewer men of
leisure likely to care for it. Nobody able to do it in addition to
his regular business or profession. Little motive for anybody,
whether leisured or not, to do the humbler and local parts of it
(*i.e.* so much as concerns the minor elections), the parts which
bring neither fame nor power.

If the work is to be done at all, some inducement, other than
fame or power, must clearly be found. Why not, some one will
say, the sense of public duty ? I will speak of public duty
presently : meantime let it suffice to remark that to rely on
public duty as the main motive power in politics is to assume
a commonwealth of angels. Men such as we know them must
have some other inducement. Even in the Christian Church
there are other than spiritual motives to lead its pastors to
spiritual work ; nor do all poets write because they seek to express the passion of their souls. In America we discover a palpable inducement to undertake the dull and toilsome work of
election politics. It is the inducement of places in the public
service. To make them attractive they must be paid. They are
paid, nearly all of them, memberships of Congress and other
Federal places, State places (including memberships of State legislatures), city and county places. Here then is the inducement,
the remuneration for political work performed in the way of
organizing and electioneering. Now add that besides the paid
administrative and legislative places which a democracy bestows
by election, judicial places are also in most of the States elective,
and held for terms of years only ; and add further, that the
holders of nearly all those administrative places, Federal, State,
and municipal, which are not held for a fixed term, are liable to
be dismissed, and have been hitherto in practice dismissed, whenever power changes from one party to another, so that those
who belong to the party out of office have a direct chance of
office when their party comes in. The inducement to undertake
political work we have been searching for is at once seen to be
adequate, and only too adequate. The men for the work are

certain to appear because remuneration is provided. Politics has now become a gainful profession, like advocacy, stockbroking, the dry goods trade, or the getting up of companies. People go into it to live by it, primarily for the sake of the salaries attached to the places they count on getting, secondarily in view of the opportunities it affords of making incidental and sometimes illegitimate gains. Every person in a high administrative post, whether Federal, State, or municipal, and, above all, every member of Congress, has opportunities of rendering services to wealthy individuals and companies for which they are willing to pay secretly in money or in money's worth. The better officials and legislators—they are the great majority, except in large cities—resist the temptation. The worst succumb to it, and the prospect of these illicit profits renders a political career distinctly more attractive to an unscrupulous man.

We find therefore that in America all the conditions exist for producing a class of men specially devoted to political work and making a livelihood by it. It is work much of which cannot be done in combination with any other kind of regular work, whether professional or commercial. Even if the man who unites wealth and leisure to high intellectual attainments were a frequent figure in America, he would not take to this work ; he would rather be a philanthropist or cultivate arts and letters. It is work which, steadily pursued by an active man, offers an income. Hence a large number of persons are drawn into it, and make it the business of their life ; and the fact that they are there as professionals has tended to keep amateurs out of it.

There are, however, two qualifications which must be added to this statement of the facts, and which it is best to add at once. One is that the mere pleasure of politics counts for something. Many people in America as well as in England undertake even the commonplace work of local canvassing and organizing for the sake of a little excitement, a little of the agreeable sense of self-importance, or from that fondness for doing something in association with others which makes a man become secretary to a cricket club or treasurer of a fund raised by subscription for some purpose he may not really care for. And the second qualification is that pecuniary motives operate with less force in rural districts than in cities, because in the former the income obtainable by public office is too small to induce men to work long in the hope of getting it. Let it therefore be understood that what is said in this chapter refers primarily to cities, and of course also to persons aiming at the higher Federal and State offices; and that I do not mean to deny that there is plenty of work done by amateurs as well as by professionals.

Having thus seen what are the causes which produce professional politicians, we may return to inquire how large this class is, compared with the corresponding class in the free countries of Europe, whom we have called the Inner Circle.

In America the Inner Circle, that is to say, the persons who make political work the chief business of their lives, includes :—

Firstly. All members of both Houses of Congress.

Secondly. All Federal office-holders except the judges, who are irremovable, and who have sometimes taken no prominent part in politics.

Thirdly. A large part of the members of State legislatures. How large a part, it is impossible to determine, for it varies greatly from State to State. I should guess that in New York, Pennsylvania, New Jersey, California, Maryland, and Louisiana, half the members were professional politicians ; in Ohio, Virginia, Illinois, Texas, less than half ; in Massachusetts, Vermont, Georgia, Kentucky, Iowa, Oregon, not more than one-fourth ; in some other States, perhaps even less. But the line between a professional and non-professional politician is too indefinite to make any satisfactory estimate possible.

Fourthly. Nearly all State office-holders, excluding all judges in a few States, and many of the judges in the rest.

Fifthly. Nearly all holders of paid offices in the greater and in many of the smaller cities, and many holders of paid offices in the counties. There are, however, great differences in this respect between different States, the New England States and the newer States of the North-west, as well as some Southern States, choosing many of their county officials from men who are not regularly employed on politics, although members of the dominant party.

Sixthly. A large number of people who hold no office but want to get one. This category includes, of course, many of the " workers " of the party which does not command the majority for the time being, in State and municipal affairs, and which has not, through the President, the patronage of Federal posts. It also includes many expectants belonging to the party for the

time being dominant, who are earning their future places by
serving the party in the meantime.

All the above may fairly be called professional or Inner Circle
politicians, but of their number I can form no estimate, save
that it must be counted by hundreds of thousands, inasmuch as
it practically includes nearly all office-holders and most expectants
of public office.

It must be remembered that the " work " of politics means in
America the business of winning elections, and that this work is
incomparably heavier and more complex than in England,
because :—

(1) The voters are a larger proportion of the population ;
(2) The government is more complex (Federal, State, and local)
and the places filled by election are therefore far more numerous;
(3) Elections come at shorter intervals; (4) The machinery of
nominating candidates is far more complete and intricate ; (5)
The methods of fighting elections are far more highly developed,
i.e. they are matters requiring more technical knowledge and
skill ; (6) Ordinary private citizens do less election work,
because they are busier than in England, and the professionals
exist to do it for them.

I have observed that there are also plenty of men engaged in
some trade or profession who interest themselves in politics and
work for their party without any definite hope of office or other
pecuniary aim. They correspond to what we have called the
Outer Circle politicians of Europe. It is hard to draw a line
between the two classes, because they shade off into one another,
there being many farmers or lawyers or saloon-keepers, for
instance, who, while pursuing their regular calling, bear a hand
in politics, and look to be some time or other rewarded for doing
so. When this expectation becomes a considerable part of the
motive for exertion, such an one may fairly be called a professional, at least for the time being, for although he has other
means of livelihood, he is apt to be impregnated with the habits
and sentiments of the professional class.

The proportion between Outer Circle and Inner Circle men
is in the United States a sort of ozonometer by which the purity
and healthiness of the political atmosphere may be tested.
Looking at the North only, for I have no tolerable data as to
the South, and excluding congressmen, the proportion of men
who exert themselves in politics without pecuniary motive is

largest in New England, in the country parts of New York, in Northern Ohio, and the North-western States, while the professional politicians most abound in the great cities—New York, Philadelphia, Boston, Baltimore, Buffalo, Cincinnati, Chicago, St. Louis, New Orleans, San Francisco.   This is because these cities have the largest masses of ignorant voters, and also because their municipal governments, handling large revenues, offer the largest facilities for illicit gains.

I shall presently return to the Outer Circle men.   Meantime let us examine the professionals somewhat more closely ; and begin with those of the humbler type, whose eye is fixed on a municipal or other local office, and seldom ranges so high as a seat in Congress.

This species, like the weeds which follow human dwellings, thrives best in cities, and even in the most crowded parts of cities.   It is known to the Americans as the "ward politician," because the city ward is the chief sphere of its activity, and the ward meeting the first scene of its triumphs.   A statesman of this type usually begins as a saloon or bar-keeper, an occupation which enables him to form a large circle of acquaintances, especially among the "loafer" class who have votes but no reason for using them one way more than another, and whose interest in political issues is therefore as limited as their stock of political knowledge.   But he may have started as a lawyer of the lowest kind, or lodging-house keeper, or have taken to politics after failure in store-keeping.   The education of this class is only that of the elementary schools : if they have come after boyhood from Europe, it is not even that.   They have of course no comprehension of political questions or zeal for political principles ; politics mean to them merely a scramble for places.   They are usually vulgar, sometimes brutal, more rarely criminal, or at least the associates of criminals.   They it is who move about the populous quarters of the great cities, form groups through whom they can reach and control the ignorant voter, pack meetings with their creatures.

Their methods and their triumphs must be reserved for a later chapter.   Those of them who are Irish, an appreciable proportion in three or four great cities, have seldom Irish patriotism to redeem the mercenary quality of their politics.   They are too strictly practical for that, being regardful of the wrongs of Ireland only so far as these furnish capital to be used with Irish voters. Their most conspicuous virtues are shrewdness, a sort of rough good-fellowship with one another, and loyalty to their chiefs, from whom they expect promotion in the ranks of the service. The plant thrives in the soil of any party, but its growth is more vigorous in whichever party is for the time dominant in a given city.

English critics, taking their cue from American pessimists, have often described these men as specimens of the whole class of politicians. This is misleading. The men are bad enough both as an actual force and as a symptom. But they are confined to a few great cities, those eight or nine I have already mentioned; it is their exploits there, and particularly in New York, where the mass of ignorant immigrants is largest, that have made them famous.

In the smaller cities, and in the country generally, the minor politicians are mostly native Americans, less ignorant and more respectable than these last-mentioned street vultures. The bar-keeping element is represented among them, but the bulk are petty lawyers, officials, Federal as well as State and county, and people who for want of a better occupation have turned office-seekers, with a fair sprinkling of store-keepers, farmers, and newspaper men. The great majority have some regular avocation, so that they are by no means wholly professionals. Law is of course the business which best fits in with politics. They are not below the level of the class to which they belong, which is what would be called in England the lower middle, or in France the *petite bourgeoisie*, and they often suppose themselves to be fighting for Republican or Democratic principles, even though in fact concerned chiefly with place hunting. It is not so much positive moral defects that are to be charged on them as a slightly sordid and selfish view of politics and a laxity in the use of electioneering methods.

These two classes do the local work and dirty work of politics. They are the rank and file. Above them stand the officers in the political army, the party managers, including the members of Congress and chief men in the State legislatures, and the editors of influential newspapers. Some of these have pushed their way up from the humbler ranks. Others are men of superior ability and education, often college graduates, lawyers who have had practice, less frequently merchants or manufacturers who have slipped into politics from business. There are all sorts among them, creatures clean and unclean, as in the sheet of St. Peter's vision, but that one may say of politicians in all countries. What characterizes them as compared with the corresponding class in Europe is that their whole time is more frequently given to political work, that most of them draw an income from politics and the rest hope to do so, that they come more largely from the poorer and less cultivated than from the higher ranks of society, and that they include but few men who have pursued any of those economical, social, or constitutional studies which form the basis of politics and legislation, although many are proficients in the arts of popular oratory, of electioneering, and of party management.

They show a high average level of practical cleverness and versatility, and a good deal of legal knowledge. They are usually correct in life, for intoxication as well as sexual immorality is condemned by American more severely than by European opinion, but are often charged with a low tone, with laxity in pecuniary matters, with a propensity to commit or to excuse jobs, with a deficient sense of the dignity which public office confers and the responsibility it implies. I shall elsewhere discuss the validity of these charges, and need only observe here that even if the last thirty years have furnished some grounds for accusing the class as a whole, there are many brilliant exceptions, many leading politicians whose honour is as stainless and patriotism as pure as that of the best European statesmen. In this general description I am simply repeating what non-political Americans themselves say. It is possible that with their half-humorous tendency to exaggerate they dwell too much on the darker side of their public life. My own belief is that things are healthier than the newspapers and common talk lead a traveller to believe, and that the blackness of the worst men in the large cities has been allowed to darken the whole class of politicians as the smoke from a few factories will darken the sky over a whole town. However, the sentiment I have described is no doubt the general sentiment. "Politician" is a term of reproach, not merely among the "superfine philosophers" of New England colleges, but among the better sort of citizens over the whole Union. "How did such a job come to be perpetrated?" I remember once asking a casual acquaintance who had been pointing out some scandalous waste of public money. "Why, what can you expect from the politicians?" was the surprised answer.

Assuming these faults to exist, to what causes are they to be ascribed ? Granted that politics has to become a gainful profession, may it not still be practised with as much integrity as other professions ? Do not the higher qualities of intellect, the ripe fruits of experience and study, win for a man ascendency here as in Europe ? Does not the suspicion of dishonour blight his influence with a public which is itself at least as morally exacting as that of any European country ? These are questions which can be better answered when the methods of party management have been described, the qualities they evoke appreciated, their reaction on men's character understood.

It remains to speak of the non-professional or Outer Circle politicians, those who work for their party without desiring office. These men were numerous and zealous shortly before and during the Civil War, when the great questions of the exclusion of slavery from the Territories and the preservation of the Union kindled the enthusiasm of the noblest spirits of the North, women as well as men. No country ever produced loftier types of dauntless courage and uncompromising devotion to principle than William Lloyd Garrison and his fellow-workers in the Abolitionist cause. Office came to Abraham Lincoln, but he would have served his party just as earnestly if there had been no office to reward him. Nor was there any want of high-souled patriotism in the South. The people gave their blood freely, and among the leaders there were many who offered up fine characters as well as brilliant talents on an altar which all but themselves deemed unhallowed. When these great issues were finally settled, and the generation whose manhood they filled began to pass away, there was less motive for ordinary citizens to trouble themselves about public affairs. Hence the professional politicians had the field left free ; and as they were ready to take the troublesome work of organizing, the ordinary citizen was contented to be superseded, and thought he did enough when he went to the poll for his party. Still there are districts where a good deal of unpaid and disinterested political work is done. In some parts of New England, New York, and Ohio, for instance, citizens of position bestir themselves to rescue the control of local elections from the ward politicians. In the main, however, the action of the Outer Circle consists in voting, and this the ordinary citizen does more steadily and intelligently than anywhere in Europe, unless perhaps in Switzerland. Doubtless much of the work which Outer Circle politicians do in Europe is in America done by professionals. But that lively interest in politics which the English Outer Circle feels, and which is not felt by the English public generally, is in America felt by almost the whole of the nation, that is to say, by the immense majority of native white Americans, and even by the better sort of immigrants, or, in other words, the American Outer Circle comes far nearer to including the whole nation than does the Outer Circle of England. Thus the influence which counterworks that of professionals is the influence of public opinion expressing itself constantly through its countless voices in the press, and more distinctly at frequent intervals by the ballot-box.

CHAPTER 4

Why the Best Men Do Not Go into Politics

" BUT," some one will say, who has read the reasons just assigned for the development of a class of professional politicians, "you allow nothing for public spirit. It is easy to show why the prize of numerous places should breed a swarm of office-seekers, not so easy to understand why the office-seekers should be allowed to have this arena of public life in a vast country, a free country, an intelligent country, all to themselves. There ought to be patriotic citizens ready to plunge into the stream and save the boat from drifting towards the rapids. They would surely have the support of the mass of the people who must desire honest and economical administration. If such citizens stand aloof, there are but two explanations possible. Either public life must be so foul that good men cannot enter it, or good men must be sadly wanting in patriotism."

This kind of observation is so common in European mouths as to need an explicit answer. The answer is two-fold.

In the first place, the arena is not wholly left to the professionals. Both the Federal and the State legislatures contain a fair proportion of upright and disinterested men, who enter chiefly, or largely, from a sense of public duty, and whose presence keeps the mere professionals in order. So does public opinion, deterring even the bad men from the tricks to which they are prone, and often driving them, when detected in a serious offence, from place and power.

However, this first answer is not a complete answer, for it must be admitted that the proportion of men of intellectual and social eminence who enter public life is smaller in America than it has been during the present century in each of the free countries of Europe. Does this fact indicate a want of public spirit ?

171

It is much to be wished that in every country public spirit were the chief motive propelling men into public life. But is it so anywhere now ? Has it been so at any time in a nation's history ? Let any one in England, dropping for the moment that self-righteous attitude of which Englishmen are commonly accused by foreigners, ask himself how many of those whom he knows as mixing in the public life of his own country have entered it from motives primarily patriotic, how many have been actuated by the love of fame or power, the hope of advancing their social pretensions or their business relations. There is nothing necessarily wrong in such forms of ambition ; but if we find that they count for much in the public life of one country, and for comparatively little in the public life of another, we must expect to find the latter able to reckon among its statesmen fewer persons of eminent intelligence and energy.

Now there are several conditions present in the United States, conditions both constitutional and social, conditions independent either of political morality or of patriotism, which make the ablest citizens less disposed to enter political life than they would otherwise be, or than persons of the same class are in Europe. I have already referred to some of these, but recapitulate them shortly here because they are specially important in this connection.

The want of a social and commercial capital is such a cause. To be a Federal politician you must live in Washington, that is, abandon your circle of home friends, your profession or business, your local public duties. But to live in Paris or London is of itself an attraction to many Englishmen and Frenchmen.

There is no class in America to which public political life comes naturally, as it still does to a certain class in England ; no families with a sort of hereditary right to serve the state. Nobody can get an early and easy start on the strength of his name and connections, as still happens in several European countries.

In Britain or France a man seeking to enter the higher walks of public life has more than five hundred seats for which he may stand. If his own town or county is impossible he goes elsewhere. In the United States he cannot. If his own district is already filled by a member of his own party, there is nothing to be done, unless he will condescend to undermine and supplant at the next nominating convention the sitting member. If he has been elected and happens to lose his own re-nomination or re-election, he cannot re-enter Congress by any other door. The fact that a man has served gives him no claim to be allowed to go on serving. In the West, rotation is the rule. No wonder that, when a political career is so precarious, men of worth and capacity hesitate to embrace it. They cannot afford to be thrown out of their life's course by a mere accident.

Politics are less interesting than in Europe. The two kinds of questions which most attract eager or ambitious minds, questions of foreign policy and of domestic constitutional change, are generally absent, happily absent. Currency and tariff questions and financial affairs generally, internal improvements, the regulation of railways and so forth, are important, no doubt, but to some minds not fascinating. How few people in the English or French legislatures have mastered them, or would relish political life if it dealt with little else! There are no class privileges or religious inequalities to be abolished. Religion, so powerful a political force in Europe, is outside politics altogether.

In most European countries there has been for many years past an upward pressure of the poorer or the unprivileged masses, a pressure which has seemed to threaten the wealthier and more particularly the landowning class. Hence members of the latter class have had a strong motive for keeping tight hold of the helm of state. They have felt a direct personal interest in sitting in the legislature and controlling the administration of their country. This has not been so in America. Its great political issues have not been class issues. On the contrary there has been so great and general a sense of economic security, whether well or ill founded I do not now inquire, that the wealthy and educated have been content to leave the active work of politics alone.

The division of legislative authority between the Federal Congress and the legislatures of the States further lessens the interest and narrows the opportunities of a political career. Some of the most useful members of the English Parliament have been led to enter it by their zeal for philanthropic schemes and social reforms. Others enter because they are interested in foreign politics or in commercial questions. In the United States foreign politics and commercial questions belong to Congress, so no one will be led by them to enter the legislature of

his State. Social reforms and philanthropic enterprises belong
to the State legislatures, so no one will be led by them to enter
Congress. The limited sphere of each body deprives it of the
services of many active spirits who would have been attracted by
it had it dealt with both these sets of matters, or with the
particular set of matters in which their own particular interest
happens to lie.

In America there are more easy and attractive openings into
other careers than in most European countries. The settlement
of the great West, the making and financing of railways, the
starting of industrial or mercantile enterprises in the newer States,
all offer a tempting field to ambition, ingenuity, and self-confidence. A man without capital or friends has a better chance
than in Europe, and as the scale of undertakings is vaster,
the prizes are more seductive. Hence much of the practical
ability which in the Old World goes to Parliamentary politics or
to the civil administration of the state, goes in America into
business, especially into railways and finance. No class strikes
one more by its splendid practical capacity than the class of
railroad men. It includes administrative rulers, generals, diplo-
matists, financiers, of the finest gifts. And in point of fact (as
will be more fully shown later) the railroad kings have of late
years swayed the fortunes of American citizens more than the
politicians.

The fascination which politics have for many people in
England is largely a social fascination. Those who belong by
birth to the upper classes like to support their position in
county society by belonging to the House of Commons, or by
procuring either a seat in the House of Lords, or the lord-
lieutenancy of their county, or perhaps a post in the royal
household. The easiest path to these latter dignities lies through
the Commons. Those who spring from the middle class expect
to find by means of politics an entrance into a more fashionable
society than they have hitherto frequented. Their wives will at
least be invited to the party receptions, or they may entertain a
party chieftain when he comes to address a meeting in their
town. Such inducements scarcely exist in America. A congressman, a State governor, a city mayor, gains nothing socially
by his position. There is indeed, except in a few Eastern cities
with exclusive sets, really nothing in the nature of a social prize
set before social ambition, while the career of political ambition

is even in those cities wholly disjoined from social success. The only exception to this rule occurs in Washington, where a senator or cabinet minister enjoys *ex officio* a certain social rank.

None of these causes is discreditable to America, yet, taken together, they go far to account for the large development of the professional element among politicians. Putting the thing broadly, one may say that in America, while politics are relatively less interesting than in Europe and lead to less, other careers are relatively more interesting and lead to more.

It may however be alleged that I have omitted one significant ground for the distaste of " the best people " for public life, viz. the bad company they would have to keep, the general vulgarity of tone in politics, the exposure to invective or ribaldry by hostile speakers and a reckless press.

I omit this ground because it seems insignificant. In every country a politician has to associate with men whom he despises and distrusts, and those whom he most despises and distrusts are sometimes those whose so-called social rank is highest—the sons or nephews of great nobles. In every country he is exposed to misrepresentation and abuse, and the most galling misrepresentations are not the coarse and incredible ones, but those which have a semblance of probability, which delicately discolour his motives and ingeniously pervert his words. A statesman must soon learn, even in decorous England or punctilious France or polished Italy, to disregard all this, and rely upon his conscience for his peace of mind, and upon his conduct for the respect of his countrymen. If he can do so in England or France or Italy, he may do so in America also. No more there than in Europe has any upright man been written down, for though the American press is unsparing, the American people are shrewd, and sometimes believe too little rather than too much evil of a man whom the press assails. Although therefore one hears the pseudo-European American complain of newspaper violence, and allege that it keeps him and his friends from doing their duty by their country, I could not learn the name of any able and high-minded man of whom it could be truly said that through this cause his gifts and virtues had been reserved for private life. The roughness of politics has, no doubt, some influence on the view which wealthy Americans take of a public career, but these are just the Americans who think that European politics are worked, to use the common phrase, " with kid gloves," and they are not the class most inclined anyhow to come to the front for the service of the nation. Without denying that there is recklessness in the American press, and a want of refinement in politics generally, I do not believe that these phenomena have anything like the importance which European visitors are taught, and willingly learn, to attribute to them. Far more weight is to be laid upon the difficulties which the organization of the party system, to be described in the following chapters, throws in the way of men who seek to enter public life. There is, as we shall see, much that is disagreeable, much that is even humiliating, in the initial stages of a political career, and doubtless many a pilgrim turns back after a short experience of this Slough of Despond.

To explain the causes which keep so much of the finest intellect of the country away from national business is one thing, to deny the unfortunate results would be quite another. Unfortunate they certainly are. But the downward tendency observable since the end of the Civil War seems to have been arrested. When the war was over, the Union saved, and the curse of slavery gone for ever, there came a season of contentment and of lassitude. A nation which had surmounted such dangers seemed to have nothing more to fear. Those who had fought with tongue and pen and rifle, might now rest on their laurels. After long-continued strain and effort, the wearied nerve and muscle sought repose. It was repose from political warfare only. For the end of the war coincided with the opening of a time of swift material growth and abounding material prosperity, in which industry and the development of the West absorbed more and more of the energy of the people. Hence a neglect of the details of politics such as had never been seen before. The last few years have brought a revival of interest in public affairs, and especially in the management of cities. There is more speaking and writing and thinking, practical and definite thinking, upon the principles of government than at any previous epoch. Good citizens are beginning to put their hands to the machinery of government; and it is noticed than those who do so are, more largely than formerly, young men, who have not contracted the bad habits which the practice of politics has engendered among many of their elders, and who will in a few years have become an even more potent force than they are now. If the path to Congress and the State legislatures and the higher municipal offices were cleared of the stumbling-blocks and dirt heaps which now encumber it, cunningly placed there by the professional politicians, a great change would soon pass upon the composition of legislative bodies, and a new spirit be felt in the management of State and municipal as well as of national affairs.

CHAPTER 5

Party Organizations

THE Americans are, to use their favourite expression, a highly executive people, with a greater ingenuity in inventing means, and a greater promptitude in adapting means to an end, than any European race. Nowhere are large undertakings organized so skilfully; nowhere is there so much order with so much complexity; nowhere such quickness in correcting a suddenly discovered defect, in supplying a suddenly arisen demand.

Government by popular vote, both local and national, is older in America than in continental Europe. It is far more complete than even in England. It deals with larger masses of men. Its methods have engaged a greater share of attention, enlisted more ingenuity and skill in their service, than anywhere else in the world. They have therefore become more elaborate and, so far as mere mechanism goes, more perfect than elsewhere.

The greatest discovery ever made in the art of war was when men began to perceive that organization and discipline count for more than numbers. This discovery gave the Spartan infantry a long career of victory in Greece, and the Swiss infantry a not less brilliant renown in the later Middle Ages. The Americans made a similar discovery in politics some fifty or sixty years ago. By degrees, for even in America great truths do not burst full-grown upon the world, it was perceived that the victories of the ballot-box, no less than of the sword, must be won by the cohesion and disciplined docility of the troops, and that these merits can only be secured by skilful organization and long-continued training. Both parties flung themselves into the task, and the result has been an extremely complicated system of party machinery, firm yet flexible, delicate yet quickly set up and capable of working well in the roughest communities.

178

Strong necessity, long practice, and the fierce competition of the two great parties, have enabled this executive people to surpass itself in the sphere of electioneering politics. Yet the principles are so simple that it will be the narrator's fault if they are not understood.

One preliminary word upon the object of a party organization. To a European politician, by which I mean one wh ɩ knows politics but does not know America, the aims of a party organization, be it local or general, seem to be four in number—

Union—to keep the party together and prevent it from wasting its strength by dissensions and schisms.

Recruiting—to bring in new voters, *e.g.* immigrants when they obtain citizenship, young men as they reach the age of suffrage, new-comers, or residents hitherto indifferent or hostile.

Enthusiasm—to excite the voters by the sympathy of numbers, and the sense of a common purpose, rousing them by speeches or literature.

Instruction—to give the voters some knowledge of the political issues they have to decide, to inform them of the virtues of their leaders, and the crimes of their opponents.

These aims, or at least the first three of them, are pursued by the party organizations of America with eminent success. But they are less important than a fifth object which has been little regarded in Europe, though in America it is the mainspring of the whole mechanism. This is the selection of party candidates ; and it is important not only because the elective places are so numerous, far more numerous than in any European country, but because they are tenable for short terms, so that elections frequently recur. Since the parties, having of late had no really distinctive principles, and therefore no well-defined aims in the direction of legislation or administration, exist practically for the sake of filling certain offices, and carrying on the machinery of government, the choice of those members of the party whom the party is to reward, and who are to strengthen it by the winning of the offices, becomes a main end of its being.

There are three ways by which in self-governing countries candidates may be brought before electors. One is by the candidate's offering himself, appealing to his fellow-citizens on the strength of his personal merits, or family connections, or wealth, or local influence. This was a common practice in most English constituencies till our own time ; and seems to be the practice over parliamentary Europe still. Another is for a group or junto of men influential in the constituency to put a candidate forward, intriguing secretly for him or openly recommending him to the electors. This also largely prevailed in England, where in counties four or five of the chief landowners used to agree as to the one of themselves who should stand for the county ; or chose the eldest son of a duke or marquis as the person whom his rank designated. So in Scotch boroughs a little knot of active bailies and other citizens combined to bring out a candidate, but generally kept their action secret, for "the clique" was always a term of reproach. The practice is common in France now, where the committees of each party recommend a candidate.

The third system is that in which the candidate is chosen neither by himself nor by the self-elected group, but by the people themselves, *i.e.* by the members of a party, whether assembled in mass or acting through representatives chosen for the purpose. This plan offers several advantages. It promises to secure a good candidate, because presumably the people will choose a suitable man. It encourages the candidate, by giving him the weight of party support, and therefore tends to induce good men to come forward. It secures the union of the party, because a previous vote has determined that the candidate is the man whom the majority prefer, and the minority are therefore likely, having had their say and been fairly outvoted, to fall into line and support him. This is the system which now prevails from Maine to California, and is indeed the keystone of trans-atlantic politics. But there is a further reason for it than those I have mentioned.

That no American dreams of offering himself for a post unless he has been chosen by the party is due not to the fact that few persons have the local pre-eminence which the social conditions of Europe bestow on the leading landowners of a neighbourhood, or on some great merchants or employers in a town, nor again to the modesty which makes an English candidate delay presenting himself as a candidate for Parliament until he has got up a requisition to himself to stand, but to the notion that the popular mind and will are and must be all in all, that the people must not only create the office-bearer by their votes, but even designate the persons for whom votes may be given. For a man to put himself before the voters is deemed presumptuous, because an encroachment on their right to say whom they will even so much as consider. The theory of popular sovereignty requires that the ruling majority must name its own standard-bearers and servants, the candidates, must define its own platform, must in every way express its own mind and will. Were it to leave these matters to the initiative of candidates offering themselves, or candidates put forward by an unauthorized clique, it would subject itself to them, would be passive instead of active, would cease to be worshipped as the source of power. A system for selecting candidates is therefore not a mere contrivance for preventing party dissensions, but an essential feature of matured democracy.

It was not however till democracy came to maturity that the system was perfected. As far back as the middle of last century it was the custom in Massachusetts, and probably in other colonies, for a coterie of leading citizens to put forward candidates for the offices of the town or colony, and their nominations, although clothed with no authority but that of the individuals making them, were generally accepted. This lasted on after the Revolution, for the structure of society still retained a certain aristocratic quality. Clubs sprang up which, especially in New York State, became the organs of groups and parties, brought out candidates, and conducted election campaigns; while in New England the clergy and the men of substance continued to act as leaders. Presently, as the democratic spirit grew, and people would no longer acquiesce in self-appointed chiefs, the legislatures began to be recognized as the bodies to make nominations for the higher Federal and State offices. Each party in Congress nominated the candidate to be run for the presidency, each party in a State legislature the candidate for governor, and often for other places also. This lasted during the first two or three decades of the present century, till the electoral suffrage began to be generally lowered, and a generation which had imbibed Jeffersonian principles had come to manhood, a generation so filled with the spirit of democratic equality that it would recognize neither the natural leaders whom social position and superior intelligence indicated, nor the official leadership of legislative bodies. As party struggles grew more bitter, a party organization became necessary, which better satisfied the claims of petty local leaders, which knit the voters in each district together and concentrated their efforts, while it expressed the absolute equality of all voters, and the right of each to share in determining his candidate and his party platform. The building up of this new organization was completed for the Democratic party about the year 1835, for the Whig party not till some years later. When the Republican party arose about 1854, it reproduced so closely, or developed on lines so similar, the methods which experience had approved, that the differences between the systems of the two great parties are now unimportant, and may be disregarded in the sketch I have to give.

The essential feature of the system is that it is from bottom to top strictly representative. This is because it has power, and power can flow only from the people. An organization which exists, like the political associations of England, solely or mainly for the sake of canvassing, conducting registration, diffusing literature, getting up courses of lectures, holding meetings and passing resolutions, has little or no power. Its object is to excite, or to persuade, or to manage such business as the defective registration system of the country leaves to be fulfilled by voluntary agencies. So too in America the committees or leagues which undertake to create or stimulate opinion have no power, and need not be strictly representative. But when an organization which the party is in the habit of obeying, chooses a party candidate, it exerts power, power often of the highest import, because it practically narrows the choice of a party, that is, of about a half of the people, to one particular person out of the many for whom they might be inclined to vote. Such power would not be yielded to any but a representative body, and it is yielded to the bodies I shall describe because they are, at least in theory, representative.

CHAPTER 6

The Machine

THE organization of an American party consists of two distinct, but intimately connected, sets of bodies, the one permanent, the other temporary. The function of the one is to manage party business, of the other to nominate party candidates.

The first of these is a system of managing committees. In some States every election district has such a committee, whose functions cover the political work of the district. Thus in country places there is a township committee, in cities a ward committee. There is a committee for every city, for every district, and for every county. In other States it is only the larger areas, cities, counties, and congressional or State Assembly districts that have committees. There is, of course, a committee for each State, with a general supervision of such political work as has to be done in the State as a whole. There is a national committee for the political business of the party in the Union as a whole, and especially for the presidential contest. The whole country is covered by this network of committees, each with a sphere of action corresponding to some constituency or local election area, so that the proper function of a city committee, for instance, is to attend to elections for city offices, of a ward committee to elections for ward offices, of a district committee to elections for district offices. Of course the city committee, while supervising the general conduct of city elections, looks to each ward organization to give special attention to the elections in its own ward; and the State committee will in State elections expect similar help from, and be entitled to issue directions to, all bodies acting for the minor areas—districts, counties, townships, cities, and wards—comprised in the State. The smaller local committees are in fact autonomous for their special local purposes, but subordinate in so far as they serve the larger purposes common to the whole party. The ordinary business of

183

these committees is to raise and apply funds for election purposes and for political agitation generally, to organize meetings when necessary, to disseminate political tracts and other information, to look after the press, to attend to the admission of immigrants as citizens and their enrolment on the party lists. At election times they have also to superintend the canvass, to procure and distribute tickets at the polls, to allot money for various election services ; but they are often aided, or virtually superseded, in this work by "campaign committees" specially created for the occasion. Finally, they have to convoke at the proper times those nominating assemblies which form the other parallel but distinct half of the party organization.

These committees are permanent bodies, that is to say, they are always in existence and capable of being called into activity at short notice. They are re-appointed annually by the Primary (hereinafter mentioned) or Convention for their local area, as the case may be, and of course their composition may be completely changed on a re-appointment. In practice it is but little changed, the same men continuing to serve year after year, because they hold the strings in their hands, because they know most and care most about the party business. In particular, the chairman is apt to be practically a permanent official, and (if the committee be one for a populous area) a powerful and important official, who has large sums to disburse and quite an army of workers under his orders. The chairmanship of the organizing committee of the county and city of New York (these areas being the same), for instance, is a post of great responsibility and in-fluence, in which high executive gifts find a worthy sphere for their exercise.

One function and one only is beyond the competence of these committees—the choice of candidates. That belongs to the other and parallel division of the party organization, the nominating assemblies.

Every election district, by which I mean every local area or constituency which chooses a person for any office, has a party meeting to select the party candidate for that office. This is called Nominating. If the district is not subdivided, *i.e.* does not contain any lesser districts, its meeting is called a Primary. A primary has two duties. One is to select the candidates for its own local district offices. Thus in the country a township primary nominates the candidates for township offices, in a city a ward primary nominates those for ward offices (if any). The other duty is to elect delegates to the nominating meetings of larger areas, such as the county or congressional district in which the township is situate, or the city to which the ward belongs. The primary is composed of all the party voters resident within the bounds of the township or ward. They are not too numerous, for in practice the majority do not attend, to meet in one room, and they are assumed to be all alike interested. But as the party voters in such a large area as a county, congressional district, or city, are too numerous to be able to meet and deliberate in one room, they must act through representatives. The choice of candidates for office in such larger areas is therefore entrusted to a body called a Nominating Convention. It is a representative body composed of delegates from all the primaries within its limits, who have been chosen at those primaries for the sole purpose of sitting in the convention and there selecting the candidates.

Sometimes a convention of this kind has itself to choose delegates to proceed to a still higher convention for a larger area. The greatest of all nominating bodies, that which is called the National Convention and nominates the party candidate for the presidency, is entirely composed of delegates from other conventions, no primary being directly represented in it. As a rule, however, there are only two sets of nominating authorities, the primary which selects candidates for its own petty offices, the convention composed of the delegates from all the primaries in the local circumscriptions of the district for which the convention acts.

A primary, of course, sends delegates to a number of different conventions, because its area, let us say the township or ward, is included in a number of different election districts, each of which has its own convention. Thus the same primary will in a city choose delegates to at least the following conventions, and probably to one or two others. (*a*) To the city convention, which nominates the mayor and other city officers. (*b*) To the Assembly district convention, which nominates candidates for the lower house of the State legislature. (*c*) To the senatorial district convention, which nominates candidates for the State Senate. (*d*) To the congressional district convention, which nominates candidates for Congress. (*e*) To the State convention, which nominates candidates for the governorship and other State offices. Sometimes, however, the nominating body for an Assembly district is a primary and not a convention. In New York City the Assembly district is the unit, and each of the twenty-four has its primary.

This seems complex : but it is a reflection of the complexity of government, there being everywhere three authorities, Federal, State, and Local (this last further subdivided), covering the same ground, yet the two former quite independent of one another, and the third for many purposes distinct from the second.

The course of business is as follows :—A township or ward primary is summoned by the local party managing committee, who fix the hour and place of meeting, or if there be not such a committee, then by some permanent officer of the organization in manner prescribed by the bye-laws. A primary for a larger area is usually summoned by the county committee. If candidates have to be chosen for local offices, various names are submitted and either accepted without a division or put to the vote, the person who gets most votes being declared chosen to be the party candidate. He is said to have received the party nomination. The selection of delegates to the various conventions is conducted in the same way. The local committee has usually prepared beforehand a list of names of persons to be chosen to serve as delegates, but any voter present may bring forward other names. All names, if not accepted by general consent, are then voted on. At the close of the proceedings the chairman signs the list of delegates chosen to the approaching convention or conventions, if more than one, and adjourns the meeting *sine die*.

The delegates so chosen proceed in due course to their respective conventions, which are usually held a few days after the primaries, and a somewhat longer period before the elections for offices. The convention is summoned by the managing. committee for the district it exists for, and when a sufficient number of delegates are present, some one proposes a temporary chairman, or the delegate appointed for the purpose by the committee of the district for which the convention is being held "calls the meeting to order" as temporary chairman. This person names a Committee on Credentials, which forthwith examines the credentials presented by the delegates from the primaries, and admits those whom it deems duly accredited. Then a permanent chairman is proposed and placed in the chair, and the convention is held to be "organized," *i.e.* duly constituted. The managing committee have almost always arranged beforehand who shall be proposed as candidates for the party nominations, and their nominees are usually adopted. However, any delegate may propose any person he thinks fit, being a recognized member of the party, and carry him on a vote if he can. The person adopted by a majority of delegates' votes becomes the party candidate, and is said to have "received the nomination." The convention sometimes, but not always, also amuses itself by passing resolutions expressive of its political sentiments; or if it is a State convention or a National convention, it adopts a platform, touching on, rather than dealing with, the main questions of the day. It then, having fulfilled its mission, adjourns *sine die*, and the rest of the election business falls to the managing committee. It must be remembered that primaries and conventions, unlike the local party associations of England, are convoked but once, make their nominations, and vanish. They are swans which sing their one song and die.

The national convention held every fourth year before a presidential election needs a fuller description, which I shall give presently. Meantime three features of the system just out lined may be adverted to.

Every voter belonging to the party in the local area for which the primary is held, is presumably entitled to appear and vote in it. In rural districts, where everybody knows everybody else, there is no difficulty about admission, for if a Democrat came into a Republican primary, or a Republican from North Adams tried to vote in the Republican primary of Lafayetteville, he would be recognized as an intruder and expelled. But in cities where people do not know their neighbours by headmark, it becomes necessary to have regular lists of the party voters entitled to a voice in the primary. These are made up by the local committee, which may exclude persons whom, though they call themselves Republicans (or Democrats, as the case may be), it deems not loyal members of the party. The usual test is, Did the claimant vote the party ticket at the last important election, generally the presidential election, or that for the State governorship? If he did not, he may be excluded. Frequently, however, the local rules of the party require every one admitted to the list of party voters to be admitted by the votes of the existing members, who may reject him at their pleasure, and also exact from each member two pledges, to obey the local committee, and to support the party nominations, the breach of either pledge

being punishable by expulsion. In many primaries voters supposed to be disagreeably independent are kept out either by the
votes of the existing members or by the application of these
strict tests. Thus it happens that three-fourths or even four-
fifths of the party voters in a primary area may not be on the
list and entitled to raise their voice in the primary for the
selection of candidates or delegates. Another regulation, restricting nominations to those who are enrolled members of the
regular organization, makes persons so kept off the list ineligible
as party candidates.

Every member of a nominating meeting, be it a primary or a
convention of delegates, is deemed to be bound by the vote of
the majority to support the candidate whom the majority select,
whether or no an express pledge to that effect has been given.
And in the case of a convention a delegate is generally held to
bind those whom he represents, *i.e.* the voters at the primary
which sent him. Of course no compulsion is possible, but long
usage and an idea of fair play have created a sentiment of honour
(so-called) and party loyalty strong enough, with most people
and in all but extreme cases, to secure for the party candidate the
support of the whole party organization in the district. It is
felt that the party must be kept together, and that he who has
come into the nominating meeting hoping to carry his own
candidate must abide by the decision of the majority. The vote
of a majority has a sacredness in America not yet reached in
Europe.

As respects the freedom left to delegates to vote at their own
pleasure or under the instructions of their primary, and to vote
individually or as a solid body, the practice is not uniform.
Sometimes they are sent up to the nominating convention without instructions, even without the obligation to "go solid."
Sometimes they are expressly directed, or it is distinctly understood by them and by the primary, that they are to support the
claims of a particular person to be selected as candidate, or that
they are at any rate to vote altogether for one person. Occasionally they are even given a list arranged in order of preference, and told to vote for A. B., failing him for C. D., failing him
for E. F., these being persons whose names have already been
mentioned as probable candidates for the nomination. This,
however, would only happen in the case of the greater offices,
such as those of member of Congress or governor of a State.

The point is in practice less important than it seems, because in most cases, whether there be any specific and avowed instruction or not, it is well settled beforehand by those who manage the choice of delegates what candidate any set of delegates are to support, or at least whose lead they are to follow in the nominating convention.

Note further how complex is the machinery needed to enable the party to concentrate its force in support of its candidates for all these places, and how large the number of persons constituting the machinery. Three sets of offices, municipal or county, State, Federal, have to be filled; three different sets of nominating bodies are therefore needed. If we add together all the members of all the conventions included in these three sets, the number of persons needed to serve as delegates will be found to reach a high total, even if some of them serve in more than one convention. Men whose time is valuable will refuse the post of delegate, gladly leaving to others who desire it the duty of selecting candidates for offices to which they seldom themselves aspire. However, as we shall see, such men are but rarely permitted to become delegates, even when they desire the function.

"Why these tedious details?" the European reader may exclaim. "Of what consequence can they be compared to the Constitution and laws of the country?" Patience. These details have more significance and make more difference to the working of the government than many of the provisions of the Constitution itself. The mariner feels the trade winds which sweep over the surface of the Pacific and does not perceive the coral insects which are at work beneath its waves, but it is by the labour of these insects that islands grow, and reefs are built up on which ships perish.

CHAPTER 7

How the Machine Works

NOTHING seems fairer or more conformable to the genius of democratic institutions than the system I have described, whereby the choice of party candidates for office is vested in the mass of the party itself. The existence of a method which selects the candidate likely to command the greatest support prevents the dissension and consequent waste of strength which the appearance of rival candidates of the same party involves; while the popular character of that method excludes the dictation of a clique, and recognizes the sovereignty of the people. It is a method simple, uniform, and agreeable throughout to its leading principle.

To understand how it actually works one must distinguish between two kinds of constituencies or voting areas. One kind is to be found in the great cities—places whose population exceeds, speaking roughly, 100,000 souls, of which there are more than thirty in the Union. The other kind includes constituencies in small cities and rural districts. What I have to say will refer chiefly to the Northern States—*i.e.* the former Free States, because the phenomena of the Southern States are still exceptional, owing to the vast population of ignorant negroes, among whom the whites, or rather the better sort of whites, still stand as an aristocracy.

The tests by which one may try the results of the system of selecting candidates are two. Is the choice of candidates for office really free—*i.e.* does it represent the unbiassed wish and mind of the voters generally? Are the offices filled by good men, men of probity and capacity sufficient for the duties?

In the country generally, *i.e.* in the rural districts and small cities, both these tests are tolerably well satisfied. It is true that many of the voters do not attend the primaries. The selection of delegates and candidates is left to be made by that

190

section of the population which chiefly interests itself in politics ; and in this section local attorneys and office-seekers have much influence. The persons who seek the post of delegate, as well as those who seek office, are seldom the most energetic and intelligent citizens; but that is because these men have something better to do. An observer from Europe who looks to see men of rank and culture holding the same place in State and local government as they do in England, especially rural England, or in Italy, or even in parts of rural France and Switzerland (one cannot explain these things except by comparisons), will be disappointed. But democracies must be democratic. Equality will have its perfect work ; and you cannot expect citizens who are pervaded by its spirit to go cap in hand to their richer neighbours begging them to act as delegates, or city or county officials, or congressmen. This much may be said, that although there is in America no difference of rank in the European sense, superior wealth or intelligence does not prejudice a man's candidature, and in most places improves its chances. If such men are not commonly chosen, it is for the same reason which makes them comparatively scarce among the town-councillors of English municipalities.

In these primaries and conventions the business is always prearranged—that is to say, the local party committee come prepared with their list of delegates or candidates. This list is usually, but not invariably, accepted, or if serious opposition appears, alterations may be made to disarm it and preserve the unity of the party. The delegates and candidates chosen are generally the members of the local committee, their friends or creatures. Except in very small places, they are rarely the best men. But neither are they the worst. In moderately-sized communities men's characters are known and the presence of a bad man in office brings on his fellow-citizens evils which they are not too numerous to feel individually. Hence tolerable nominations are made, the general sentiment of the locality is not outraged ; and although the nominating machinery is worked rather in the name of the people than by the people, the people are willing to have it so, knowing that they can interfere if necessary to prevent serious harm.

In large cities the results are different because the circumstances are different. We find there, besides the conditions previously enumerated, viz. numerous offices, frequent elections, universal suffrage, an absence of stimulating issues, three others of great moment—

A vast population of ignorant immigrants.

The leading men all intensely occupied with business.

Communities so large that people know little of one another, and that the interest of each individual in good government is comparatively small.

Any one can see how these conditions affect the problem. The immigrants vote, that is, they obtain votes after three or four years' residence at most, and often less, but they are not fit for the suffrage. They know nothing of the institutions of the country, of its statesmen, of its political issues. Neither from Germany nor from Ireland do they bring much knowledge of the methods of free government, and from Ireland they bring a suspicion of all government. Incompetent to give an intelligent vote, but soon finding that their vote has a value, they fall into the hands of the party organizations, whose officers enrol them in their lists, and undertake to fetch them to the polls. I was taken to watch the process of admitting to citizenship in New York. Droves of squalid men, who looked as if they had just emerged from an emigrant ship, and had perhaps done so only a few weeks before, for the law prescribing a certain term of residence is frequently violated, were brought up to a magistrate by the ward agent of the party which had captured them, declared their allegiance to the United States, and were forthwith placed on the roll. Such a sacrifice of common sense to abstract principles has seldom been made by any country. Nobody pretends that such persons are fit for civic duty, or will be dangerous if kept for a time in pupilage, but neither party will incur the odium of proposing to exclude them. The real reason for admitting them, besides democratic theory, was that the party which ruled New York expected to gain their votes. It is an afterthought to argue that they will sooner become good citizens by being immediately made full citizens. A stranger must not presume to say that the Americans have been imprudent, but he may doubt whether the possible ultimate gain compensates the direct and certain danger.

In these great transatlantic cities, population is far less settled and permanent than in the cities of Europe. In New York, Brooklyn, Chicago, St. Louis, San Francisco, a very small part of the inhabitants are natives of the city, or have resided in it for twenty years. Hence they know but little of one another, or even of those who would in Europe be called the leading men.

There are scarcely any old families, families associated with the city, whose name recommends one of their scions to the confidence of his fellow-citizens. There are few persons who have had any chance of becoming generally known, except through their wealth ; and the wealthy have neither time nor taste for political work. Political work is a bigger and heavier affair than in small communities : hence ordinary citizens cannot attend to it in addition to their regular business. Moreover, the population is so large that an individual citizen feels himself a drop in the ocean. His power of affecting public affairs by his own intervention seems insignificant. His pecuniary loss through overtaxation, or jobbery, or malversation, is trivial in comparison with the trouble of trying to prevent such evils.

As party machinery is in great cities most easily perverted, so the temptation to pervert it is there strongest, because the prizes are great. The offices are well paid, the patronage is large, the opportunities for jobs, commissions on contracts, pickings, and even stealings, are enormous. Hence it is well worth the while of unscrupulous men to gain control of the machinery by which these prizes may be won.

Such men, the professional politicians of the great cities, have two objects in view. One is to seize the local city and county offices. A great city of course controls the county in which it is situate. The other is so to command the local party vote as to make good terms with the party managers of the State, and get from them a share in State offices, together with such legislation as is desired from the State legislature, and similarly to make good terms with the Federal party managers, thus securing a share in Federal offices, and the means of influencing legislation in Congress. How do the city professionals move towards these objects ?

There are two stages in an election campaign. The first is to nominate the candidates you desire : the second to carry them at the polls. The first of these is often the more important, because in many cities the party majority inclines so decidedly one way or the other (*e.g.* New York City is steadily Democratic, Philadelphia Republican), that nomination is in the case of the dominant party equivalent to election. Now to nominate your candidates you must, above all things, secure the primaries. They require and deserve unsparing exertion, for everything turns upon them.

The first thing is to have the kind of primary you want. Now the composition of a primary is determined by the roll or "check list," as it is called, of ward voters entitled to appear in it. This is prepared by the managing committee of the ward, who are naturally desirous to have on it only such men as they can trust or control. They are aided in securing this by the rules requiring members to be admitted by the votes of those already on the list, and exacting from persons admitted a pledge to obey the committee, and abide by the party nominations. Men of independent temper often refuse this pledge, and are excluded. Many of the ward voters do not apply for admission. Of those who do apply and take the pledge, some can be plausibly rejected by the primary on the ground that they have on some recent occasion failed to vote the party ticket. Thus it is easy for an active committee to obtain a subservient primary, composed of persons in sympathy with it or obedient to it. In point of fact the rolls of membership of many primaries are largely bogus rolls. Names of former members are kept on when these men have left the district or died : names are put on of men who do not belong to the district at all, and both sets of names are so much "voting stock," applicable at the will and needs of the local party managers, who can admit the latter to vote, and recognize men personating the former. In fact, their control of the lists enables them to have practically whatever primary they desire.

The next thing is to get the delegates chosen whom you wish for. The committee when it summons the primary settles in secret conclave the names of the delegates to be proposed, of course selecting men it can trust, particularly office-holders bound to the party which has put them in, and "workers" whom the prospect of office will keep faithful. When the meeting assembles a chairman is suggested by the committee and usually accepted. Then the list of delegates, which the committee has brought down cut and dry, is put forward. If the meeting is entirely composed of professionals, office-holders, and their friends, it is accepted without debate. If opponents are present, they may propose other names, but the official majority is almost always sufficient to carry the official list, and the chairman is prepared to exert, in favour of his friends, his power of ruling points of order. In extreme cases a disturbance will be got up, in the midst of which the chairman may plausibly declare the official list carried, or the meeting is adjourned in the hope that the opposition will not be at the trouble of coming next time, a hope likely to be realized, if the opposition consists of respectable citizens who dislike spending an evening in such company. Sometimes the professionals will bring in roughs from other districts to shout down opponents, and if necessary threaten them with violence. One way or another the "official" or committee's list of delegates is almost invariably carried.

The scene now shifts to the Nominating Convention, which is also summoned by the appropriate committee. When it is "called to order" a temporary chairman is installed, the importance of whose position consists in his having (usually) the naming of a committee on credentials, or contested seats, which examines the titles of the delegates from the various primaries to vote in the convention. Being himself in the interest of the professionals, he names a committee in their interest, and this committee does what it can to exclude delegates who are suspected of an intention to oppose the candidates whom the professionals have prearranged. The primaries have almost always been so carefully packed, and so skilfully "run," that a majority of trusty delegates has been secured; but sometimes a few primaries have sent delegates belonging to another faction of the party, or to some independent section of the party, and then there may be trouble. Occasionally two sets of delegates appear, each claiming to represent their primary. The dispute generally ends by the exclusion of the Independents or of the hostile faction, the committee discovering a flaw in their credentials, but sometimes, though rarely, the case is so clear that they must be admitted. In doubtful cases a partisan chairman is valuable, for, as it is expressed, "he is a solid 8 to 7 man all the time." When the credentials have been examined the convention is deemed to be duly organized, a permanent chairman is appointed, and the business of nominating candidates proceeds. A spokesman of the professionals proposes A. B. in a speech, dwelling on his services to the party. If the convention has been properly packed, he is nominated by acclamation. If there be a rival faction represented, or if independent citizens who dislike him have been sent up by some primary which the professionals have failed to secure, another candidate is proposed and a vote taken. Here also there is often room for a partial chairman to influence the result; here, as in the primary, a tumult or a hocus pocus may in extreme cases be got up to enable the chairman to decide in favour of his allies.

Americans are, however, so well versed in the rules which govern public meetings, and so prepared to encounter all sorts of tricks, that the managers do not consider success certain unless they have a majority behind them. This they almost certainly have; at least it reflects discredit on their handling of the primaries if they have not. The chief hope of an opposition therefore is not to carry its own candidate but so to frighten the professionals as to make them abandon theirs, and substitute some less objectionable name. The candidate chosen, who, ninety-nine times out of a hundred, is the person predetermined by the managers, becomes the party nominee, entitled to the support of the whole party. He has received "the regular nomination." If there are other offices whereto nominations have to be made, the convention goes on to these, which being despatched, it adjourns and disappears for ever.

I once witnessed such a convention, a State convention, held at Rochester, N.Y., by the Democrats of New York State, at that time under the control of the Tammany Ring of New York City. The most prominent figure was the famous Mr. William M. Tweed, then in the zenith of his power. There was, however, little or nothing in the public proceedings from which an observer could learn anything of the subterranean forces at work. During the morning, a tremendous coming and going and chattering and clattering of crowds of men who looked at once sordid and flashy, faces shrewd but mean and sometimes brutal, vulgar figures in good coats forming into small groups and talking eagerly, and then dissolving to form fresh groups, a universal *camaraderie*, with no touch of friendship about it; something between a betting-ring and the flags outside the Liverpool Exchange. It reminded one of the swarming of bees in tree boughs, a ceaseless humming and buzzing which betokens immense excitement over proceedings which the bystander does not comprehend. After some hours all this settled down; the meeting was duly organized; speeches were made, all dull and thinly declamatory, except one by an eloquent Irishman; the candidates for State offices were proposed and carried by acclamation; and the business ended. Everything had evidently been prearranged; and the discontented, if any there were, had been talked over during the swarming hours.

After each of the greater conventions it is usual to hold one or more public gatherings, at which the candidates chosen are solemnly adopted by the crowd present, and rousing speeches are delivered. Such a gathering is called a "ratification" meeting. It has no practical importance, being of course attended only by those prepared to support the nominations made. The candidate is now launched, and what remains is to win the election.

The above may be thought, as it is thought by many Americans, a travesty of popular choice. Observing the forms of consulting the voters, it substantially ignores them, and forces on them persons whom they do not know, and would dislike if they knew them. It substitutes for the party voters generally a small number of professionals and their creatures, extracts prearranged nominations from packed meetings, and calls this consulting the pleasure of the sovereign people.

Yet every feature of the Machine is the result of patent causes. The elective offices are so numerous that ordinary citizens cannot watch them, and cease to care who gets them. The conventions come so often that busy men cannot serve in them. The minor offices are so unattractive that able men do not stand for them. The primary lists are so contrived that only a fraction of the party get on them; and of this fraction many are too lazy or too busy or too careless to attend. The mass of the voters are ignorant; knowing nothing about the personal merits of the candidates, they are ready to follow their leaders like sheep. Even the better class, however they may grumble, are swayed by the inveterate habit of party loyalty and prefer a bad candidate of their own party to a (probably no better) candidate of the other party. It is less trouble to put up with impure officials, costly city government, a jobbing State legislature, an inferior sort of congressman, than to sacrifice one's own business in the effort to set things right. Thus the Machine works on, and grinds out places, power, and the opportunities for illicit gain to those who manage it.

CHAPTER 8

Rings and Bosses

THIS is the external aspect of the Machine; these the phenomena which a visitor taken round to see a number of Primaries
and Nominating Conventions would record.   But the reader
will ask, How is the Machine run ?   What are the inner springs
that move it ?   What is the source of the power the committees
wield ?   What force of cohesion keeps leaders and followers
together ?   What kind of government prevails among this army
of professional politicians ?

The source of power and the cohesive force is the desire for
office, and for office as a means of gain.   This one cause is sufficient to account for everything, when it acts, as it does in these
cities, under the condition of the suffrage of a host of ignorant
and pliable voters.

Those who in great cities form the committees and work the
machine are persons whose chief aim in life is to make their
living by office.   Such a man generally begins by acquiring influence among a knot of voters who live in his neighbourhood,
or work under the same employer, or frequent the same grog-
shop or beer saloon, which perhaps he keeps himself.   He becomes a member of his primary, attends regularly, attaches himself to some leader in that body, and is forward to render service by voting as his leader wishes, and by doing duty at
elections.   He has entered the large and active class called,
technically, "workers," or more affectionately, "the Boys."   Soon
he becomes conspicuous in the primary, being recognized as controlling the votes of others—"owning them" is the technical
term—and is chosen delegate to a convention.   Loyalty to the
party there and continued service at elections mark him out for
further promotion.   He is appointed to some petty office in one
of the city departments, and presently is himself nominated for

an elective office. By this time he has also found his way on to the ward committee, whence by degrees he rises to sit on the central committee, having carefully nursed his local connection and surrounded himself with a band of adherents, who are called his "heelers," and whose loyalty to him in the primary, secured by the hope of "something good," gives weight to his words. Once a member of the central committee he discovers what everybody who gets on in the world discovers sooner or later, by how few persons the world is governed. He is one of a small knot of persons who pull the wires for the whole city, controlling the primaries, selecting candidates, "running" conventions, organizing elections, treating on behalf of the party in the city with the leaders of the party in the State. Each of this knot, which is probably smaller than the committee, because every committee includes some ciphers put on to support a leader, and which may include one or two strong men not on the committee, has acquired in his upward course a knowledge of men and their weaknesses, a familiarity with the wheels, shafts, and bands of the party machine, together with a skill in working it. Each can command some primaries, each has attached to himself a group of dependants who owe some place to him, or hope for some place from him. The aim of the knot is not only to get good posts for themselves, but to rivet their yoke upon the city by garrisoning the departments with their own creatures, and so controlling elections to the State legislature that they can procure such statutes as they desire, and prevent the passing of statutes likely to expose or injure them. They cement their dominion by combination, each placing his influence at the disposal of the others, and settle all important measures in secret conclave.

Such a combination is called a Ring.

The power of such a combination is immense, for it ramifies over the whole city. There are, in New York City, for instance, over ten thousand persons employed by the city authorities, all dismissible by their superiors at short notice and without cause assigned. There are two thousand five hundred persons employed in the Custom-House, Post-Office, and other branches of the Federal service, most of whom are similarly dismissible by the proper Federal authority ; and there are also State servants, responsible to and dismissible by the State authority. If the same party happens to be supreme in city politics, in the Federal government, and in the State government, all this army of employés is expected to work for the party leaders of the city, in city primaries, conventions, and elections, and is virtually amenable to the orders of these leaders. If the other party holds the reins of Federal government, or of both the Federal government and State government, then the city wirepullers have at any rate their own ten thousand or more, while other thousands swell the army of "workers" for the opposite party. Add those who expect to get offices, and it will be seen how great and how disciplined a force is available to garrison the city and how effective it becomes under strict discipline. Yet it is not larger than is needed, for the work is heavy. *Tantae molis erat Romanam condere gentem.*

In a Ring there is usually some one person who holds more strings in his hand than do the others. Like them he has worked himself up to power from small beginnings, gradually extending the range of his influence over the mass of workers, and knitting close bonds with influential men outside as well as inside politics, perhaps with great financiers or railway magnates, whom he can oblige, and who can furnish him with funds. At length his superior skill, courage, and force of will make him, as such gifts always do make their possessor, dominant among his fellows. An army led by a council seldom conquers : it must have a commander-in-chief, who settles disputes, decides in emergencies, inspires fear or attachment. The head of the Ring is such a general. He dispenses places, rewards the loyal, punishes the mutinous, concocts schemes, negotiates treaties. He generally avoids publicity, preferring the substance to the pomp of power, and is all the more dangerous because he sits, like a spider, hidden in the midst of his web. He is a Boss.

Although the career I have sketched is that whereby most Bosses have risen to greatness, some attain it by a shorter path. There have been brilliant instances of persons stepping at once on to the higher rungs of the ladder in virtue of their audacity and energy, especially if coupled with oratorical power. The first theatre of such a man's successes may have been the stump rather than the primary : he will then become potent in conventions, and either by hectoring or by plausible address, for both have their value, spring into popular favour, and make himself necessary to the party managers. It is of course a gain to a

Ring to have among them a man of popular gifts, because he helps to conceal the odious features of their rule, gilding it by his rhetoric, and winning the applause of the masses who stand outside the circle of workers. However, the position of the rhetorical boss is less firmly rooted than that of the intriguing boss, and there have been instances of his suddenly falling to rise no more.

A great city is the best soil for the growth of a Boss, because it contains the largest masses of manageable voters as well as numerous offices, and plentiful opportunities for jobbing. But a whole State sometimes falls under the dominion of one intriguer. To govern so large a territory needs high abilities; and the State boss is always an able man, somewhat more of a politician, in the European sense, than a city boss need be. He dictates State nominations, and through his lieutenants controls State and sometimes Congressional conventions, being in diplomatic relations with the chief city bosses and local rings in different parts of the State. His power over them mainly springs from his influence with the Federal executive and in Congress. He is usually, almost necessarily, a member of Congress, probably a senator, and can procure, or at any rate can hinder, such legislation as the local leaders desire or dislike. The President cannot ignore him, and the President's ministers, however little they may like him, find it worth while to gratify him with Federal appointments for persons he recommends, because the local votes he controls may make all the difference to their own prospects of getting some day a nomination for the presidency. Thus he uses his Congressional position to secure State influence, and his State influence to strengthen his Federal position. Sometimes however he is rebuffed by the powers at Washington and then his State thanes fly from him. Sometimes he quarrels with a powerful city boss, and then honest men come by their own.

It must not be supposed that the members of Rings, or the great Boss himself, are wicked men. They are the offspring of a system. Their morality is that of their surroundings. They see a door open to wealth and power, and they walk in. The obligations of patriotism or duty to the public are not disregarded by them, for these obligations have never been present to their minds. A State boss is usually a native American and a person of some education, who avoids the grosser forms of corruption, though he has to wink at them when practised by his friends. He may be a man of personal integrity. A city boss is often of foreign birth and humble origin; he has grown up in an atmosphere of oaths and cocktails : ideas of honour and purity are as strange to him as ideas about the nature of the currency and the incidence of taxation : politics is merely a means for getting and distributing places. "What," said an ingenuous delegate at one of the National Conventions at Chicago in 1880, "what are we here for except the offices?" It is no wonder if he helps himself from the city treasury and allows his minions to do so. Sometimes he does not rob, and, like Clive, wonders at his own moderation. And even he improves as he rises in the world. Like a tree growing out of a dust heap, the higher he gets, the cleaner do his boughs and leaves become. America is a country where vulgarity is scaled off more easily than in England, and where the general air of good nature softens the asperities of power. Some city bosses are men from whose decorous exterior and unobtrusive manners no one would divine either their sordid beginnings or their noxious trade. As for the State boss, whose talents are probably greater to begin with, he must be of very coarse metal if he does not take a polish from the society of Washington.

A city Ring works somewhat as follows. When the annual or biennial city or State elections come round, its members meet to discuss the apportionment of offices. Each may desire something for himself, unless indeed he is already fully provided for, and anyhow desires something for his friends. The common sort are provided for with small places in the gift of some official, down to the place of a policeman or doorkeeper or messenger, which is thought good enough for a common " ward worker." Better men receive clerkships or the promise of a place in the custom-house or post-office to be obtained from the Federal authorities. Men still more important aspire to the elective posts, seats in the State legislature, a city aldermanship or commissionership, perhaps even a seat in Congress. All the posts that will have to be filled at the coming elections are considered with the object of bringing out a party ticket, *i.e.* a list of candidates to be supported by the party at the polls when its various nominations have been successfully run through the proper conventions. Some leading man, or probably the Boss himself, sketches out an allotment of places ; and when this allotment has been worked out fully, it results in a Slate, *i.e.* a complete draft list of candidates to be proposed for the various offices. It may happen that the slate does not meet everybody's wishes. Some member of the ring or some local boss—most members of a ring are bosses each in his own district, as the members of a cabinet are heads of the departments of state, or as the cardinals are bishops of dioceses near Rome and priests and deacons of her parish churches—may complain that he and his friends have not been adequately provided for, and may demand more. In that case the slate will probably be modified a little to ensure good feeling and content; and will then be presented to the Convention.

But there is sometimes a more serious difficulty to surmount. A party in a State or city may be divided into two or more factions. Success in the election will be possible only by uniting these factions upon the same nominees for office. Occasionally the factions may each make its list and then come together in the party convention to fight out their differences. But the more prudent course is for the chiefs of each faction to arrange matters in a private conference. Each comes wishing to get the most he can for his clansmen, but feels the need for a compromise. By a process of "dickering" (*i.e.* bargaining by way of barter), various offers and suggestions being made all round, a list is settled on which the high contracting parties agree. This is a Deal, or Trade, a treaty which terminates hostilities for the time, and brings about "harmony." The list so settled is now a Slate, unless some discontented magnate objects and threatens to withdraw. To do so is called "breaking the slate." If such a "sore-head" persists, a schism may follow, with horrible disaster to the party; but usually a new slate is prepared and finally agreed upon. The accepted Slate is now ready to be turned by the Machine into a Ticket, and nothing further remains but the comparatively easy process of getting the proper delegates chosen by packed primaries, and running the various parts of the ticket through the conventions to which the respective nominations belong. Internal dissension among the chiefs is the one great danger; the party must at all hazards be kept together, for the power of a united party is enormous. It has not only a large but a thoroughly trained and disciplined army in its office-holders and office-seekers; and it can concentrate its force upon any point where opposition is threatened to the regular party nominations. All these office-holders and office-seekers have not only the spirit of self-interest to rouse them, but the bridle of fear to check any stirrings of independence. Discipline is very strict in this army. Even city politicians must have a moral code and

moral standard.   It is not the code of an ordinary unprofessional
citizen.   It does not forbid falsehood, or malversation, or ballot
stuffing, or "repeating."   But it denounces apathy or cowardice,
disobedience, and above all, treason to the party.   Its typical
virtue is "solidity," unity of heart, mind, and effort among the
workers, unquestioning loyalty to the party leaders, and devotion to the party ticket.   He who takes his own course is a
Kicker or Bolter ; and is punished not only sternly but vindic-
tively.   The path of promotion is closed to him ; he is turned out
of the primary, and forbidden to hope for a delegacy to a convention ; he is dismissed from any office he holds which the Ring
can command.   Dark stories are even told of a secret police
which will pursue the culprit who has betrayed his party, and of
mysterious disappearances of men whose testimony against the
Ring was feared.   Whether there is any foundation for such tales
I do not undertake to say.   But true it is that the bond between
the party chiefs and their followers is very close and very seldom
broken.   What the client was to his patron at Rome, what the
vassal was to his lord in the Middle Ages, that the heelers and
workers are to their boss in these great transatlantic cities.   They
render a personal feudal service, which their suzerain repays with
the gift of a livelihood ; and the relation is all the more cordial
because the lord bestows what costs him nothing, while the vassal
feels that he can keep his post only by the favour of the lord.

European readers must again be cautioned against drawing for
themselves too dark a picture of the Boss.   He is not a demon.
He is not regarded with horror even by those "good citizens"
who strive to shake off his yoke.   He is not necessarily either
corrupt or mendacious, though he grasps at place, power, and
wealth.   He is a leader to whom certain peculiar social and political conditions have given a character dissimilar from the party
leaders whom Europe knows.   It is worth while to point out in
what the dissimilarity consists.

A Boss needs fewer showy gifts than a European demagogue.
His special theatre is neither the halls of the legislature nor the
platform, but the committee-room.   A power of rough and ready
repartee, or a turn for florid declamation, will help him ; but he
can dispense with both.   What he needs are the arts of intrigue
and that knowledge of men which teaches him when to bully,
when to cajole, whom to attract by the hope of gain, whom by
appeals to party loyalty.   Nor are so-called "social gifts"

unimportant. The lower sort of city politicians congregate in clubs and bar-rooms ; and as much of the cohesive strength of the smaller party organizations arises from their being also social bodies, so also much of the power which liquor dealers exercise is due to the fact that "heelers" and "workers" spend their evenings in drinking places, and that meetings for political purposes are held there. Of the 1007 primaries and conventions of all parties held in New York City preparatory to the elections of 1884, 633 took place in liquor saloons. A Boss ought therefore to be hail fellow well met with those who frequent these places, not fastidious in his tastes, fond of a drink and willing to stand one, jovial in manners, and ready to oblige even a humble friend.

The aim of a Boss is not so much fame as power, and not so much power over the conduct of affairs as over persons. Patronage is the sort of power he seeks, patronage understood in the largest sense in which it covers the disposal of lucrative contracts and other modes of enrichment as well as salaried places. The dependants who surround him desire wealth, or at least a livelihood ; his business is to find this for them, and in doing so he strengthens his own position. It is as the bestower of riches that he holds his position, like the leader of a band of condottieri in the fifteenth century.

The interest of a Boss in political questions is usually quite secondary. Here and there one may be found who is a politician in the European sense, who, whether sincerely or not, purports and professes to be interested in some principle or measure affecting the welfare of the country. But the attachment of the ringster is usually given wholly to the concrete party, that is to the men who compose it, regarded as office-holders or office-seekers ; and there is often not even a profession of zeal for any party doctrine. As a noted politician happily observed to a friend of mine, "You know, Mr. R., there are no politics in politics." Among bosses, therefore, there is little warmth of party spirit. The typical boss regards the boss of the other party much as counsel for the plaintiff regards counsel for the defendant. They are professionally opposed, but not necessarily personally hostile. Between bosses there need be no more enmity than results from the fact that the one has got what the other wishes to have. Accordingly it sometimes happens that there is a good understanding between the chiefs of opposite parties in cities ; they will even go the length of making (of course secretly) a joint "deal," *i.e.* of arranging for a distribution of offices whereby some of the friends of one shall get places, the residue being left for the friends of the other. A well-organized city party has usually a disposable vote which can be so cast under the directions of the managers as to effect this, or any other desired result. The appearance of hostility must, of course, be maintained for the benefit of the public; but as it is for the interest of both parties to make and keep these private bargains, they are usually kept when made, though of course it is seldom possible to prove the fact.

The real hostility of the Boss is not to the opposite party, but to other factions within his own party. Often he has a rival leading some other organization, and demanding, in respect of the votes which that organization controls, a share of the good things going. The greatest cities can support more than one faction within the same party; thus New York has long had three democratic organizations, two of which are powerful and often angrily hostile. If neither can crush the other, it finds itself obliged to treat, and to consent to lose part of the spoils to its rival. Still more bitter, however, is the hatred of Boss and Ring towards those members of the party who do not desire and are not to be appeased by a share of the spoils, but who agitate for what they call reform. They are natural and permanent enemies; nothing but the extinction of the Boss himself and of bossdom altogether will satisfy them. They are moreover the common enemies of both parties, that is, of bossdom in both parties. Hence in ring-governed cities professionals of both parties will sometimes unite against the reformers, or will rather let their opponents secure a place than win it for themselves by the help of the "independent vote." Devotion to "party government," as they understand it, can hardly go farther.

This great army of workers is mobilized for elections, the methods of which form a wide and instructive department of political science. Here I have to refer only to their financial side, because that is intimately connected with the Machine. Elections need money, in America a great deal of money. Where, then, does the money come from, seeing that the politicians themselves belong to, or emerge from, a needy class?

The revenues of a Ring, that is, their collective, or, as one may say, corporate revenues, available for party purposes, flow from five sources.

I. The first is public subscriptions. For important elections such as the biennial elections of State officers, or perhaps for that of the State legislature, a "campaign fund," as it is called, is raised by an appeal to wealthy members of the party. So strong is party feeling that many respond, even though they suspect the men who compose the Ring, disapprove its methods, and have no great liking for the candidates.

II. Contributions are sometimes privately obtained from rich men who, though not directly connected with the Ring, may expect something from its action. Contractors, for instance, have an interest in getting pieces of work from the city authorities. Railroad men have an interest in preventing State legislation hostile to their lines. Both, therefore, may be willing to help those who can so effectively help them. This source of income is only available for important elections. Its incidental mischief in enabling wealth to control a legislature through a Ring is serious.

III. An exceptionally audacious Ring will sometimes make an appropriation from the city or (more rarely) from the State treasury for the purposes not of the city or the State, but of its own election funds. It is not thought necessary to bring such an appropriation into the regular accounts to be laid before the public ; in fact, pains are taken to prevent the item from appearing, and the accounts have often to be manipulated for that purpose. The justification, if any, of conduct not authorized by the law, must be sought in precedent, in the belief that the other side would do the same, and in the benefits which the Ring expects to confer upon the city it administers It is a method of course available only when Ring officials have the control of the public funds, and cannot be resorted to by an opposition.

IV. A tax is levied upon the office-holders of the party, varying from one to four or even five per cent upon the amount of their annual salaries. The aggregate annual salaries of the city officials in New York City amount to $11,000,000 (£2,200,000 sterling), and those of the two thousand five hundred Federal officials, who, if of the same party, might also be required to contribute, to $2,500,000 (£500,000 sterling). An assessment at two per cent on these amounts would produce over £45,000 and £10,000 respectively, quite a respectable sum for election expenses. Even policemen in cities, even office boys, and workmen in Federal dockyards, have been assessed by their respective parties. As a tenant had in the days of feudalism to make occasional money payments to his lord in addition to the military service he rendered, so now the American vassal must render his aids in money as well as give knightly service at the primaries, in the canvass, at the polls. His liabilities are indeed heavier than those of the feudal tenant, for the latter could relieve himself from duty in the field by the payment of scutage, while under the Machine a money payment never discharges from the obligation to serve in the army of "workers." As in the days of the Anglo-Norman kings, forfeiture and the being proclaimed as "nithing" is the penalty for failure to discharge the duties by which the vassal holds. Efforts which began with an order issued by President Hayes in 1877 applying to Federal offices, have lately been made to prevent by administrative action and by legislation the levying of this tribute on officials, but they have not as yet proved completely successful, for the subordinate fears to offend his superiors.

V. Another useful expedient has been borrowed from European monarchies in the sale of nominations and occasionally of offices themselves. A person who seeks to be nominated as candidate for one of the more important offices, such as a judgeship or a seat in the State Senate, or in Congress, is often required to contribute to the election fund a sum proportioned to the importance of the place he seeks, the excuse given for the practice being the cost of elections ; and the same principle is occasionally applied to the gift of non-elective offices, the right of appointing to which is vested in some official member of a Ring—*e.g.* a mayor. The price of a nomination for a seat in the State legislature is said to run from $500 up to $1000, and for one of the better judgeships as high as $5000 ; but this is largely matter of conjecture. Of course much less will be given if the prospects of carrying the election are doubtful : the prices quoted must be taken to represent cases where the party majority makes success certain. Naturally, the salaries of officials have to be raised in order to enable them to bear this charge, so that in the long run it may be thrown upon the public ; and a recent eminent boss of New York City defended, before a committee of the legislature, the large salaries paid to aldermen, on the ground that "heavy demands were made on them by their party."

Chapter 9

Spoils

An illustration of the familiar dictum regarding the wisdom with which the world is governed may be found in the fact that the greatest changes are often those introduced with the least notion of their consequence, and the most fatal those which encounter least resistance. So the system of removals from Federal office which began some sixty years ago, though disapproved of by some of the leading statesmen of the time, including Clay, Webster, and Calhoun, excited comparatively little attention in the country, nor did its advocates foresee a tithe of its far-reaching results.

The Constitution of the United States vests the right of appointing to Federal offices in the President, requiring the consent of the Senate in the case of the more important, and permitting Congress to vest the appointment of inferior officers in the President alone, in the courts, or in the heads of departments. It was assumed that this clause gave officials a tenure at the pleasure of the President—*i.e.* that he had the legal right of removing them without cause assigned. But the earlier Presidents considered the tenure as being practically for life or during good behaviour, and did not remove, except for some solid reason, persons appointed by their predecessors. Washington in his eight years displaced only nine persons, and all for cause, John Adams nine in four years, and those not on political grounds. Jefferson in his eight years removed thirty-nine, but many of these were persons whom Adams had unfairly put in just before quitting office; and in the twenty years that followed (1808-28) there were but sixteen removals. In 1820, however, a bill was run through Congress fixing four years as the term for a large number of offices. This was ominous of evil, and called forth the displeasure of both Jefferson and Madison. The

President, however, and his heads of departments did not remove, so the tenure of good behaviour generally remained. But a new era began with the hot and heady Jackson, who reached the presidential chair in 1829. He was a raw rude Western, a man of the people, borne into power by a popular movement, incensed against all who were connected with his predecessor, a warm friend and a bitter enemy, anxious to repay services rendered to himself. Penetrated by extreme theories of equality, he proclaimed in his Message that rotation in office was a principle in the Republican creed, and obeyed both his doctrine and his passions by displacing five hundred post-masters in his first year, and appointing partisans in their room. The plan of using office as a mere engine in partisan warfare had already been tried in New York, where the stress of party contests had led to an early development of many devices in party organization; and it was a New York adherent of Jackson, Marcy, who, speaking in the Senate in 1832, condensed the new doctrine in a phrase that has become famous—"To the victor belong the spoils."

From 1828 till a few years ago the rule with both parties has been that on a change of President nearly all Federal offices, from the legations to European Courts down to village post-masterships, are deemed to be vacant. The present holders may of course be continued or reappointed (if their term has expired); and if the new President belongs to the same party as his predecessor, many of them will be; but they are not held to have either a legal or a moral claim. The choice of the President or departmental head has been absolutely free, no qualifications, except the citizenship of the nominee, being required, nor any check imposed on him, except that the Senate's consent is needed to the more important posts.

The want of knowledge on the part of the President and his ministers of the persons who applied for places at a distance, obliged them to seek information and advice from those who, belonging to the neighbourhood, could give it. It was natural for the senators from a State or the representative in Congress from a district within which a vacant office lay, to recommend to the President candidates for it, natural for the President or his ministers to be guided by this recommendation, of course, in both cases, only when they belonged to the same party as the President. Although this usage received no sanction from the Constitution, senators and representatives maintained it so persistently, since it strengthened themselves and their party in the locality, that the executive virtually admitted the rights they claimed, and suffered its patronage to be prostituted to the purpose of rewarding local party service and conciliating local party support. Now and then a President, or a strong Minister controlling the President, has proved restive; yet the usage continues, being grounded on the natural wish of the executive to have the good-will and help of the senators in getting treaties and appointments confirmed, and on the feeling that the party in every district must be strengthened by a distribution of good things, in the way which the local leader thinks most serviceable. The essential features of the system are, that a place in the public service is held at the absolute pleasure of the appointing authority; that it is invariably bestowed from party motives on a party man, as a reward for party services (whether of the appointee or of some one who pushes him); that no man expects to hold it any longer than his party holds power; and that he has therefore the strongest personal reasons for fighting in the party ranks. Thus the conception of office among politicians came to be not the ideal one, of its involving a duty to the community, nor the "practical" one, of its being a snug berth in which a man may live if he does not positively neglect his work, but the perverted one, of its being a salary paid in respect of party services, past, present, and future.

The politicians, however, could hardly have riveted this system on the country but for certain notions which had become current among the mass of the people. "Rotation in office" was, and indeed by most men still is, held to be conformable to the genius of a democracy. It gives every man an equal chance of power and salary, resembling herein the Athenian and Florentine system of choosing officers by lot. It is supposed to stimulate men to exertion, to foster a laudable ambition to serve the country or the neighbourhood, to prevent the growth of an official caste, with its habits of routine, its stiffness, its arrogance. It recognizes that equality which is so dear to the American mind, bidding an official remember that he is the servant of the people and not their master, like the bureaucrats of Europe. It forbids him to fancy that he has any right to be where he is, any ground for expecting to stay there. It ministers in an odd kind of way to that fondness for novelty and change in persons and surroundings which is natural in the constantly-moving communities of the West. The habit which grew up of electing State and city officers for short terms tended in the same direction. If those whom the people itself chose were to hold office only for a year or two, why should those who were appointed by Federal authority have a longer tenure? And the use of patronage for political purposes was further justified by the example of England, whose government was believed by the Americans of fifty years ago to be worked, as in last century it largely was worked, by the Patronage Secretary of the Treasury in his function of distributing places to members of the House of Commons, and honours (such as orders, and steps in the peerage) to members of the House of Lords, ecclesiastical preferments to the relatives of both.

Another and a potent reason why the rotation plan commended itself to the Americans is to be found in the belief that one man is as good as another, and will do well enough any work you set him to, a belief happily expressed by their old enemy King George the Third when he said that " every man is good enough for any place he can get." In America every smart man is expected to be able to do anything that he turns his hand to, and the fact that a man has worked himself into a place is some evidence of his smartness. He is a " practical man." This is at bottom George the Third's idea; if you are clever enough to make people give you a place, you are clever enough to discharge its duties, or to conceal the fact that you are not discharging them. It may be added that most of these Federal places, and those which come most before the eyes of the ordinary citizen, require little special fitness. Any careful and honest man does fairly well for a tide-waiter or a lighthouse keeper. Able and active men had no great interest in advocating appointment by merit or security of tenure, for they seldom wanted places themselves; and they had, or thought they had, an interest in jobbing their poor relatives and unprosperous friends into the public service. It is true that the relative or friend ran the risk of being turned out. But hope is stronger than fear. The prospect of getting a place affects ten people for one who is affected by the prospect of losing it, for aspirants are many and places relatively few.

Hitherto we have been considering Federal offices only, the immense majority whereof are such petty posts as those of postmaster in a village, custom-house officer at a seaport, and so forth, although they also include clerkships in the departments at Washington, foreign ambassadorships and consulates, and governorships of the Territories. The system of rotation had however laid such a hold on the mind of the country that it soon extended itself over State offices and city offices also, in so far as such offices remained appointive, and were not, like the higher administrative posts and (in most of the States and the larger cities) the judicial offices, handed over to popular election. Thus appointment by favour and tenure at the pleasure of the appointer became the rule in every sphere and branch of government, National, State, and municipal, down to that very recent time of which I shall speak presently. It may seem strange that a people so eminently practical as the Americans acquiesced in a system which perverts public office from its proper function of serving the public, destroys the prospect of that skill which comes with experience, and gives nobody the least security that he will gain a higher post, or even retain the one he holds, by displaying the highest efficiency. The explanation is that administration used to be conducted in a happy-go-lucky way, that the citizens, accustomed to help themselves, relied very little on their functionaries, and did not care whether they were skilful or not, and that it was so easy and so common for a man who fell out of one kind of business to take to and make his living by another that deprivation seemed to involve little hardship. However, the main reason was that there was no party and no set of persons specially interested in putting an end to the system, whereas there soon came to be a set specially concerned to defend it. It developed, I might almost say created, the class of professional politicians, and they maintained it, because it exactly suited them. That great and growing volume of political work to be done in managing primaries, conventions, and elections for the city, State, and National governments, whereof I have already spoken, and which the advance of democratic sentiment and the needs of party warfare evolved from 1820 down to about 1850, needed men who should give to it constant and undivided attention. These men the plan of rotation in office provided. Persons who had nothing to gain for themselves would soon have tired of the work. The members of a permanent civil service would have had no motive for interfering in politics, because the political defeat of a public officer's friends would have left his position the same as before, and the civil service not being all of one party, but composed of persons appointed at different times by executives of different hues, would not have acted together as a whole. Those, however, whose bread and butter depend on their party may be trusted to work for their party, to enlist recruits, look after the organization, play electioneering tricks from which ordinary party spirit might recoil. The class of professional politicians was therefore the first crop which the spoils system, the system of using public office as private plunder, bore. Bosses were the second crop. In the old Scandinavian poetry the special title of the king or chieftain is "the giver of rings." He attracts followers and rewards the services, whether of the warrior or the skald, by liberal gifts. So the Boss wins and holds power by the bestowal of patronage. Places are the prize of victory in election warfare; he divides this spoil before as well as after the battle, promising the higher elective offices to the strongest among his fighting men, and dispensing the minor appointive offices which lie in his own gift, or that of his lieutenants, to combatants of less note but equal loyalty. Thus the chieftain consolidates, extends, fortifies his power by rewarding his supporters. He garrisons the outposts with his squires and henchmen, who are bound fast to him by the hope of getting something more, and the fear of losing what they have. Most of these appointive offices are too poorly paid to attract able men; but they form a stepping-stone to the higher ones obtained by popular election; and the desire to get them and keep them provides that numerous rank and file which the American system requires to work the Machine. In a country like England office is an object of desire to a few prominent men, but only to a few, because the places which are vacated on a change of government are less than fifty in all, while vacancies in other places happen only by death or promotion. Hence an insignificant number of persons out of the whole population have a personal pecuniary interest in the triumph of their party. In England, therefore, one has what may be called the general officers and headquarters staff of an army of professional politicians, but few subalterns and no privates. And in England most of these general officers are rich men, independent of official salaries. In America the privates are proportioned in number to the officers. They are a great host. As nearly all live by politics, they are held together by a strong personal motive. When their party is kept out of the spoils of the Federal government, as the Democrats were out from 1861 till 1885, they have a second chance in the State spoils, a third chance in the city spoils; and the prospect of winning at least one of these two latter sets of places maintains their discipline and whets their appetite, however slight may be their chance of capturing the Federal offices.

It is these spoilsmen who have depraved and distorted the mechanism of politics. It is they who pack the primaries and run the conventions so as to destroy the freedom of popular choice, they who contrive and execute the election frauds which disgrace some States and cities,—repeating and ballot stuffing, obstruction of the polls, and fraudulent countings in.

In making every administrative appointment a matter of party claim and personal favour, the system has lowered the general tone of public morals, for it has taught men to neglect the interests of the community, and made insincerity ripen into cynicism. Nobody supposes that merit has anything to do with promotion, or believes the pretext alleged for an appointment. Politics has been turned into the art of distributing salaries so as to secure the maximum of support from friends with the minimum of offence to opponents. To this art able men have been forced to bend their minds: on this Presidents and ministers have spent those hours which were demanded by the real problems of the country. The rising politician must think of obscure supporters seeking petty places as well as of those greater appointments by which his knowledge of men and his honesty deserve to be judged. It is hardly a caricature in Mr. Lowell's satire when the intending presidential candidate writes to his maritime friend in New England,—

> "If you git me inside the White House,
> Your head with ile I'll kinder 'nint,
> By gittin' you inside the light-house,
> Down to the end of Jaalam pint."

After this, it seems a small thing to add that rotation in office has not improved the quality of the civil service. Men selected for their services at elections or in primaries have not proved the most capable servants of the public. As most of the posts they fill need nothing more than such ordinary business qualities as the average American possesses, the mischief has not come home to the citizens generally, but it has sometimes been serious in the higher grades, such as the departments at Washington and some of the greater custom-houses. Moreover, the official is not free to attend to his official duties. More important, because more influential on his fortunes, is the duty to his party of looking after its interests at the election, and his duty to his chiefs, the Boss and Ring, of seeing that the candidate they favour gets the party nomination. Such an official, whom democratic theory seeks to remind of his dependence on the public, does not feel himself bound to the public, but to the city boss or senator or congressman who has procured his appointment. Gratitude, duty, service, are all for the patron. So far from making the official zealous in the performance of his functions, insecurity of tenure has discouraged sedulous application to work, since it is not by such application that office is retained and promotion won. The administration of some among the public departments in Federal and city government is more behind that of private enterprises than is the case in European countries; the ingenuity and executive talent which the nation justly boasts, are least visible in national or municipal business. In short, the civil service is not in America, and cannot under the system of rotation become, a career. Place-hunting is the career, and an office is not a public trust, but a means of requiting party services, and also, under the method of assessments previously described, a source whence party funds may be raised for election purposes.

Some of these evils were observed as far back as 1853, when an Act was passed by Congress requiring clerks appointed to the departments at Washington to pass a qualifying examination. Neither this nor subsequent legislative efforts in the same direction produced any improvement, for the men in office who ought to have given effect to the law were hostile to it. Similar causes defeated the system of competitive examination, inaugurated by an Act of Congress in 1871, when the present agitation for civil service reform had begun to lay hold of the public mind. Mr. Hayes (1877-81) was the first President who seems to have honestly desired to reform the civil service, but the opposition of the politicians, and the indifference of Congress, which had legislated merely in deference to the pressure of enlightened opinion outside, proved too much for him. A real step in advance was however made in 1883, by the passage of what is called from its author (late senator from Ohio) the Pendleton Act, which instituted a board of civil service commissioners (to be named by the

President), directing them to apply a system of competitive examinations to a considerable number of offices in the departments at Washington, and a smaller number in other parts of the country. President Arthur named a good commission, and under the rules framed by it some improvement was effected. When Mr. Cleveland became President in 1885 it was feared that the hungry Democrats, having been out of power since 1861, would fall like wolves upon the offices, compelling the President to dismiss the present place-holders to make room for his own partisans. Mr. Cleveland, however, if he did much less good than sanguine reformers hoped, seems to have acquiesced in less evil than many reformers expected. That he did not make a clean sweep of office-holders, whether belonging to the classes covered by the Pendleton Act or to any others, may be gathered from the complaints that arose from Democratic spoilsmen, who thought the presidency hardly worth winning if it did not bear fruit for the class they belong to. The action of President Harrison, who succeeded in 1889, cannot as yet be fully judged.

The Act of 1883 originally applied to only 14,000 (now however to 28,000) out of about 120,000 posts. But its moral effect has been greater than this proportion represents, and entitles it to the description given of it at the time as "a sad blow to the pessimists." It strengthens the hands of any President who may desire reform, and has stimulated the civil service reform movement in States and municipalities. Several States have now instituted examinations for admission to their civil service ; and similar legislation has been applied to New York, Brooklyn, Boston, and other cities. Some years must pass before the result of these changes upon the purification of politics can be fairly judged. It is for the present enough to say that while the state of things above described has been generally true both of Federal and of State and city administration during the last sixty years, there is now reason to hope that the practice of appointing for short terms, and dismissing in order to fill vacancies with political adherents, has been shaken ; and that the extension of examinations will tend more and more to exclude mere spoilsmen from the public service.

CHAPTER 10

Corruption

No impression regarding American politics is more generally diffused in Europe than that contained in the question which the traveller who has returned from the United States becomes so weary of being asked, "Isn't everybody corrupt there?" It is an impression for which the Americans themselves, with their airy way of talking about their own country, their fondness for broad effects, their enjoyment of a good story and humorous pleasure in exaggerations generally, are largely responsible. European visitors who, generally belonging to the wealthier classes, are generally reactionary in politics, and glad to find occasion for disparaging popular government, eagerly catch up and repeat the stories they are told in New York or San Francisco. European readers take literally the highly-coloured pictures of some American novels and assume that the descriptions there given of certain men and groups "inside politics" —descriptions legitimate enough in a novel—hold true of all men and groups following that unsavoury trade. Europeans, moreover, and Englishmen certainly not less than other Europeans, have a useful knack of forgetting their own shortcomings when contemplating those of their neighbours; so you may hear men wax eloquent over the depravity of transatlantic politicians who will sail very near the wind in giving deceptive pledges to their own constituents, who will support flagrant jobs done on behalf of their own party, who will accept favours from, and dine with, and receive at their own houses, financial speculators and members of the legislature whose aims are just as base, and whose standard is just as low as those of the worst congressman that ever came to push his fortune in Washington.

I am sensible of the extreme difficulty of estimating the amount of corruption that prevails in the United States. If a native American does not know—as few do—how deep it goes nor how widely it is spread, much less can a stranger. I have, however, submitted the impressions I formed to the judgment of some fair-minded and experienced American friends, and am assured by them that these impressions are substantially correct; that is to say, that they give a view of the facts such as they have themselves formed from an observation incomparably wider than that of a European traveller could be.

The word " corruption " needs to be analyzed. It is used to cover several different kinds of political unsoundness.

One sense, the most obvious, is the taking or giving of money bribes. Another sense is the taking or giving of bribes in kind, *e.g.* the allotment of a certain quantity of stock or shares in a company, or of an interest in a profitable contract, or of a land grant. The offence is essentially the same as where a money bribe passes, but to most people it does not seem the same, partly because the taking of money is a more unmistakable selling of one's self, partly because it is usually uncertain how the bribe given in kind will turn out, and a man excuses himself by thinking that its value will depend on how he develops the interest he has obtained. A third sense of the word includes the doing of a job, *e.g.* promising a contractor that he shall have the clothing of the police or the cleaning of the city thoroughfares in return for his political support; giving official advertisements to a particular newspaper which puffs you; promising a railroad president, whose subscription to party funds is hoped for, to secure the defeat of a bill seeking to regulate the freight charges of his road or threatening its land grants. These cases shade off into those of the last preceding group, but they seem less black, because the act done is one which would probably be done anyhow by some one else from no better motive, and because the turpitude consists not in getting a private gain but in misusing a public position to secure a man's own political advancement. Hence the virtue that will resist a bribe will often succumb to these temptations.

There is also the sense in which the bestowal of places of power and profit from personal motives is said to be a corrupt exercise of patronage. Opinion has in all countries been lenient to such action when the place is given as a reward of party services, but the line between a party and a personal service cannot be easily drawn.

Then, lastly, one sometimes hears the term stretched to cover insincerity in professions of political faith. To give pledges and advocate measures which one inwardly dislikes and deems opposed to the public interest is a form of misconduct which seems far less gross than to sell one's vote or influence, but it may be, in a given instance, no less injurious to the state.

Although these two latter sets of cases do not fall within the proper meaning and common use of the word corruption, it seems worth while to mention them, because derelictions of duty which a man thinks trivial in the form with which custom has made him familiar in his own country, where perhaps they are matter for merriment, shock him when they appear in a different form in another country. They get mixed up in his mind with venality, and are cited to prove that the country is corrupt and its politicians profligate. A European who does not blame a minister for making a man governor of a colony because he has done some back-stairs parliamentary work, will be shocked at seeing in New York some one put into the custom-house in order that he may organize primaries in the district of the congressman who has got him the place. English members of Parliament condemn the senator who moves a resolution intended to "placate" the Irish vote, while they forget their own professions of ardent interest in schemes which they think economically unsound but likely to rouse the flagging interest of the agricultural labourer. Distinguishing these senses in which the word corruption is used, let us attempt to inquire how far it is chargeable on the men who compose each of the branches of the American Federal and State Government.

No President has ever been seriously charged with pecuniary corruption. The Presidents have been men very different in their moral standard, and sometimes neither scrupulous nor patriotic, but money or money's worth they have never touched for themselves, great as the temptations must have been to persons with small means and heavy expenses. They have doubtless often made bad appointments from party motives, have sought to strengthen themselves by the use of their patronage, have talked insincerely and tolerated jobs ; but all these things have also been done within the last thirty years by sundry English, French, and Italian prime ministers, some of whom have since been canonized.

The standard of honour maintained by the Presidents has not

always been maintained by the leading members of recent administrations, several of whom have been suspected of complicity in railroad jobs, and even in frauds upon the revenue. They may not have, probably they did not, put any part of the plunder into their own pockets, but they have winked at the misdeeds of their subordinates, and allowed the party funds to be replenished, not by direct malversation, yet by rendering services to influential individuals or corporations which a strict sense of public duty would have forbidden. On the other hand, it is fair to say that there seems to be no case since the war—although there was a bad case in President Buchanan's Cabinet just before the war—in which a member of the Cabinet has received money, or its equivalent, as the price of either an executive act or an appointment, while inferior officials, who have been detected in so doing (and this occasionally happens), have been dismissed and disgraced.

Next, as to Congress. It is particularly hard to discover the truth about Congress, for few of the abundant suspicions excited and accusations brought against senators or members of the House have been, or could have been, sifted to the bottom. Among four hundred men there will be the clean and the unclean. The opportunities for private gain are large, the chances of detection small; few members keep their seats for three or four successive congresses, and one half are changed every two years, so the temptation to make hay while the sun shines is all the stronger.

There are several forms which temptation takes in the Federal legislature. One is afforded by the position a member holds on a committee. All bills and many resolutions are referred to some one of the committees, and it is in the committee-room that their fate is practically decided. In a small body each member has great power, and the exercise of power (as observed already) is safeguarded by little responsibility. He may materially advance a bill promoted by an influential manufacturer, or financier, or railroad president. He may obstruct it. He may help, or may oppose, a bill directed against a railroad or other wealthy corporation, which has something to gain or lose from Federal legislation. No small part of the business of Congress is what would be called in England private business; and although the individual railroads which come directly into relation with the Federal government are not numerous,—the great transcontinental lines which have received land grants or other subventions are the most important,—questions affecting these roads do frequently come up and involve large amounts of money. The tariff on imports opens another enormous sphere in which legislative intervention affects private pecuniary interests; for it makes all the difference to many sets of manufacturers whether duties on certain classes of goods are raised, or maintained, or lowered. Hence the doors of Congress are besieged by a whole army of commercial or railroad men and their agents, to whom, since they have come to form a sort of profession, the name of Lobbyists is given. Many congressmen are personally interested, and lobby for themselves among their colleagues from the vantage-ground of their official positions.

Thus a vast deal of solicitation and bargaining goes on. Lobbyists offer considerations for help in passing a bill which is desired or in stopping a bill which is feared. Two members, each of whom has a bill to get through, or one of whom desires to prevent his railroad from being interfered with while the other wishes the tariff on an article which he manufactures kept up, make a compact by which each aids the other. This is Logrolling: You help me to roll my log, which is too heavy for my unaided strength, and I help you to roll yours. Sometimes a member brings in a bill directed against some railroad or other great corporation, merely in order to levy blackmail upon it. This is technically called a Strike. An eminent railroad president told me that for some years a certain senator regularly practised this trick. When he had brought in his bill he came straight to New York, called at the railroad offices, and asked the president what he would give him to withdraw the bill. That the Capitol and the hotels at Washington are a nest of such intrigues and machinations, while Congress is sitting, is admitted on all hands; but how many of the members are tainted no one can tell. Sometimes when money passes it goes not to the member of Congress himself, but to some Boss who can and does put pressure on him. Sometimes, again, a lobbyist will demand a sum for the purpose of bribing a member who is really honest, and, having ascertained that the member is going to vote in the way desired, will keep the sum in his own pocket. Bribery often takes the form of a transfer of stocks or shares, nor have even free passes on railroads been scorned by some of the more needy legislators. The abuse on this head had grown so serious that the bestowal of passes on inter-State lines was forbidden by statute in 1887.   In the end of 1883 portions of a correspondence in the years 1876-78 between Mr. Huntington, one of the proprietors and directors of the Central Pacific Railroad, who then represented that powerful corporation at Washington, and one of his agents in California, were published ; and from these it appeared that the company, whose land grants were frequently threatened by hostile bills, and which was exposed to the competition of rival enterprises, which (because they were to run through Territories) Congress was asked to sanction, defended itself by constant dealings with senators and representatives— dealings in the course of which it offered money and bonds to those whose support it needed.   Mr. Huntington comments freely on the character of various members of both Houses, and describes not only his own operations, but those of Mr. Scott, his able and active opponent, who had the great advantage of being able to command passes on some railways running out of Washington.

It does not seem, from what one hears on the spot, that money is often given, or, I should rather say, it seems that the men to whom it is given are few in number.   But considerations of some kind pretty often pass, so that corruption in both the first and second of the above senses must be admitted to exist and to affect a portion, though only a small portion of Congress.   A position of some delicacy is occupied by eminent lawyers who sit in Congress and receive retainers from powerful corporations whose interests may be affected by congressional legislation, retainers for which they are often not expected to render any forensic service.   There are various ways in which members of Congress can use their position to advance their personal interests.   They have access to the executive, and can obtain favours from it ; not so much because the executive cares what legislation they pass, for it has little to do with legislation, but that the members of the Cabinet are on their promotion, and anxious to stand well with persons whose influence covers any considerable local area, who may perhaps be even able to control the delegation of a State in a nominating convention.   Hence a senator or congressman may now and then sway the executive towards a course it would not otherwise have taken, and the resulting gain to himself, or to some person who has invoked his influence, may be an illicit gain, probably not in the form of money, but as a job out of which something may be made.

Again, it has been hitherto an important part of a member's duty to obtain places for his constituents in the Federal civil service. There are about 120,000 of such places. Here is a vast field, if not for pecuniary gain, for appointments are not sold, yet for the gratification of personal and party interests. Nor does the mischief stop with the making of inferior appointments, for the habit of ignoring public duty which is formed blunts men's sense of honour, and makes them more apt to yield to some grosser form of temptation. Similar causes produced similar effects during the last century in England, and it is said that the French legislature now suffers from the like malady, members of the Chamber being incessantly occupied in wheedling or threatening the executive into conferring places or decorations upon their constituents.

The rank and file of the Federal civil service attain a level of integrity as high as that of England or Germany. The State civil service is comparatively small, and in most States one hears little said against its purity. Taking one part of the country with another, a citizen who has business with a government department, such as the customs or excise, or with a State treasurer's office, or with a poor law or school authority, has as much expectation of finding honest men to deal with as he has of finding trustworthy agents to conduct a piece of private commercial business. Instances of dishonesty are more noticed when they occur in a public department, but I do not think they are more frequent.

It is hard to form a general judgment regarding the State legislatures, because they differ so much among themselves. Those of Massachusetts, Vermont, and several of the North-western States, such as Michigan, are pure, *i.e.* the members who would take a bribe are excessively few, and those who would push through a job for some other sort of consideration a small fraction of the whole. On the other hand, New York and Pennsylvania have so bad a name that people profess to be surprised when a good act passes, and a strong governor is kept constantly at work vetoing bills corruptly obtained or mischievous in themselves. Several causes have contributed to degrade the legislature of New York State. It is comparatively small in number, the Assembly having but 128 members, the Senate 32. It includes, besides New York and Brooklyn, several smaller ring-governed cities whence bad members come. It has to deal with immensely powerful corporations, such as the great railroads which traverse it on their way to the West. These corporations are the bane of State politics, for their management is secret, being usually in the hands of one or two capitalists, and their wealth is so great that they can offer bribes at which ordinary virtue grows pale. There are many honest men in the Assembly, and a few are rich men who do not need a *douceur*, but the proportion of tainted men is large enough to pollute the whole lump. Of what the bribe-taker gets he keeps a part for himself, using the rest to buy the doubtful votes of purchaseable people ; to others he promises his assistance when they need it, and when by such log-rolling he has secured a considerable backing, he goes to the honest men, among whom, of course, he has a considerable acquaintance, puts the matter to them in a plausible way—they are probably plain farmers from the rural districts—and so gains his majority. Each great corporation keeps an agent at Albany, the capital of the State, who has authority to buy off the promoters of hostile bills, and to employ the requisite professional lobbyists. Such a lobbyist, who may or may not be himself a member, bargains for a sum down, $5000 or $10,000 (£1000 or £2000), in case he succeeds in getting the bill in question passed or defeated, as the case may be ; and when the session ends he comes for his money, and no questions are asked. This sort of thing now goes on, or has lately gone on, in several other States, though nowhere on so grand a scale. Virginia, Maryland, California, Illinois, Missouri, are all more or less impure ; Louisiana is said to be now worse than New York. But the lowest point was reached in some of the Southern States shortly after the war, when, the negroes having received the suffrage, the white inhabitants were still excluded as rebels, and the executive government was conducted by Northern carpet-baggers under the protection of Federal troops. In some States the treasury was pilfered ; huge State debts were run up ; negroes voted farms to themselves ; all kinds of robbery and jobbery went on unchecked. South Carolina, for instance, was a perfect Tartarus of corruption, as much below the Hades of Illinois or Missouri as the heaven of ideal purity is above the ordinary earth of Boston and Westminster. In its legislature there was an old darkey, jet black and with venerable white hair, a Methodist preacher, and influential among his brother states-men, who kept a stall for legislation, where he dealt in statutes at prices varying from $100 to $400. Since those days there has been a peaceful revolution for the better at the South, but some of its legislative bodies have still much leeway to make up.

Of city governments I have spoken in previous chapters. They begin to be bad when the population begins to exceed 100,000, and includes a large proportion of recent immigrants. They are generally pure in smaller places, that is to say, they are as pure as those of an average English, French, or German city.

The form which corruption usually takes in the populous cities is the sale of "franchises" (especially monopolies in the use of public thoroughfares), the jobbing of contracts, and the bestowal of places upon personal adherents, both of them faults not unknown in large European municipalities, and said to be specially rife in Paris, though no rifer than under Louis Napoleon, when the reconstruction of the city under Prefect Haussman provided unequalled opportunities for the enrichment of individuals at the public expense. English vestries, local boards, and even, though much more rarely, town councils, do some quiet jobbery. No European city has, however, witnessed scandals approaching those of New York or Philadelphia, where the public till has been robbed on a vast scale, and accounts have been systematically cooked to conceal the thefts.

Last of all we come to the ordinary voter and the question of bribery at elections. Here, again, there is the widest possible difference between different regions of the country. The greater part of the Union is pure, as pure as Scotland, where from 1868 till 1885 there was only one election petition for alleged bribery. Other parts are no better than the small boroughs of Southern England were before the Corrupt Practices Act of 1883. No place, however, not even the poorest ward in New York City, sinks below the level of such constituencies as Yarmouth, Sandwich, or Canterbury were in England. Bribery is not practised in America in the same way as it was recently in some parts of England, or as anciently at Rome, by distributing small sums among a large mass of poor electors, or even, as in many English boroughs, among a section of voters (not always the poorest) known to be venal, and accustomed to reserve their votes till shortly before the close of the poll. The American practice has been to give sums of from $20 to $50 (£4 to £10) to an active local "worker," who undertakes to bring up a certain number of voters, perhaps twenty or thirty, whom he "owns" or can get at. He is not required to account for the money, and probably spends very little of it in direct bribes, though something in drinks to the lower sort of elector. This kind of expenditure belongs rather to the category of paid canvassing than of bribery, yet sometimes the true European species occurs. In a New Hampshire town not long ago, $10 (£2) were paid to each of two hundred doubtful voters. In some districts of New York the friends of a candidate will undertake, in case he is returned, to pay the rent of the poorest voters who occupy tenement houses, and the candidate subsequently makes up the amount. The expenses of congressional and presidential elections are often heavy, and though the larger part goes in organization and demonstrations, meetings, torchlight processions, and so forth, a part is likely to go in some illicit way. A member of Congress for a poor district in a great city told me that his expenses ran from $8000 up to $10,000 (£1600 to £2000), which is just about what a parliamentary contest used to cost in an English borough constituency of equal area. In America the number of voters in a constituency is more than five times as great as it now is in England, but the official expenses of polling-booths and clerks are not borne by the candidate. In a corrupt district along the Hudson River above New York I have heard of as much as $50,000 (£10,000) being spent at a single congressional election, when in some other districts of the State the expenses did not exceed $2000 (£400). In a presidential election great sums are spent in doubtful, or, as they are called, "pivotal" States. Indiana was "drenched with money" in 1880, much of it contributed by great corporations, yet one is told that little of this went in bribery. How much ever does go it is the harder to determine, because elections are rarely impeached on this ground, both parties tacitly agreeing that bygones shall be bygones. The election of 1888 was one of the worst on record, so large was the expenditure in doubtful States.

Well-informed Americans do not consider bribery at elections to be a growing evil in their country. Serious it is, but not comparable for the mischief it does either to Bossism or to election frauds. Probably the disease is no more diffused than in England before 1883. In most rural districts it is practically unknown : the only thing approaching it is the farmer's notion, that when he drives in five or six miles to a polling place he ought to get his dinner for nothing.

On a review of the whole matter, the following conclusions may be found not very wide of the truth.

Bribery exists in Congress, but is confined to a few members, say five per cent of the whole number. It is more common in the legislatures of a few, but only a few States, practically absent from the higher walks of the Federal civil service and among the chief State officials, rare among the lower officials, unknown among the Federal judges, rare among State judges.[1]

The taking of other considerations than money, such as a share in a lucrative contract, or a railway pass, or a "good thing" to be secured for a friend, prevails among legislators to a somewhat larger extent. Being less coarsely palpable than the receipt of money, it is thought more venal. One may roughly conjecture that from fifteen to twenty per cent of the members of Congress or of an average State legislature would allow themselves to be influenced by inducements of this kind.

Malversation of public funds occurs occasionally in cities, rarely among Federal or State officers.

Jobbery of various kinds, *i.e.* the misuse of a public position for the benefit of individuals, is pretty frequent. It is often disguised as a desire to render some service to the party, and the same excuse is sometimes found for a misappropriation of public money.

Patronage is usually dispensed with a view to party considerations or to win personal support. But this remark is equally true of England and France, the chief difference being that owing to the short terms and frequent removals the quantity of patronage is relatively greater in the United States.

If this is not a bright picture, neither is it so dark as that which most Europeans have drawn, and which the loose language of many Americans sanctions. What makes it seem dark is the contrast between the deficiencies which the government shows in this respect, and the excellence, on the one hand of the frame of the Constitution, on the other of the tone and sentiment of the people. The European reader may, however, complain that the picture is vague in its outlines. I cannot make it more definite. The facts are not easy to ascertain, and it is hard to say what standard one is to apply to them. In the case of America men are inclined to apply an ideal standard, because she is a republic, professing to have made a new departure in politics, and setting before her a higher ideal than most European monarchies. Yet it must be remembered that in a new and large country, where the temptations are enormous and the persons tempted have many of them no social position to forfeit, the conditions are not the most favourable to virtue. If, recognizing the fact that the path of the politician is in all countries thickly set with snares, we leave ideals out of sight and try America by an actual standard, we shall find that while her legislative bodies fall below the level of purity maintained in England and Germany, probably also in France and Italy, her Federal and State administration, in spite of the evils flowing from an uncertain tenure, is not, in point of integrity, at this moment sensibly inferior to the administrations of European countries.

Chapter 11

Nominating Conventions

In every American election there are two acts of choice, two periods of contest. The first is the selection of the candidate from within the party by the party ; the other is the struggle between the parties for the place. Frequently the former of these is more important, more keenly fought over, than the latter, for there are many districts in which the predominance of one party is so marked that its candidate is sure of success, and therefore the choice of a candidate is virtually the choice of the officer or representative.

Preceding chapters have described the machinery which exists for choosing and nominating a candidate. The process is similar in every State of the Union, and through all elections to office, from the lowest to the highest, from that of common councilman for a city ward up to that of President of the United States. But, of course, the higher the office, and the larger the area over which the election extends, the greater are the efforts made to secure the nomination, and the hotter the passions it excites.

Like most political institutions, the system of nominating the President by a popular convention is the result of a long process of evolution.

In the first two elections, those of 1789 and 1792, there was no need for nominations of candidates, because the whole nation wished and expected George Washington to be elected. So too, when in 1796 Washington declared his retirement, the dominant feeling of one party was for John Adams, that of the other for Thomas Jefferson, and nobody thought of setting out formally what was so generally understood.

In 1800, however, the year of the fourth election, there was somewhat less unanimity. The prevailing sentiment of the Federalists went for re-electing Adams, and the small conclave of Federalist members of Congress which met to promote his

interest was deemed scarcely necessary. The Republicans, however (for that was the name then borne by the party which now
calls itself Democratic), while united in desiring to make Jefferson
President, hesitated as to their candidate for the vice-presidency,
and a meeting of Republican members of Congress was therefore
called to recommend Aaron Burr for this office. It was a small
meeting and a secret meeting, but it is memorable not only as the
first congressional caucus but as the first attempt to arrange in
any way a party nomination.

In 1804 a more regular gathering for the same purpose was
held. All the Republican members of Congress were summoned
to meet; and they unanimously nominated Jefferson for President, and George Clinton of New York for Vice-President. So
in 1808 nearly all the Republican majority in both Houses of
Congress met and formally nominated Madison and Clinton.
The same course was followed in 1812, and again in 1816.
But the objections which were from the first made to this
action of the party in Congress, as being an arrogant usurpation of the rights of the people—for no one dreamed of leaving
freedom to the presidential electors—gained rather than lost
strength on each successive occasion, so much so that in 1820
the few who met made no nomination, and in 1824, out of the
Democratic members of both Houses of Congress summoned to
the "nominating caucus," as it was called, only sixty-six attended,
many of the remainder having announced their disapproval of
the practice. The nominee of this caucus came in only third at
the polls, and this failure gave the *coup de grâce* to a plan which
the levelling tendencies of the time, and the disposition to refer
everything to the arbitrament of the masses, would in any case
have soon extinguished. No congressional caucus was ever
again held for the choice of candidates.

A new method, however, was not at once discovered. In 1828
Jackson was recommended as candidate by the legislature of
Tennessee and by a number of popular gatherings in different
places, while his opponents accepted, without any formal nomination, the then President, J. Q. Adams, as their candidate. In
1831, however, and again in 1832, assemblies were held by two
great parties (the Anti-Masons and the National Republicans,
afterwards called Whigs) consisting of delegates from most of
the States; and each of these conventions nominated its candidates for the presidency and vice-presidency. A third "national

convention" of young men, which met later in 1832, adopted the Whig nominations, and added to them a series of ten resolutions, constituting the first political platform ever put forth by a nominating body. The friends of Jackson followed suit by holding their convention which nominated him and Van Buren. For the election of 1836, a similar convention was held by the Jacksonian Democrats, none by their opponents. But for that of 1840, national conventions of delegates from nearly all the States were held by both Democrats and Whigs, as well as by the (then young and very small) party of the Abolitionists. This precedent has been followed in every subsequent contest, so that the national nominating conventions of the great parties are now as much a part of the regular machinery of politics as the election rules contained in the Constitution itself. The establishment of the system coincides with and represents the complete social democratization of politics in Jackson's time. It suits both the professionals, for whom it finds occupation and whose power it secures, and the ordinary citizen who, not having time himself to attend to politics, likes to think that his right of selecting candidates is duly recognized in the selection of candidates by delegates whom he is entitled to vote for. But it was soon seen to be liable to fall under the control of selfish intriguers and to destroy the chances of able and independent men, and was denounced as early as 1844 by Calhoun, who then refused to allow his name to be submitted to a nominating convention. He observed that he would never have joined in breaking down the old congressional caucus had he foreseen that its successor would prove so much more pernicious.

Thus from 1789 till 1800 there were no formal nominations; from 1800 till 1824, nominations were made by congressional caucuses; from 1824 till 1840, nominations irregularly made by State legislatures and popular meetings were gradually ripening towards the method of a special gathering of delegates from the whole country. This last plan has held its ground from 1840 till the present day, and is so exactly conformable to the political habits of the people that it is not likely soon to disappear.

Its perfection, however, was not reached at once. The early conventions were to a large extent mass meetings. The later and present ones are regularly-constituted representative bodies, composed exclusively of delegates, each of whom has been duly elected at a party meeting in his own State, and brings with him his credentials. It would be tedious to trace the process whereby the present system was created, so I shall be content with describing it in outline as it now stands.

The Constitution provides that each State shall choose as many presidential electors as it has persons representing it in Congress, *i.e.* two electors to correspond to the two senators from each State, and as many more as the State sends members to the House of Representatives. Thus Delaware and Oregon have each three electoral votes, because they have each only one representative besides their two senators. New York has thirty-six electoral votes : two corresponding to its two senators, thirty-four corresponding to its thirty-four representatives in the House.

Now in the nominating convention each State is allowed twice as many delegates as it has electoral votes, *e.g.* Delaware and Oregon have each six delegates, New York has seventy-two. The delegates are chosen by local conventions in their several States, viz. two for each congressional district by the party convention of that district, and four for the whole State (called delegates-at-large) by the State convention. As each convention is composed of delegates from primaries, it is the composition of the primaries which determines that of the local conventions, and the composition of the local conventions which determines that of the national. To every delegate there is added a person called his " alternate," chosen by the local convention at the same time, and empowered to replace him in case he cannot be present in the national convention. If the delegate is present to vote the alternate is silent ; if from any cause the delegate is absent, the alternate steps into his shoes.

Respecting the freedom of the delegate to vote for whom he will, there have been differences both of doctrine and of practice. A local convention or State convention may instruct its delegates which aspirant shall be their first choice, or even in case he cannot be carried, for whom their subsequent votes shall be cast. Such instructions are frequently given, and still more frequently implied, because a delegate is often chosen expressly as being the supporter of one or other of the aspirants whose names are most prominent. But the delegate is not absolutely bound to follow his instructions. He may vote even on the first ballot for some other aspirant than the one desired by his own local or State convention. Much more, of course, may he, though not so instructed, change his vote when it is plain that that aspirant will not succeed. His vote is always a valid one, even when given in the teeth of his instructions; but how far he will be held censurable for breaking them depends on a variety of circumstances. His motives may be corrupt; perhaps something has been given him. They may be pardonable; a party chief may have put pressure on him, or he may desire to be on the safe side, and go with the majority. They may be laudable; he really seeks to do the best for the party, or has been convinced by facts lately brought to his knowledge that the man for whom he is instructed is unworthy. Where motives are doubtful, it may be charitable, but it is not safe, to assume that they are of the higher order. Each " State delegation " has its chairman, and is expected to keep together during the convention. It usually travels together to the place of meeting; takes rooms in the same hotel; has a recognized headquarters there ; sits in a particular place allotted to it in the convention hall ; holds meetings of its members during the progress of the convention to decide on the course which it shall from time to time take. These meetings, if the State be a large and doubtful one, excite great interest, and the sharp-eared reporter prowls round them, eager to learn how the votes will go. Each State delegation votes by its chairman, who announces how his delegates vote ; but if his report is challenged the roll of delegates is called, and they vote individually. Whether the votes of a State delegation shall be given solid for the aspirant whom the majority of the delegation favours, or by the delegates individually according to their preferences, is a point which has excited bitter controversy. The present practice of the Republican party (so settled in 1876 and again in 1880) allows the delegates to vote individually, even when they have been instructed by a State convention to cast a solid vote. The Democratic party, on the other hand, sustains any such instruction given to the delegation, and records the vote of all the State delegates for the aspirant whom the majority among them approve. This is the so-called Unit Rule. If, however, the State convention has not imposed the unit rule, the delegates vote individually.

For the sake of keeping up party life in the Territories and in the Federal District of Columbia, delegates from them are admitted to the national convention, although the Territories and District have no votes in a presidential election. Delegations

of States which are known to be in the hands of the opposite
party, and whose preference of one aspirant to another will not
really tell upon the result of the presidential election, are
admitted to vote equally with the delegations of the States sure
to go for the party which holds the convention. This arrangement is justified on the ground that it sustains the interest and
energy of the party in States where it is in a minority. But it
permits the choice to be determined by districts whose own
action will not tell in any way on the election itself, and the
delegates from these districts are apt to belong to a lower class
of politicians than those from the States where the party holds
a majority, and to be swayed by more sordid motives.

So much for the composition of the national convention : we
may now go on to describe its proceedings.

It is held in the summer immediately preceding a presidential
election, usually in June or July, the election falling in November. A large city is always chosen, in order to obtain adequate
hotel accommodation, and easy railroad access. Formerly, conventions were commonly held in Baltimore or Philadelphia, but
since the centre of population has shifted to the Mississippi valley,
Cincinnati, St. Louis, and especially Chicago, have become the
favourite spots.

Business begins by the "calling of the convention to order"
by the chairman of the National Party committee. Then a
temporary chairman is nominated, and, if opposed, voted on ;
the vote sometimes giving an indication of the respective strength
of the factions present. Then the secretaries and the clerks are
appointed, and the rules which are to govern the business are
adopted. After this, the committees, particularly those on credentials and resolutions, are nominated, and the convention
adjourns till their report can be presented.

The next sitting usually opens, after the customary prayer,
with the appointment of the permanent chairman, who inaugu-
rates the proceedings with a speech. Then the report of the
committee on resolutions (if completed) is presented. It contains
what is called the platform, a long series of resolutions embodying
the principles and programme of the party, which has usually
been so drawn as to conciliate every section, and avoid or treat
with prudent ambiguity those questions on which opinion within
the party is divided. Any delegate who objects to a resolution
can move to strike it out or amend it ; but it is generally

sustained in the shape it has received from the practised hands of the committee.

Next follows the nomination of aspirants for the post of party candidate. The roll of States is called, and when a State is reached to which an aspirant intended to be nominated belongs, a prominent delegate from that State mounts the platform, and proposes him in a speech extolling his merits, and sometimes indirectly disparaging the other aspirants. Another delegate seconds the nomination, sometimes a third follows; and then the roll-call goes on till all the States have been despatched, and all the aspirants nominated. The average number of nominations is seven or eight; it rarely exceeds twelve.

Thus the final stage is reached, for which all else has been but preparation—that of balloting between the aspirants. The clerks call the roll of States from Alabama to Wisconsin, and as each is called the chairman of its delegation announces the votes, *e.g.* six for A, five for B, three for C, unless, of course, under the unit rule, the whole vote is cast for that one aspirant whom the majority of the delegation supports. When all have voted, the totals are made up and announced. If one competitor has an absolute majority of the whole number voting, according to the Republican rule, a majority of two-thirds of the number voting, according to the Democratic rule, he has been duly chosen, and nothing remains but formally to make his nomination unanimous. If, however, as has usually happened of late years, no one obtains the requisite majority, the roll is called again, in order that individual delegates and delegations (if the unit rule prevails) may have the opportunity of changing their votes; and the process is repeated until some one of the aspirants put forward has received the required number of votes. Sometimes many roll-calls take place. In 1852 the Democrats nominated Franklin Pierce on the forty-ninth ballot, and the Whigs General Scott on the fifty-third. In 1880, thirty-six ballots were taken before General Garfield was nominated. But, in 1835, Martin Van Buren; in 1844, Henry Clay; in 1868 and 1872, Ulysses S. Grant, were unanimously nominated, the two former by acclamation, the latter on the first ballot. In 1884 Mr. Blaine was nominated by the Republicans on the fourth ballot, Mr. Cleveland by the Democrats on the second. Thus it sometimes happens that the voting is over in an hour or two, while at other times it may last for days.

When a candidate for the presidency has been thus found, the convention proceeds to similarly determine its candidate for the vice-presidency. The inferiority of the office, and the exhaustion which has by this time overcome the delegates, make the second struggle a less exciting and protracted one. Frequently one of the defeated aspirants is consoled by this minor nomination, especially if he has retired at the nick of time in favour of the rival who has been chosen. The work of the convention is then complete, and votes of thanks to the chairman and other officials conclude the proceedings. The two nominees are now the party candidates, entitled to the support of the party organizations and of loyal party men over the length and breadth of the Union.

Entitled to that support, but not necessarily sure to receive it. Even in America, party discipline cannot compel an individual voter to cast his ballot for the party nominee. All that the convention can do is to recommend the candidate to the party; all that opinion can do is to brand as a Kicker or Bolter whoever breaks away; all that the local party organization can do is to strike the bolter off its lists. But how stands it, the reader will ask, with the delegates who have been present in the convention, have had their chance of carrying their man, and have been beaten? are they not held absolutely bound to support the candidate chosen?

This is a question which has excited much controversy. The impulse and effort of the successful majority has always been to impose such an obligation on the defeated minority, and the chief motive which has prevented it from being always formally enforced by a rule or resolution of the convention has been the fear that it might precipitate hostilities, might induce men of independent character, or strongly opposed to some particular aspirant, to refuse to attend as delegates, or to secede early in the proceedings when they saw that a person whom they disapproved was likely to win.

At the Republican national convention at Chicago in June 1880 an attempt was successfully made to impose the obligation by the following resolution, commonly called the "Iron clad Pledge":—

"That every member of this convention is bound in honour to support its nominee, whoever that nominee may be, and that no man should hold his seat here who is not ready so to agree."

This was carried by 716 votes to 3. But at the Republican national convention at Chicago in June 1884, when a similar resolution was presented, the opposition developed was strong enough to compel its withdrawal; and in point of fact, several conspicuous delegates at that convention strenuously opposed its nominee at the subsequent presidential election, themselves voting, and inducing others to vote, for the candidate of the Democratic party.

CHAPTER 12

The Nominating Convention at Work

WE have examined the composition of a national convention and the normal order of business in it. The more difficult task remains of describing the actual character and features of such an assembly, the motives which sway it, the temper it displays, the passions it elicits, the wiles by which its members are lured or driven to their goal.

A national convention has two objects, the formal declaration of the principles, views, and practical proposals of the party, and the choice of its candidates for the executive headship of the nation.

Of these objects the former has in critical times, such as the two elections preceding the Civil War, been of great importance. In the Democratic Convention at Charleston in 1860, a debate on resolutions led to a secession, and to the break-up of the Democratic party. But of late years the adoption of platforms, drafted in a somewhat vague and pompous style by the committee, has been almost a matter of form. Some observations on these enunciations of doctrine will be found in another chapter.

The second object is of absorbing interest and importance, because the presidency is the great prize of politics, the goal of every statesman's ambition. The President can by his veto stop legislation adverse to the wishes of the party he represents. The President is the universal dispenser of patronage.

One may therefore say that the task of a convention is to choose the party candidate. And it is a task difficult enough to tax all the resources of the host of delegates and their leaders. Who is the man fittest to be adopted as candidate? Not even a novice in politics will suppose that it is the best man, *i.e.* the wisest, strongest, and most upright. Plainly, it is the man most likely to win, the man who, to use the technical term, is most "available." What a party wants is not a good President but a good candidate. The party managers have therefore to look out for the person likely to gain most support, and at the same time excite least opposition. Their search is rendered more troublesome by the fact that many of them, being themselves either aspirants or the close allies of aspirants, are not disinterested, and are distrusted by their fellow-searchers.

Many things have to be considered. The ability of a statesman, the length of time he has been before the people, his oratorical gifts, his "magnetism" (personal attractiveness), his family connections, his face and figure, the purity of his private life, his "record" (the chronicle of his conduct) as regards integrity—all these are matters needing to be weighed. To have served with distinction in the Federal ranks during the War of Secession, endears a man to the still numerous veterans of the Northern armies, and does not damage him in the South. Account must be taken of the personal jealousies and hatreds which a man has excited. To have incurred the enmity of a leading statesman, of a powerful boss or ring, or of an influential newspaper, is serious. Several such feuds may be fatal.

Finally, much depends on the State whence a possible candidate comes. Local feeling leads a State to support one of its own citizens; it increases the vote of his own party in that State, and reduces the vote of the opposite party. Where the State is decidedly of one political colour, *e.g.* so steadily Republican as Vermont, so steadily Democratic as Maryland, this consideration is weak, for the choice of a Democratic candidate from the former, or of a Republican candidate from the latter, would not make the difference of the State's vote. It is therefore from a doubtful State that a candidate may with most advantage be selected ; and the larger the doubtful State the better   California, with her five electoral votes, is just worth "placating"; Indiana, with her fifteen votes, more so; New York, with her thirty-six votes, most so of all. Hence an aspirant who belongs to a great and doubtful State is *prima facie* the most eligible candidate. The force of this consideration is shown by the fact that during the last thirty years nearly all leading aspirants have come from great States, though some of the most eminent statesmen have been citizens of small ones such as Vermont and Delaware.

Aspirants hoping to obtain the party nomination from a national convention may be divided into three classes, the two last of which, as will appear presently, are not mutually exclusive, viz.—

Favourites.　　　Dark Horses.　　　Favourite Sons.

A Favourite is always a politician well known over the Union, and drawing support from all or most of its sections. He is a man who has distinguished himself in Congress, or in the war, or in the politics of some State so large that its politics are matter of knowledge and interest to the whole nation. He is usually a person of conspicuous gifts, whether as a speaker, or a party manager, or an administrator. The drawback to him is that in making friends he has also made enemies.

A Dark Horse is a person not very widely known in the country at large, but known rather for good than for evil. He has probably sat in Congress, been useful on committees, and gained some credit among those who dealt with him in Washington. Or he has approved himself a safe and assiduous party man in the political campaigns of his own and neighbouring States, yet without reaching national prominence. Sometimes he is a really able man, but without the special talents that win popularity. Still, speaking generally, the note of the Dark Horse is respectability, verging on colourlessness; and he is therefore a good sort of person to fall back upon when able but dangerous Favourites have proved impossible. That native mediocrity rather than adverse fortune has prevented him from winning fame is proved by the fact that the Dark Horses who have reached the White House, if they have seldom turned out bad presidents, have even more seldom turned out distinguished ones.

A Favourite Son is a politician respected or admired in his own State, but little regarded beyond it. He may not be, like the Dark Horse, little known to the nation at large, but he has not fixed its eye or filled its ear. He is usually a man who has sat in the State legislature; filled with credit the post of State governor; perhaps gone as senator or representative to Washington, and there approved himself an active promoter of local interests. Probably he possesses the qualities which gain local popularity — geniality, activity, sympathy with the dominant sentiment and habits of his State; or while endowed with gifts excellent in their way, he has lacked the audacity and tenacity which push a man to the front through a jostling crowd. More rarely he is a demagogue who has raised himself by flattering the masses of his State on some local questions, or a skilful handler of party organizations who has made local bosses and spoilsmen believe that their interests are safe in his hands. Anyhow, his personality is such as to be more effective with neighbours than with the nation, as a lamp whose glow fills the side chapel of a cathedral sinks to a spark of light when carried into the nave.

A Favourite Son may be also a Dark Horse ; that is to say, he may be well known in his own State, but so little known out of it as to be an unlikely candidate. But he need not be. The types are different, for as there are Favourite Sons whom the nation knows but does not care for, so there are Dark Horses whose reputation, such as it is, has not been made in State affairs, and who rely very little on State favour.

There are seldom more than two, never more than three Favourites in the running at the same convention. Favourite Sons are more numerous—it is not uncommon to have four or five, or even six, though perhaps not all these are actually started in the race. The number of Dark Horses is practically unlimited, because many talked of beforehand are not actually started, while others not considered before the convention begins are discovered as it goes on. This happened in the leading and most instructive case of James A. Garfield, who was not voted for at all on the first ballot in the Republican Convention of 1880, and had, on no ballot up to the thirty-fourth, received more than two votes. On the thirty-sixth he was nominated by 399. So, in 1868, Horatio Seymour, who had been so little thought of as a candidate that he was chairman of the Democratic Convention, was first voted for on the twenty-second ballot. He refused to be nominated, but was induced to leave the chair and nominated on that very ballot.

To carry the analysis farther, it may be observed that four sets of motives are at work upon those who direct or vote in a convention, acting with different degrees of force on different persons. There is the wish to carry a particular aspirant. There is the wish to defeat a particular aspirant, a wish sometimes stronger than any predilection. There is the desire to get something for one's self out of the struggle—*e.g.* by trading one's vote or influence for the prospect of a Federal office. There is the wish to find the man who, be he good or bad, friend or foe, will give the party its best chance of victory. These motives

cross one another, get mixed, vary in relative strength from hour
to hour as the convention goes on and new possibilities are disclosed. To forecast their joint effect on the minds of particular
persons and sections of a party needs wide knowledge and
eminent acuteness, to play upon them is a matter of the finest
skill.

The proceedings of a nominating convention can be best·
understood by regarding the three periods into which they fall :
the transactions which precede the opening of its sittings ; the
preliminary business of passing rules and resolutions and deliver-
ing the nominating speeches ; and, finally, the balloting.

A President has scarcely been elected before the newspapers
begin to discuss his probable successor. Little, however, is done
towards the ascertainment of candidates till about a year before
the next election, when the factions of the chief aspirants prepare to fall into line, newspapers take up their parable in favour
of one or other, and bosses begin the work of "subsoiling," *i.e.*
manipulating primaries and local conventions so as to secure the
choice of such delegates to the next national convention as they
desire. In most of the conventions which appoint delegates, the
claims of the several aspirants are canvassed, and the delegates
chosen are usually chosen in the interest of one particular
aspirant. The newspapers, with their quick sense of what is
beginning to stir men's thoughts, redouble their advocacy, and
the "boom" of one or two of the probable favourites is thus
fairly started. Before the delegates leave their homes for the
national convention, most of them have fixed on their candidate,
many having indeed received positive instructions as to how their
vote shall be cast. All appears to be spontaneous, but in reality
both the choice of particular men as delegates, and the instructions given, are usually the result of untiring underground work
among local politicians, directed, or even personally conducted,
by two or three skilful agents and emissaries of a leading
aspirant, or of the knot which seeks to run him.

Four or five days before the day fixed for the opening of the
convention the delegations begin to flock into the city where it
is to be held. Some come attended by a host of friends and
camp-followers, and are received at the depôt (railway terminus)
by the politicians of the city, with a band of music and an admir-
ing crowd. Thus Tammany Hall, the famous Democratic club
of New York City, came six hundred strong to Chicago in July

1884, filling two special trains. A great crowd met it at the station, and it marched, following its Boss, from the cars to its headquarters at the Palmer House in procession, each member wearing his badge, just as the retainers of Earl Warwick the King-maker used to follow him through the streets of London with the Bear and Ragged Staff upon their sleeves. Less than twenty of the six hundred were delegates; the rest ordinary members of the organization, who had accompanied to give it moral and vocal support.

Before the great day dawns many thousands of politicians, newspaper men, and sight-seers have filled to overflowing every hotel in the city, and crowded the main thoroughfares so that the horse-cars can scarcely penetrate the throng. It is like a mediæval pilgrimage, or the mustering of a great army. When the chief delegations have arrived the work begins in earnest. Not only each large delegation, but the faction of each leading aspirant to the candidacy, has its headquarters, where the managers hold perpetual session, reckoning up their numbers, starting rumours meant to exaggerate their resources, and dishearten their opponents, organizing raids upon the less experienced delegates as they arrive. Some fill the entrance halls and bars of the hotels, talk to the busy reporters, extemporize meetings with tumultuous cheering for their favourite. The common "worker" is good enough to raise the boom by these devices. Meanwhile, the more skilful leaders begin (as it is expressed) to "plough around" among the delegations of the newer Western and Southern States, usually (at least among the Republicans) more malleable, because they come from regions where the strength of the factions supporting the various aspirants is less accurately known, and are themselves more easily "captured" by bold assertions or seductive promises. Sometimes an expert intriguer will "break into" one of these wavering delegations, and make havoc like a fox in a hen-roost. "Missionaries" are sent out to bring over individuals; embassies are accredited from one delegation to another to endeavour to arrange combinations by coaxing the weaker party to drop its own aspirant, and add its votes to those of the stronger party. All is conducted with perfect order and good-humour, for the least approach to violence would recoil upon its authors; and the only breach of courtesy is where a delegation refuses to receive the ambassadors of an organization whose evil fame has made it odious.

It is against etiquette for the aspirants themselves to appear upon the scene, whether from some lingering respect for the notion that a man must not ask the people to choose him, but accept the proffered honour, or on the principle that the attorney who conducts his own case has a fool for a client. But from Washington, if he is an official or a senator, or perhaps from his own home in some distant State, each aspirant keeps up hourly communication with his managers in the convention city, having probably a private wire laid on for the purpose. Not only may officials, including the President himself, become aspirants, but Federal office-holders may be, and very largely are, delegates, especially among the Southern Republicans when that party is in power. They have the strongest personal interest in the issue; and the heads of departments can, by promises of places, exert a potent influence. One hears in America, just as one used to hear in France under Louis Napoleon or Marshal MacMahon, of the " candidate of the Administration."

As the hour when the convention is to open approaches, each faction strains its energy to the utmost. The larger delegations hold meetings to determine their course in the event of the man they chiefly favour proving "unavailable." Conferences take place between different delegations. Lists are published in the newspapers of the strength of each aspirant. Sea and land are compassed to gain one influential delegate, who " owns " other delegates. If he resists other persuasions, he is " switched on " to the private wire of some magnate at Washington, who " talks to him," and suggests inducements more effective than those he has hitherto withstood. The air is thick with tales of plots and treasons, so that no politician trusts his neighbour, for rumour spares none.

At length the period of expectation and preparation is over, and the summer sun rises upon the fateful day to which every politician in the party has looked forward for three years. Long before the time (usually 11 A.M.) fixed for the beginning of business, every part of the hall, erected specially for the gather-ing—a hall often large enough to hold from ten to fifteen thousand persons—is crowded. The delegates—who in 1884 were 820 in number—are a mere drop in the ocean of faces. Eminent politicians from every State of the Union, senators and representatives from Washington not a few, journalists and reporters, ladies, sight-seers from distant cities, as well as a swarm

of partisans from the city itself, press in ; some semblance of
order being kept by the sergeant-at-arms and his marshals.
Some wear devices, sometimes the badge of their State, or of
their organization ; sometimes the colours or emblem of their
favourite aspirant. Each State delegation has its allotted place
marked by the flag of the State floating from a pole ; but leaders
may be seen passing from one group to another, while the spectators listen to the band playing popular airs, and cheer any well-
known figure that enters.

When the assembly is " called to order," a prayer is offered
—each day's sitting begins with a prayer by some clergyman of
local eminence, the susceptibilities of various denominations
being duly respected in the selection—and business proceeds according to the order described in the last chapter. First come the
preliminaries, appointment of committees and chairman, then the
platform, and probably on the second day, but perhaps later, the
nominations and balloting, the latter sometimes extending over
several days. There is usually both a forenoon and an afternoon
session.

A European is astonished to see eight hundred men prepare
to transact the two most difficult pieces of business an assembly
can undertake, the solemn consideration of their principles, and
the selection of the person they wish to place at the head of the
nation, in the sight and hearing of twelve thousand other men
and women. Observation of what follows does not lessen the
astonishment. The convention presents in sharp contrast and
frequent alternation, the two most striking features of Americans
in public—their orderliness and their excitability. Everything
is done according to strict rule, with a scrupulous observance of
small formalities which European meetings would ignore or
despise. Points of order almost too fine for a parliament are
taken, argued, decided on by the chair, to whom every one bows.
Yet the passions that sway the multitude are constantly bursting
forth in storms of cheering or hissing at an allusion to a favourite
aspirant or an obnoxious name, and five or six speakers often
take the floor together, shouting and gesticulating at each other
till the chairman obtains a hearing for one of them. Of course
it depends on the chairman whether or no the convention sinks
into a mob. A chairman with a weak voice, or a want of prompt
decision, or a suspicion of partisanship, may bring the assembly
to the verge of disaster, and it has more than once happened that

when the confusion that prevailed would have led to an irregular vote which might have been subsequently disputed, the action of the manager acting for the winning horse has, by waiving some point of order or consenting to an adjournment, saved the party from disruption. Even in the noisiest scenes the singular good sense and underlying love of fair-play—fair-play according to the rules of the game, which do not exclude some dodges repugnant to an honourable man—will often reassert itself, and pull back the vehicle from the edge of the precipice.

The chief interest of the earlier proceedings lies in the indications which speeches and votings give of the relative strength of the factions. Sometimes a division on the choice of a chairman, or on the adoption of a rule, reveals the tendencies of the majority, or of influential leaders, in a way which sends the chances of an aspirant swiftly up or down the barometer of opinion. So when the nominating speeches come, it is not so much their eloquence that helps a nominee as the warmth with which the audience receives them, the volume of cheering and the length of time, sometimes fifteen minutes, during which the transport lasts. As might be guessed from the size of the audience which he addresses, an orator is expected to "soar into the blue empyrean" at once. The rhetoric is usually pompous and impassioned. To read a speech, even a short speech, from copious notes, is neither irregular nor rare.

While forenoon and evening, perhaps even late evening, are occupied with the sittings of the convention, canvassing and intrigue go on more briskly than ever during the rest of the day and night. Conferences are held between delegations anxious to arrange for a union of forces on one candidate. Divided delegations hold meetings of their own members, meetings often long and stormy, behind closed doors, outside which a curious crowd listens to the angry voices within, and snatches at the reports which the dispersing members give of the result. Sometimes the whole issue of the convention hinges on the action of the delegates of a great State, which, like New York, under the unit rule, can throw seventy-two votes into the trembling scale. It may even happen, although this is against a well-settled custom, that a brazen aspirant himself goes the round of several delegations and tries to harangue them into supporting him.

As it rarely happens that any aspirant is able to command at starting a majority of the whole convention, the object of each

is to arrange a combination whereby he may gather from the
supporters of other aspirants votes sufficient to make up the
requisite majority, be it two-thirds, according to the Democratic
rule, or a little more than a half, according to the Republican.
Let us take the total number of votes at 820—the figure in
1884. There are usually two aspirants commanding each from
230 to 330; one or two others with from 50 to 100, and the
rest with much smaller figures, 10 to 30 each. A combination
can succeed in one of two ways : (a) One of the stronger aspirants
may pick up votes, sometimes quickly, sometimes by slow
degrees, from the weaker candidates, sufficient to overpower the
rival Favourite ; (b) Each of the strongest aspirants may hold
his forces so well together that after repeated ballotings it becomes clear that neither can win against the resistance of the
other. Neither faction will, however, give way, because there
is usually bitterness between them, because each would feel
humiliated, and because each aspirant has so many friends that
his patronage will no more than suffice for the clients to whom
he is pledged already. Hence one or other of the baffled
Favourites suddenly transfers the votes he commands to some
one of the weaker men, who then so rapidly "develops strength"
that the rest of the minor factions go over to him, and he obtains
the requisite majority. Experience has so well prepared the
tacticians for one or other of these issues that the game is always
played with a view to them. The first effort of the managers of
a Favourite is to capture the minor groups of delegates who
support one or other of the Favourite Sons and Dark Horses.
Not till this proves hopeless do they decide to sell themselves as
dear as they can by taking up and carrying to victory a Dark
Horse or perhaps even a Favourite Son, thereby retaining the
pleasure of defeating the rival Favourite, while at the same time
establishing a claim for themselves and their faction on the
aspirant whom they carry.

It may be asked why a Dark Horse often prevails against
the Favourites, seeing that either of the latter has a much larger
number of delegates in his favour. Ought not the wish of a
very large group to have so much weight with the minor groups
as to induce them to come over and carry the man whom a
powerful section of the party obviously desires ? The reason
why this does not happen is that a Favourite is often as much
hated by one strong section as he is liked by another, and if the

hostile section is not strong enough to keep him out by its un-aided vote, it is sure to be able to do so by transferring itself to some other aspirant. Moreover, a Favourite has often less chance with the minor groups than a Dark Horse may have. He has not the charm of novelty. His "ins and outs" are known ; the delegations weighed his merits before they left their own State, and if they, or the State convention that instructed them, decided against him then, they are slow to adopt him now. They have formed a habit of "antagonizing" him, whereas they have no hostility to some new and hitherto inconspicuous aspirant.

Let us now suppose resolutions and nominating speeches despatched, and the curtain raised for the third act of the convention. The chairman raps loudly with his gavel, announcing the call of States for the vote. A hush falls on the multitude, a long deep breath is drawn, tally books are opened and pencils grasped, while the clerk reads slowly the names of State after State. As each is called, the chairman of its delegation rises and announces the votes it gives, bursts of cheering from each faction in the audience welcoming the votes given to the object of its wishes. Inasmuch as the disposition of most of the delegates has become known beforehand, not only to the managers, but to the public through the press, the loudest welcome is given to a delegate or delegation whose vote turns out better than had been predicted.

In the first scene of this third and decisive act the Favourites have, of course, the leading parts. Their object is to produce an impression of overwhelming strength, so the whole of this strength is displayed, unless, as occasionally happens, an astute manager holds back a few votes. This is also the bright hour of the Favourite Sons. Each receives the vote of his State, but each usually finds that he has little to expect from external help, and his friends begin to consider into what other camp they had better march over. The Dark Horses are in the background, nor is it yet possible to say which (if any) of them will come to the front.

The first ballot seldom decides much, yet it gives a new aspect to the battlefield, for the dispositions of some groups of voters who had remained doubtful is now revealed, and the managers of each aspirant are better able to tell, from the way in which certain delegations are divided, in what quarters they are most likely to gain or lose votes on the subsequent ballots. They whisper hastily together, and try, in the few moments they have before the second ballot is upon them, to prepare some new line of defence or attack.

The second ballot, taken in the same way, sometimes reveals even more than the first. The smaller and more timid delegations, smitten with the sense of their weakness, despairing of their own aspirant, and anxious to be on the winning side, begin to give way ; or if this does not happen on the second ballot, it may do so on the third. Rifts open in their ranks, individuals or groups of delegates go over to one of the stronger candidates, some having all along meant to do so, and thrown their first vote merely to obey instructions received or fulfil the letter of a promise given. The gain of even twenty or thirty votes for one of the leading candidates over his strength on the preceding ballot so much inspirits his friends, and is so likely to bring fresh recruits to his standard, that a wily manager will often, on the first ballot, throw away some of his votes on a harmless antagonist that he may by rallying them increase the total of his candidate on the second, and so convey the impression of growing strength.

The breathing space between each ballot and that which follows is used by the managers for hurried consultations. Aides-de-camp are sent to confirm a wavering delegation, or to urge one which has been supporting a now hopeless aspirant to seize this moment for dropping him and coming over to the winning standard. Or the aspirant himself, who, hundreds of miles away, sits listening to the click of the busy wires, is told how matters stand, and asked to advise forthwith what course his friends shall take. Forthwith it must be, for the next ballot is come, and may give the battlefield a new aspect, promising victory or presaging irretrievable defeat.

Any one who has taken part in an election, be it the election of a pope by cardinals, of a town-clerk by the city council, of a fellow by the dons of a college, of a schoolmaster by the board of trustees, of a pastor by a congregation, knows how much depends on generalship. In every body of electors there are men who have no minds of their own ; others who cannot make up their minds till the decisive moment, and are determined by the last word or incident ; others whose wavering inclination yields to the pressure or follows the example of a stronger colleague. There are therefore chances of running in by surprise an aspirant whom few may have desired, but still fewer have positively disliked, chances specially valuable when controversy has spent itself between two equally-matched competitors, so that the majority are ready to jump at a new suggestion. The wary tactician awaits his opportunity; he improves the brightening prospects of his aspirant to carry him with a run before the opposition is ready with a counter move; or if he sees a strong antagonist, he invents pretexts for delay till he has arranged a combination by which that antagonist may be foiled. Sometimes he will put forward an aspirant destined to be abandoned, and reserve till several votings have been taken the man with whom he means to win. All these arts are familiar to the convention manager, whose power is seen not merely in the dealing with so large a number of individuals and groups whose dispositions he must grasp and remember, but in the cool promptitude with which he decides on his course amid the noise and passion and distractions of twelve thousand shouting spectators. Scarcely greater are the faculties of combination and coolness of head needed by a general in the midst of a battle, who has to bear in mind the position of every one of his own corps and to divine the positions of those of the enemy's corps which remain concealed, who must vary his plan from hour to hour according to the success or failure of each of his movements and the new facts that are successively disclosed, and who does all this under the roar and through the smoke of cannon.

One balloting follows another till what is called "the break" comes. It comes when the weaker factions, perceiving that the men of their first preference cannot succeed, transfer their votes to that one among the aspirants whom they like best, or whose strength they see growing. When the faction of one aspirant has set the example, others are quick to follow, and thus it may happen that after thirty or forty ballots have been taken with few changes of strength as between the two leading competitors, a single ballot, once the break has begun, and the column of one or both of these competitors has been "staggered," decides the battle.

If one Favourite is much stronger from the first than any other, the break may come soon and come gently, *i.e.* each ballot shows a gain for him on the preceding ballot, and he marches so steadily to victory that resistance is felt to be useless. But if two well-matched rivals have maintained the struggle through twenty or thirty ballots, so that the long strain has wrought up all minds to unwonted excitement, the break, when it comes, comes with fierce intensity, like that which used to mark the charge of the Old Guard. The defeat becomes a rout. Battalion after battalion goes over to the victors, while the vanquished, ashamed of their candidate, try to conceal themselves by throwing away their colours and joining in the cheers that acclaim the conqueror. In the picturesquely technical language of politicians, it is a Stampede.

To stampede a convention is the steadily contemplated aim of every manager who knows he cannot win on the first ballot. He enjoys it as the most dramatic form of victory, he values it because it evokes an enthusiasm whose echo reverberates all over the Union, and dilates the party heart with something like that sense of supernatural guidance which Rome used to have when the cardinals chose a pope by the sudden inspiration of the Holy Spirit. Sometimes it comes of itself, when various delegations, smitten at the same moment by the sense that one of the aspirants is destined to conquer, go over to him all at once. Sometimes it is due to the action of the aspirant himself. In 1880 Mr. Blaine, who was one of the two leading Favourites, perceiving that he could not be carried against the resistance of the Grant men, suddenly telegraphed to his friends to transfer their votes to General Garfield, till then a scarcely considered candidate. In 1884 General Logan, also by telegraph, turned over his votes to Mr. Blaine between the third and fourth ballot, thereby assuring the already probable triumph of that Favourite.

When a stampede is imminent, only one means exists of averting it, that of adjourning the convention so as to stop the panic and gain time for a combination against the winning aspirant. A resolute manager always tries this device, but he seldom succeeds, for the winning side resists the motion for adjournment, and the vote which it casts on that issue is practically a vote for its aspirant, against so much of the field as has any fight left in it. This is the most critical and exciting moment of the whole battle. A dozen speakers rise at once, some to support, some to resist the adjournment, some to protest against debate upon it, some to take points of order, few of which can be heard over the din of the howling multitude. Meanwhile, the managers who have kept their heads rush swiftly about through

friendly delegations, trying at this supreme moment to rig
up a combination which may resist the advancing tempest.
Tremendous efforts are made to get the second Favourite's
men to abandon their chief and "swing into line" for some Dark
Horse or Favourite Son, with whose votes they may make head
till other factions rally to them.

> " In vain, in vain, the all-consuming hour
> Relentless falls."

The battle is already lost, the ranks are broken and cannot be
rallied, nothing remains for brave men but to cast their last votes
against the winner and fall gloriously around their still waving
banner.   The motion to adjourn is defeated, and the next ballot
ends the strife with a hurricane of cheering for the chosen leader.
Then a sudden calm falls on the troubled sea.   What is done is
done, and whether done for good or for ill, the best face must be
put upon it.   Accordingly the proposer of one of the defeated
aspirants moves that the nomination be made unanimous, and the
more conspicuous friends of other aspirants hasten to show their
good-humour and their loyalty to the party as a whole by
seconding this proposition.   Then, perhaps, a gigantic portrait of
the candidate, provided by anticipation, is hoisted up, a signal
for fresh enthusiasm, or a stuffed eagle is carried in procession
round the hall.

Nothing further remains but to nominate a candidate for the
vice-presidency, a matter of small moment now that the great
issue has been settled.   This nomination is frequently used to
console one of the defeated aspirants for the presidential nomination, or is handed over to his friends to be given to some politician of their choice.   If there be a contest, it is seldom prolonged
beyond two or three ballots.   The convention is at an end, and
in another day the whole host of exhausted delegates and camp-
followers, hoarse with shouting, is streaming home along the
railways.

The fever heat of the convention is almost matched by that of
the great cities, and indeed of every spot over the Union to which
there runs an electric wire.   Every incident, speech, vote, is
instantly telegraphed to all the cities.   Crowds gather round the
newspaper offices, where frequent editions are supplemented by
boards displaying the latest bulletins.   In Washington, Congress
can hardly be kept together, because every politician is personally

interested in every move of the game. When at last the result is announced, the partisans of the chosen candidate go wild with delight ; salvos of artillery are fired off, processions with bands parade the streets, ratification meetings are announced for the same evening, "campaign clubs" bearing the candidate's name are organized on the spot. The excitement is of course greatest in the victor's own State, or in the city where he happens to be resident. A crowd rushes to his house, squeezes his hand to a quivering pulp, congratulates him on being virtually President, while the keen-eyed reporter telegraphs far and wide how he smiled and spoke when the news was brought. Defeated aspirants telegraph to their luckier rival their congratulations on his success, promising him support in the campaign. Interviewers fly to prominent politicians, and cross-examine them as to what they think of the nomination. But in two days all is still again, and a lull of exhaustion follows till the real business of the contest begins some while later with the issue of the letter of acceptance, in which the candidate declares his views and outlines his policy.

Chapter 13

The Presidential Campaign

A PRESIDENTIAL election in America is something to which Europe can show nothing similar. Though the issues which fall to be decided by the election of a Chamber in France or Italy, or of a House of Commons in England, are often far graver than those involved in the choice of A or B to be executive chief magistrate for four years, the commotion and excitement, the amount of "organization," of speaking, writing, telegraphing, and shouting, is incomparably greater in the United States. It is only the salient features of these contests that I shall attempt to sketch, for the detail is infinite.

The canvass usually lasts about four months. It begins soon after both of the great parties have chosen their candidate, *i.e.* before the middle of July; and it ends early in November, on the day when the presidential electors are chosen simultaneously in and by all the States. The summer heats and the absence of the richer sort of people at the seaside or mountain resorts keep down the excitement during July and August; it rises in September, and boils furiously through October.

The first step is for each nominated candidate to accept his nomination in a letter, sometimes as long as a pamphlet, setting forth his views of the condition of the nation and the policy which the times require. Such a letter is meant to strike the keynote for the whole orchestra of orators. It is, of course, published everywhere, extolled by friendly and dissected by hostile journals. Together with the "platform" adopted at the national party convention, it is the official declaration of party principles, to be referred to as putting the party case, no less than the candidate himself, before the nation.

While the candidate is composing his address, the work of organization goes briskly forward, for in American elections everything is held to depend on organization. A central or national party committee nominated by the national convention, and consisting of one member from each State, gets its members together and forms a plan for the conduct of the canvass. It raises money by appealing to the wealthy and zealous men of the party for subscriptions, and, of course, presses those above all who have received something in the way of an office or other gratification from the party. It communicates with the leading statesmen and orators of the party, and arranges in what district of the country each shall take the stump. It issues shoals of pamphlets, and forms relations with party newspapers. It allots grants from the "campaign fund" to particular persons and State committees, to be spent by them for "campaign purposes," an elastic term which may cover a good deal of illicit expenditure. Enormous sums are sometimes gathered and disbursed by this committee, and the accounts submitted do not, as may be supposed, answer all the questions they suggest. The committee directs its speakers and its funds chiefly to the doubtful States, those in which eloquence or expenditure may turn the balance either way. There are seldom more than six or seven such States at any one election, possibly fewer.

The efforts of the national committee are seconded not only by State committees, but by an infinite number of minor organizations over the country, in the rural districts no less than in the cities. Some of these are permanent. Others are created for the election alone; and as they contemplate a short life, they make it a merry one. These "campaign clubs," which usually bear the candidates' names, are formed on every imaginable basis, that of locality, of race, of trade or profession, of university affiliation. There are Irish clubs, Italian clubs, German clubs, Scandinavian clubs, Polish clubs, coloured (*i.e.* negro) clubs, Orange clubs. There are young men's clubs, lawyers' clubs, dry-goods clubs, insurance men's clubs, shoe and leather clubs. There are clubs of the graduates of various colleges. Their work consists in canvassing the voters, making up lists of friends, opponents, and doubtfuls, getting up processions and parades, holding meetings, and generally "booming all the time."

This is mostly unpaid labour. But there are also thousands of paid agents at work, canvassing, distributing pamphlets or leaflets, lecturing on behalf of the candidate. It is in America no reproach to a political speaker that he receives a fee or a salary. Even men of eminence are permitted to receive not only their travelling expenses, but a round sum. Whether the candidate himself takes the field depends on his popular gifts. If he is a brilliant speaker his services are too valuable to be lost; and he is sent on a tour through the doubtful States, where he speaks for weeks together twice or thrice on most days, filling up the intervals with "receptions" at which he has to shake hands with hundreds of male callers, and be presented to ladies scarcely less numerous. The leading men of the party are, of course, pressed into the service. Even if they dislike and have opposed the nomination of the particular candidate, party loyalty and a lively sense of favours to come force them to work for the person whom the party has chosen. An eminent Irishmen or an eminent German is especially valuable for a stumping tour, because he influences the vote of his countrymen. Similarly each senator is expected to labour assiduously at his own State, where presumably his influence is greatest, and any refusal to do so is deemed a pointed disapproval of the candidate.

The committees print and distribute great quantities of campaign literature, pamphlets, speeches, letters, leaflets, and one can believe that this printed matter is more serviceable than it would be in England, because a larger part of the voters live in quiet country places, and like something to read in the evening. Even novelettes are composed in the interests of a candidate. I found mention of one, written by a literary colonel, in which "the lovers, while in the most romantic situation, are made to talk about the protective tariff. One-third of the book consists of love and tragedy, and the remainder is an argument for protection. (This is a large proportion of powder to jam.) Thousands of these have been distributed as campaign documents." Sometimes a less ingenuous use is made of the press. On the very eve of the election of 1880, too late for a contradiction to obtain equal publicity, a forged letter, purporting to come from Mr. Garfield, and expressing views on Chinese immigration and labour, distasteful to the Pacific States, was lithographed and scattered broadcast over California, where it told heavily against him. And in 1884, an extract, purporting to come from a pamphlet issued by the "London Free Trade Club" was circulated, in which that (non-existent) body was represented as declaring that "the salvation of England depends on the destruction of American manufactures, and this must be effected by means of free trade and the Democratic party."

Most constant and effective of all is the action of the news-papers. The chief journals have for two or three months a daily leading article recommending their own and assailing the hostile candidate, with a swarm of minor editorial paragraphs bearing on the election. Besides these there are reports of speeches delivered, letters to the editor with the editor's comments at the end, stories about the candidates, statements as to the strength of each party in particular States, counties, and cities. An examination of a few of the chief newspapers during the months of September and October 1884, showed that their " campaign matter " of all kinds formed between one-half and one-third of the total letterpress of the paper (excluding advertisements), and this, be it remembered, every day during those two months. The most readable part of this matter consists in the reports of the opinion of individual persons, more or less prominent, on the candidate. You find, for instance, a paragraph stating that the Rev. Dr. A., president of such and such a college, or Mr. B., the philanthropist who is head of the Y Z Bank, or ex-Governor C., or Judge D., has said he thinks the candidate a model of chivalric virtue, or fit only for a felon's cell, as the case may be, and that he will vote for or against him accordingly. Occasionally the prominent man is called on by an interviewer and gives a full statement of his views, or he writes to a young friend who has asked his advice a private letter, which is immediately published. The abundance of these expressions or citations of the opinions of private citizens supplies a curious evidence of the disposition of some sections in a demo-cracy to look up to its intellectual and moral leaders. For the men thus appealed to are nearly all persons eminent by their character, ability, learning, or success in business ; the merely rich man is cited but rarely, and as if his opinion did not matter, though of course his subscription may. Judges and lawyers, university dignitaries and literary men, are, next to the clergy, the persons most often quoted.

The function of the clergy in elections is very charac-teristic of the country and the occasion. They used during the period from 1820 to 1856 to give politics a wide berth, for not only would their advocacy of any particular cause have offended a section among their flocks, but the general sentiment condemned the immixture in politics of a clerical element. The struggle against slavery, being a moral issue, brought them into more frequent public activity. Since the close of that struggle they have again tended to retire. However, the excitement of a presidential election suspends all rules ; and it sometimes happens that the charges brought against a candidate involve moral issues which are deemed, at least by partisans, to justify clerical intervention. In the contest of 1884, at any rate, ecclesiastics came well to the front. For months the newspapers were full of the opinions of clergymen. Sermons were reported if they seemed to bear upon the issue. Paragraphs appeared saying that such and such a pastor would carry three-fourths of his congregation with him, whereas the conduct of another in appearing at a meeting on behalf of the opposing candidate was much blamed by his flock. Not many ministers actually took the platform, though there was a general wish to have them as chairmen. But one, the late Mr. Henry Ward Beecher, did great execution by his powerful oratory, artillery all the more formidable because it was turned against the candidate of the party to which he had through his long life belonged. Nor was there any feature in the canvass of that same candidate more remarkable than the assembly of 1018 clergymen of all denominations (including a Jewish rabbi), which gathered at the Fifth Avenue Hotel in New York, to meet him and assure him of their support on moral grounds immediately before the election day.

From a class usually excluded from politics by custom to a class excluded by law, the transition is easy. Women as a rule keep as much aloof from electoral contests in America as in continental Europe, and certainly more than in England, for I have never heard of their forming an organization to canvass the voters of a district in America, as the (Conservative) Primrose League has done all over England for four years past, and as several women's associations belonging to the Liberal party are now doing in London. Nor are women appointed delegates from any ward primary,[1] as ladies have lately been in some divisions of London. In no State of the Union can they vote at any State election, and therefore neither can they vote at Federal elections. However, the excitement of 1884 drew even women into the vortex. In various cities receptions were tendered by the ladies of each party to the candidate, receptions reported in the public press as politically significant. And a good many of the letters which appeared in the newspapers attacking or defending the candidate bore female signatures. The Women's Suffrage jour-

[1] Women, however, appear as delegates at the conventions of the Prohibition party.

nal gave its support to the Republican party, but a section of the suffragists, incensed at the faithlessness or indifference of both of the parties to their claims, started a presidential candidate of their own, Mrs. Belva C. Lockwood, a lady practising law at Washington. She took the stump on her own behalf, but did not ultimately go to the poll.

Speaking and writing and canvassing are common to elections all over the world. What is peculiar to America is the amazing development of the "demonstration" as a means for raising enthusiasm. For three months, processions, usually with brass bands, flags, badges, crowds of cheering spectators, are the order of the day and night from end to end of the country. The Young Men's Pioneer Club of a village in the woods of Michigan turns out in the summer evening; the Democrats or Republicans of Chicago or Philadelphia leave their business to march through the streets of these great cities many thousands strong.

When a procession is exceptionally large it is called a Parade. In New York City, on the 29th of October 1884, the business men who supported Mr. James Gillespie Blaine held such a demonstration. They were organized by profession or occupation: the lawyers, 800 strong, forming one battalion, the dry-goods men another, the Produce Exchange a third, the bankers a fourth, the brokers a fifth, the jewellers a sixth, the Petroleum Exchange a seventh, and so on *ad infinitum*. They started from the Bowling-green near the south end of Manhattan Island, and marched right up the city along Broadway to Madison Square, where Mr. Blaine reviewed and addressed them. Rain fell incessantly, and the streets were deep with mud, but neither rain above nor mud below damped the spirits of this great army, which tramped steadily along, chanting various "campaign refrains," such as

> " Five, Five, Five Cent Fare ; "

but most frequently

> " Blaine, Blaine, James G. Blaine
> We don't care a bit for the rain,
> O—O—O—O—HI—O."

There were said to have been 25,000 business men in this parade, which was followed soon after by another more miscellaneous Blaine parade of 60,000 Republicans, as well as (of course) by counter parades of Democrats. A European, who stands amazed at the magnitude of these demonstrations, is apt to ask whether the result attained is commensurate with the money, time, and effort given to them. His American friends answer that, as with advertising, it is not to be supposed that shrewd and experienced men would thus spend their money unless convinced that the expenditure was reproductive. The parade and procession business, the crowds, the torches, the badges, the flags, the shouting, all this pleases the participants by making them believe they are effecting something; it impresses the spectators by showing them that other people are in earnest, it strikes the imagination of those who in country hamlets read of the doings in the great city. In short, it keeps up the "boom," and an American election is held to be, truly or falsely, largely a matter of booming.

If the cynical visitor smiles at these displays, he is constrained to admire the good-humour and good order which prevail. Neither party in the Northern, Middle, and Western States dreams of disturbing the parades or meetings of the other. You might believe, from the acclamations which accompany a procession, that the whole population was with it, for if opponents are present they do not hoot or hiss, and there are always enough sympathizers to cheer. During the hotly-contested elections of 1880 and 1884 there were hardly any collisions or disturbances reported from California to Maine. Even in Virginia, Maryland, Missouri, where the old Southern party is apt to let its angry passions rise against the negroes and their white Republican allies, the breaches of order were in 1884 neither numerous nor serious. There is a large and vicious mob in New York, Chicago, and Cincinnati, but it behaved perfectly well in the two former cities, though badly in the third at the October State elections. Over four-fifths of the Southern States perfect quiet prevailed. It is true that one party could there count on an overwhelming majority, so that there was no excuse for the one to bully nor any inducement for the other to show fight.

The maxim that nothing succeeds like success is nowhere so cordially and consistently accepted as in America. It is the corner-stone of all election work. The main effort of a candidate's orators and newspapers is to convince the people that their side is the winning one, for there are sure to be plenty of voters anxious to be on that side, not so much from any advantage to be gained for themselves as because reverence for "the People" makes them believe that the majority are right. Hence the exertions to prove that the Germans, or the Irish, or the working men are going for candidate X. or candidate Y. Hence the reports of specimen canvasses showing that seventy per cent of the clerks in a particular bank or eighty per cent of the professors in a particular theological college have declared themselves for X. Hence the announcements of the betting odds for a particular candidate, and the assertion that the supporters of the other man who had put large sums on him are now beginning to hedge. But the best evidence to which a party can appeal is its winning minor elections which come off shortly before the great presidential one. In two States the choice of a governor and other State officers took place, till lately, within the month prior to the 8th of November, in two or three it still takes place in September. If the State is a safe one for the Republicans or the Democrats (as the case may be), the votes cast are compared with those cast at the last preceding similar election, and the inference drawn that one or other party is gaining. If it is a doubtful State, the interest is still more keen, and every nerve is strained to carry an election whose issue will presage, and by presaging contribute to, success in the presidential struggle. Possibly the candidate or some of his ablest speakers stump this State ; probably also it is drenched with money. The inferences from such a contest may be thought uncertain, because State elections are always complicated with local questions, and with the character of the particular candidates for State offices. But it is a maxim among politicians that in a presidential year local issues vanish, the voters being so warmed with party spirit that they go solid for their party in spite of all local or personal obstacles. The truth of this view was illustrated by the fact that Ohio often returns a majority of Democrats to Congress and has a Democratic majority in her own legislature, but has for several elections given a majority for the presidential candidate of the Republican party. The eagerness shown to carry the October elections in this great and often doubtful State used to be scarcely second to that displayed in the presidential contest. She has now put her fall elections later, and makes them coincide (every second term) with the presidential election, in order to avoid the tremendous strain which they had been forced to bear. Before this change it was often made an argument why the party should select its candidate from Ohio, that this would give a better chance of winning the preliminary canter, and thereby securing the advantage of a presageful victory.

So far I have described the contest as one between two parties and two candidates only. But it is usually complicated by the appearance of other minor parties and minor candidates who, although they have no chance of success, affect the main struggle by drawing off strength from one side or the other. In the elections of 1876, 1880, and 1884, the Prohibitionist party and the Greenback (now the Labour) party each held a national convention, nominated candidates for presidency and vice-presidency, and obtained at the polls a number of votes far too small to carry any single State, and therefore, of course, too small to choose any presidential electors, but sufficient to affect, perhaps to turn, the balance of strength between Republicans and Democrats in two or three of the doubtful States. The Prohibitionist candidate draws most of his votes from the Republican side ; the Greenbacker or Labour man from the Democratic : hence there is a sort of tacit alliance during the campaign between the Republican organs and the Greenback party, between the Democratic organs and the Prohibitionists ; and conversely much ill blood between Republicans and Prohibitionists, between Democrats and Greenbackers. In 1884, the Democrats charged the Republicans with secretly encouraging and supporting by money the candidature of General Benjamin F. Butler, nominated by the Greenbackers and Labour men, while the Republicans bitterly reproached the temperance people with playing into the hands of the liquor-loving Democrats. Any one can see what an opening these complications give for intrigue, and how much they add to the difficulty of predicting the result.

Chapter 14

Further Observations on Nominations and Elections

SEVERAL questions may have occurred to the European reader who has followed the foregoing account of presidential nominations and elections.

The most obvious is—How comes it that a system of nomination by huge party assemblies has grown up so unlike anything which the free countries of Europe have seen ?

The nominating convention is the natural and legitimate outgrowth of two features of the Constitution, the restricted functions of Congress and the absolute sovereignty of the people. It was soon perceived that under the rule of party, a party must be united on its candidate in order to have a prospect of success. There was therefore need for a method of selecting the candidate which the whole of a party would recognize as fair and entitled to respect. At first the representatives of the party in Congress assumed the right of nomination. But it was presently felt that they were not entitled to it, for they had not been chosen for any such purpose, and the President was not constitutionally responsible to them, but rather set up to check them. When the congressional caucus had been discredited, the State legislatures tried their hands at nominations ; but acting irregularly, and with a primary regard to local sentiment, they failed to win obedience. It began to be seen that whom the people were to elect the people must also nominate. Thus presently the tumultuous assemblies of active politicians were developed into regular representative bodies, modelled after Congress, and giving to the party in each State exactly the same weight in nominating as the State possessed in voting. The elaborate nominating scheme of primaries and conventions which was being constructed for the purpose of city, State, and congressional elections, was applied to the election of the President and the

264

national convention was the result. We may call it an effort of nature to fill the void left in America by the absence of the European parliamentary or cabinet system, under which an executive is called into being out of the legislature by the majority of the legislature. In the European system no single act of nomination is necessary, because the leader of the majority comes gradually to the top in virtue of his own strength. In America there must be a single and formal act : and this act must emanate from the people, since it is to them that the party leader, when he becomes chief magistrate, will be responsible. There is not quite so strong a reason for entrusting to the convention the function of declaring the aims and tenets of the party in its platform, for this might properly be done by a caucus of the legislature. But as the President is, through his veto power, an independent branch of the legislature, the moment of nominating him is apt for a declaration of the doctrines, whereof the party makes him the standard-bearer.

What effects has the practice of nomination by conventions had upon the public life of the country ? Out of several I select two. It makes political struggles turn more upon men and less upon measures than might have been expected in a country where equality is so fully established, and the citizens are so keenly interested in public questions. The victory of a party in a presidential election depends upon its being unanimous in its support of a particular candidate. It must therefore use every effort to find, not necessarily the best man, but the man who will best unite it. In the pursuit of him, it is distracted from its consideration of the questions on which it ought to appeal to the country, and may form its views on them hastily or loosely. The convention is the only body authorized to declare the tenets and practical programme of the party. But the duty of declaring them is commonly overshadowed by the other duty of choosing the candidate, which naturally excites warmer feelings in the hearts of actual or potential office-holders. Accordingly delegates are chosen by local conventions rather as the partisans of this or that aspirant than as persons of political ability or moral weight; and the function of formulating the views of the party may be left to, and ill-discharged by, men of an inferior type.

A further result will have been foreseen by those who have realized what these conventions are like. They are monster meetings. Besides the eight hundred delegates there are some ten to fourteen thousand spectators on the floor and in the galleries. It goes without saying that such a meeting is capable neither of discussing political questions and settling a political programme, nor of deliberately weighing the merits of rival aspirants for the nomination. Its programme must be presented to it cut and dry, and this is the work of a small committee. In choosing a candidate, it must follow a few leaders. And what sort of leaders do conventions tend to produce? Two sorts—the intriguer and the declaimer. There is the man who manipulates delegates, and devises skilful combinations. There is also the orator, whose physical gifts, courage, and readiness enable him to browbeat antagonists, overawe the chairman, and perhaps, if he be possessed of eloquence, carry the multitude away in a fit of enthusiasm. For men of wisdom and knowledge, not seconded by a commanding voice and presence, there is no demand, and little chance of usefulness, in these tempestuous halls.

Why, however, it may also be asked, should conventions be so pre-eminently tempestuous, considering that they are not casual concourses, but consist of persons duly elected, and are governed by a regular code of procedure? The reason may be found in the fact that in them are united the two conditions which generate excitement, viz. very large numbers and important issues to be determined. In no other modern assemblies do these conditions concur. Modern deliberative assemblies are comparatively small—the House of Representatives has only 325 members; the French Chamber 584; while in the British House of Commons there is sitting space for only 400. Large popular gatherings, on the other hand, such as mass meetings, are excitable in virtue of their size, but have nothing to do but pass resolutions, and there is seldom controversy over these, because such meetings are attended only by those who agree with the summoners. But a national convention consists of more than eight hundred delegates, as many alternates, and some twelve thousand spectators. It is the hugest mass meeting the world knows of. Not only, therefore, does the sympathy of numbers exert an unequalled force, but this host, larger than the army with which the Greeks conquered at Marathon, has an issue of the highest and most exciting nature to decide, an issue which quickens the pulse even of those who read in cold blood afterwards how the votes fell as the roll of States was called, and which thrills those who see and listen, and, most of all, those who are themselves concerned as delegates, with an intensity of emotion surpassing, in proportion to the magnitude of the issue, that which attends the finish of a well-contested boat race. If you wish to realize the passionate eagerness of an American convention, take the House of Commons or the French Chamber during a division which is to decide the fate of a ministry and a policy, and raising the numbers present twenty-fold, imagine the excitement twenty-fold hotter. Wanting those wonderful scenes which a great debate and division in Parliament provide the English with, America has evolved others not less dramatic. The contrast between the two countries is perhaps most marked in this, that in Parliament the strife is between two parties, in an American Convention between the adherents of different leaders belonging to the same party. We might have expected that in the more democratic country more would turn upon principles, less upon men. It is exactly the other way. The struggle in a convention is over men, not over principles.

These considerations may serve to explain to a European the strange phenomena of a convention. But his inquiry probably extends itself to the electoral campaign which follows. "Why," he asks, "is the contest so much longer, more strenuous, and more absorbing than the congressional elections, or than any election struggle in Europe, although Europe is agitated by graver problems than now occupy America? And why does a people externally so cool, self-contained, and unimpulsive as the American work itself up into a fever of enthusiasm over an issue of little permanent importance between two men, neither of whom will do much good or can do much harm?"

The length of the contest is a survival. The Americans themselves regret it, for it sadly interrupts both business and pleasure. It is due to the fact that when communication was difficult over a rough and thinly-settled country, several months were needed to enable the candidates and their orators to go round. Now railways and telegraphs have drawn the continent so much together that five or six weeks would be sufficient. That the presidential election is fought more vehemently than congressional elections seems due to its coming only half as often; to the fact that the President is the dispenser of Federal patronage, and to the habit formed in days when the President was the real head of the party, and his action in foreign affairs was important, of looking on his election as the great trial of party strength. Besides, it is the choice of one officer by the whole country, a supreme political act in which every voter has a share, and the same share ; an act which fills the whole of the party in all of the States with the sense that it is feeling and thinking and willing as one heart and mind. This simultaneity of effort, this concentration of interest upon one person and one polling day, gives to the struggle a sort of tension not to be looked for where a number of elections of different persons are going on in as many different spots, nor always at the same time. In congressional elections each constituency has to think first of itself and its own candidate. In the presidential elections all eyes are fixed on the same figure ; the same personal as well as political issue is presented to the nation. Each polling district in a State, each State in the Union, emulates every other in the efforts it puts forth to carry the party ticket.

To explain why the hard-headed self-possessed Americans go so wild with excitement at election times is a more difficult task. See what the facts are : There has not been a single presidential candidate, since Abraham Lincoln's re-election in 1864 (always excepting General Grant), of whom his friends could say that he had done anything to command the gratitude of the nation. Some of these candidates had been skilful party leaders, others had served with credit in the Civil War. None could be called distinguished in the sense in which, I will not say, Hamilton, Jefferson, Marshall, Webster, but J. Q. Adams, Clay, Benton, Calhoun, Seward, Stanton, and Chase, were distinguished men. However, let us take Mr. Blaine and Mr. Cleveland. One had been Speaker of the House, and was unquestionably a skilful debater in Congress, an effective speaker on a platform, a man socially attractive, never forgetting a face or a service. The other had made a shrewd and upright Mayor of Buffalo and Governor of New York State. Compare the services rendered to the country by them, or by any other candidate of recent times, with those of Mazzini, Garibaldi, Cavour, and Victor Emmanuel to Italy, of Bismarck and Moltke to Germany, even of Thiers and Gambetta to France in her hour of peril. Yet the enthusiasm shown for Mr. Blaine (who seems to have drawn out the precious fluid at a higher temperature than his rival), the demonstrations made in his honour wherever he appeared, equalled anything done, in their several countries, for these heroes of Italy, Germany, or France. As for England, where two great political leaders, towering far above their fellows, have of late years excited the warmest admiration and the bitterest dislike from friends and foes, imagine eight hundred English barristers turning out from the Temple and Lincoln's Inn to walk in slow procession from London Bridge to South Kensington, shouting themselves hoarse for Gladstone or Disraeli !

In trying to account for this fact, it is well to begin by taking the bull by the horns. Is the world right in deeming the Americans a cool and sober people? The American is shrewd and keen, his passion seldom obscures his reason ; he keeps his head in moments when a Frenchman, or an Italian, or even a German, would lose it. Yet he is also of an excitable temper, with emotions capable of being quickly and strongly stirred. That there is no contradiction between these qualities appears from the case of the Scotch, who are both more logical and more cautious in affairs than the English, but are also more enthusiastic, more apt to be swept away by a passionate movement. Moreover, the Americans like excitement. They like it for its own sake, and go wherever they can find it. They surrender themselves to the enjoyment of this pleasure the more willingly because it is comparatively rare, and relieves the level tenor of their ordinary life. Add to this the further delight which they find in any form of competition. The passion which in England expresses itself in the popular eagerness over a boat race or a horse race, extends more widely in America to every kind of rivalry and struggle. The presidential election, in which two men are pitted against one another over a four months' course for the great prize of politics, stirs them like any other trial of strength and speed ; sets them betting on the issue, disposes them to make efforts for a cause in which their deeper feelings may be little engaged.

These tendencies are intensified by the vast area over which the contest extends, and the enormous multitude that bears a part in it. The American imagination is peculiarily sensitive to the impression of great size. " A big thing " is their habitual phrase of admiration. In Europe, antiquity is what chiefly commands the respect of some minds, novelty what rouses the interest of others. Beyond the Atlantic, the sense of immensity, the sense that the same thought and purpose are animating millions of other men in sympathy with himself, lifts a man out of himself, and sends him into transports of eagerness and zeal about things intrinsically small, but great through the volume of human feeling they have attracted. It is not the profundity of an idea or emotion, but its lateral extension which most quickly touches the American imagination. For one man who can feel the former a hundred are struck by the latter; and he who describes America must remember that he has always to think first of the masses.

These considerations may help to explain the disproportion that strikes a European between the merits of the presidential candidate and the blazing enthusiasm which he evokes. It is not really given to him as an individual, it is given to the party personified in him, because he bears its banner, and its fervour is due, not even so much to party passion as to the impressionist character of the people, who desire to be excited, desire to demonstrate, desire, as English undergraduates say, "to run with the boats," and cheer the efforts of the rowers. As regards the details of the demonstrations, the parades and receptions, the badges and brass bands and triumphal arches, any one can understand why the masses of the people—those who in Europe would be called the lower middle and working classes—should relish these things, which break the monotony of their lives, and give them a sense of personal participation in a great movement. Even in London, least externally picturesque among European cities, when the working men turn out for a Hyde Park meeting they come marshalled in companies under the banners of their trade unions or other societies, carrying devices, and preceded by music. They make a somewhat scrubby show, for England does not know how to light up the dulness of her skies and streets by colour in costume or variety in design. But the taste for display is there as it is in human nature everywhere. In England, the upper class is shy of joining in any such " functions," even when they have a religious tinge. Its fastidiousness and sense of class dignity are offended. But in America, the sentiment of equality is so pervading that the rich and cultivated do not think of scorning the popular procession ; or if some do feel such scorn, they are careful to conceal it. The habit of demonstrating with bands and banners and emblems was formed in days when the upper class was very small, and would not have dreamt of standing aloof from anything which interested the crowd ; and now, when the rich and cultivated have grown to be as numerous, and, in most respects, as fastidious as the parallel class in Europe, the habit is too deeply rooted to be shaken. Nobody thinks of sneering. To do as the people do is a tribute to the people's majesty. And the thousand lawyers who shout "James G. Blaine, O-h-i-o," as they march through the October mud of Broadway, have no more sense that they are making themselves ridiculous than the European noble who backs with repeated obeisances out of the presence of his sovereign.

Chapter 15

Types of American Statesmen

As trees are known by their fruits, and as different systems of government evidently tend to produce different types of statesmanship, it is pertinent to our examination of the American party system to inquire what are the kinds of statesmen which it engenders and ripens to maturity. A democracy, not less than any other form of government, needs great men to lead and inspire the people. The excellence therefore of the methods democracy employs may fairly enough be tested by the excellence of the statesmen whom these methods call forth. Europeans are wont to go farther, and reason from the character of the statesmen to the character of the people, a convenient process, because it seems easier to know the careers and judge the merits of persons than of nations, yet one not universally applicable. In the free countries of Europe, the men who take the lead in public affairs may be deemed fair specimens of its best talent and character, and fair types, possibly of the virtues of the nation, though the temptations of politics are great, and certainly of its practical gifts. But in two sorts of countries one cannot so reason from the statesmen to the masses. In despotic monarchies the minister is often merely the king's favourite, who has risen by unworthy arts, or, at any rate, not by merit; and in a democracy where birth and education give a man little advantage in the race, a political career may have become so unattractive as compared with other pursuits that the finest or most ambitious spirits do not strive for its prizes, but generally leave them to men of the second order.

This second case is, as we have seen, to some extent the case of America. We must not therefore take her statesmen as types of the highest or strongest American manhood. The national qualities come out fully in them, but not always in their best form. I speak of the generations that have grown up since the great men of the Revolution epoch died off. Some of those men were the peers of the best European statesmen of the time : one of them rises in moral dignity above all his European contemporaries. The generation to which J. Q. Adams, Jackson, Webster, Clay, Calhoun, and Benton belonged is less impressive, perhaps because they failed to solve a question which may have been too hard for any one to solve. Yet the men I have mentioned were striking personalities who would have made a figure in any country. Few of the statesmen of the third or Civil War period enjoyed more than a local reputation when it began, but in its course several of them developed remarkable powers, and one became a national hero. The fourth generation is now upon the stage. The Americans confess that not many who belong to it have as yet won fame. The times, they remark, are comparatively quiet. What is wanted is not so much an impassioned popular leader nor a great philosophic legislator as men who will administer the affairs of the nation with skill and rectitude, and who, fortified by careful study and observation, will grapple with the economic problems which the growth of the country makes urgent. I admit this, but think that much must also be ascribed to the character of the party system which, as we have seen, is unfavourable to the development of the finest gifts. Let us note what are the types which that system displays to us.

In such countries as England, France, Germany, and Italy there is room and need for five sorts of statesmen. Men are wanted for the management of foreign and colonial policy, men combining the talents of a diplomatist with a wide outlook over the world's horizon. The needs of social and economic reform, grave in old countries with the mistakes of the past to undo, require a second kind of statesman with an aptitude for constructive legislation. Thirdly there is the administrator who can manage a department with diligence and skill and economy. Fourthly comes the parliamentary tactician, whose function it is to understand men, who frames cabinets and is dexterous in humouring or spurring a representative assembly. Lastly we have the leader of the masses, who, whether or no he be a skilful parliamentarian, thinks rather of the country than of the chamber, knows how to watch and rouse the feelings of the multitude, and rally a great party to the standard which he bears aloft. The first of these has no need for eloquence; the second and third can get on without it; to the fourth it is almost, yet not absolutely, essential; it is the life breath of the fifth.

Let us turn to America. In America there are few occasions for the first sort of statesman, while the conditions of a Federal government, with its limited legislative sphere, are unfavourable to the second, as frequently changing cabinets are to the third. It is chiefly for persons of the fourth and fifth classes we must look. Persons of those classes we shall find, but in a different shape and guise from what they would assume in Europe. American politics seem at this moment to tend to the production of two types, the one of whom may be called *par excellence* the man of the desk or of the legislature, the other the man of the convention and the stump. They resemble the fourth and fifth of our European types, but with instructive differences.

The first of these types is usually a shrewd, cool, hard-headed man of business. He is such a man as one would find successful in the law or in commerce if he had applied his faculties to those vocations. He has mostly been, is often still, a practising counsel and attorney. He may lack imagination and width of view; but he has a tight grip of facts, a keen insight into men, and probably also tact in dealing with them. That he has come to the front shows him to possess a resolute and tenacious will, for without it he must have been trodden down in the fierce competition of a political career. His independence is limited by the necessity of keeping step with his party, for isolated action counts for little in America, but the tendency to go with one's party is so inbred there that a man feels less humiliated by waiving his private views than would be the case in Europe. Such compliance does not argue want of strength. As to what is called " culture," he has often at least a susceptibility to it, with a wish to acquire it which, if he has risen from humble beginnings, may contrast oddly with the superficial roughness of his manner. He is a ready and effective rather than a polished speaker, and is least agreeable when, forsaking the solid ground of his legal or administrative knowledge, he attempts the higher flights of eloquence.

Such a man does not necessarily make his first reputation in an assembly. He may begin as governor of a State or mayor of a large city, and if he earns a reputation there, can make pretty sure of going on to Congress if he desires it. In any case, it is in

administration and the legislative work which deals with administration that he wins his spurs. The sphere of local government
is especially fitted to develop such talents, and to give that
peculiar quality I have been trying to describe. It makes able
men of affairs; men fit for the kind of work which needs the
combination of a sound business head and the power of working
along with others. One may go further and say, that this sort
of talent is the talent which during the last half-century has been
most characteristic of the American people. Their greatest
achievements have lain in the internal development of their
country by administrative shrewdness, ingenuity, promptitude,
and an unequalled dexterity in applying the principle of association, whether by means of private corporations or of local public
or quasi-public organisms. These national characteristics reappear
in Federal politics, not always accompanied by the largeness of
vision and mastery of the political and economic sciences which
that wider sphere demands.

The type I am trying to describe is less brilliant than those
modern Europe has learned to admire in men like Bismarck or
Cavour, Thiers or Gambetta, perhaps one may add, Tisza or
Minghetti. But then the conditions required for the rise of the
last-named men do not exist in America, nor is her need for them
pressing. America would have all she wants if such statesmen
as I have described were more numerous; and if a philosophic
mind, capable of taking in the whole phenomena of transatlantic
society, and propounding comprehensive solutions for its problems,
were more common among the best of them. Persons of this
type have hitherto been most frequently found in the Senate, to
which they usually rise from the House of Representatives or from
a State legislature. They are very useful there; indeed, it is
they who have given it that, apparently now declining, authority
which it has enjoyed.

The other kind of statesman is the product of two factors
which give to American politics their peculiar character, viz. an
enormous multitude of voting citizens and the existence of a
wonderful network of party organizations for the purpose of
selecting and carrying candidates for office. To move the masses,
a man must have the gifts of oratory; to rule party committees,
he must be a master of intrigue. The stump and the committee-
room are his sphere. There is a great deal of campaign speaking
to be done at State elections, at congressional elections, above

all, in presidential campaigns. It does not flow in such a perennial torrent as in England, for England has since 1876 become the most speech-flooded country in the world, but it is more copious than in France, Italy, or Germany. The audiences are less ignorant than those of Europe, but their critical standard is not higher; and whereas in England it is Parliament that forms most speakers and creates the type of political oratory, Congress renders no such service to America. There is therefore, I think, less presumption in America than in Europe that the politician who makes his way by oratory is a man either of real eloquence or of vigorous thinking power. Able, however, he must be. He is sure to have fluency, a power of touching either the emotions or the imagination, a command of sonorous rhetoric. Probably he has also humour and a turn for quick retort. In fact, he must have the arts—we all know what they are—which please the multitude; arts not blamable in themselves, but needing to be corrected by occasional appearances before a critical audience. These arts joined to a powerful voice and a forcible personality will carry a man far. If he can join to them a ready and winning address, a geniality of manner if not of heart, he becomes what is called magnetic. Now, magnetism is among the highest qualities which an American popular leader can possess. Its presence may bring him to the top. Its absence may prevent him from getting there. It makes friends for him wherever he goes. It immensely enhances his powers in the region of backstairs politics.

For besides the visible work on the stump, there is the invisible work of the committee-room, or rather of the inner conclave, whose resolves are afterwards registered in the committee, to be still later laid before the convention. The same talent for intrigue which in monarchies or oligarchies is spent within the limits of a court or a knot of ruling families, here occupies itself with bosses and rings and leaders of political groups. To manipulate these men and groups, to know their weaknesses, their ambitions, their jealousies, to play upon their hopes and fears, attaching some by promises, entrapping others through their vanity, browbeating others into submission, forming combinations in which each partisan's interest is so bound up with that of the aspiring statesman that he is sure to stand faithfully by his chief—all this goes a long way to secure advancement under the party system.

It may be thought that between such aptitudes and the art of oratory there is no necessary connection. There are intriguers who are nothing but intriguers, useless on the stump or on the platform of a convention. But fluent oratory, as distinguished from eloquence, is an art which most able men can acquire with practice. In popularly-governed countries it is as common as it is worthless. And a link between the platform and the committee-room is found in the quality of magnetism. The magnetic man attracts individuals just as he captivates masses. Where oratory does not need either knowledge or reflection, because the people are not intent upon great questions, or because the parties evade them, where power of voice and skill in words, and ready sympathy with the feelings and prejudices of the crowd, are enough to command the ear of monster meetings, there the successful speaker will pass for a statesman. He will seem a fit man to put forward for high office, if he can but persuade the managers to run him; and therefore the other side of his activity is spent among and upon the managers.

It sometimes happens that the owner of these gifts is also a shrewd, keen, practical man, so that the first type is blended with the second. Nor is there anything to prevent the popular speaker and skilled intriguer from also possessing the higher attributes of statesmanship. This generation has seen the conjunction both in America and in France. But the conjunction is rare; not only because these last-named attributes are themselves rare, but because the practice of party intrigue is unfavourable to their development. It narrows a man's mind and distorts his vision. His eye, accustomed to the obscurity of committee-rooms, cannot range over the wide landscape of national questions. Habits of argument formed on the stump seldom fit a man to guide a legislature. In none of the greatest public men that have adorned America do we discern the features of the type just sketched. Hamilton was no intriguer, though he once executed a brilliant piece of strategy.[1] Neither was Clay or Webster. Jefferson, who added an eminent talent for party organization and management to his powers as a thinker and writer, was no speaker; and one might go through the whole list without finding one man of the first historic rank in whom

[1] In agreeing that the national capital should be placed in the South in return for the support of two Southern men to his plan for the settlement of the public debt.

have now brought it. National conventions offer the best field for the display of the peculiar kind of talent which this type of statesman exhibits. To rouse eight hundred delegates and ten thousand spectators needs powerful lungs, a striking presence, address, and courage. A man capable enough in Congress may fail in this arena. But less than half the work of a convention is done on the public stage. Delegates have to be seen in private, combinations arranged, mines laid and those of the opponent discovered and countermined, a distribution of the good things in the gift of the party settled with swarms of hungry aspirants. Easy manners, tact, and suppleness, a reputation for remembering and requiting good turns and ill turns—in fact, many of the qualities which make a courtier are the qualities which the intrigues of a convention require, develop, and perfect.

Besides such causes inherent in the present party system as check the growth of first-class statesmen in America, there are two springing from her constitutional arrangements which must not be forgotten. One is the disconnection of Congress from the executive. Another is the existence of States, each of which has a political life and distinct party organization of its own. Men often rise to eminence in a State without making their mark in national politics. They may become virtual masters of the State either in a legitimate way by good service to it or in an illegitimate way as its bosses. In either case they have to be reckoned with when a presidential election comes round, and are able, if the State be a doubtful one, to dictate their terms. Thus they push their way to the front without having ever shown the qualities needed for guiding the nation; they crowd out better men, and they make party leadership and management even more of a game than under the spoils system and the convention system it naturally becomes. The State vote comes to be in national politics what the ward vote is in city politics, a commodity which a boss or ring can dispose of; the power of a man who can influence it is greater than his personal merits entitle him to; and the kind of skill which can make friends of these State bosses and bring them into a "pool" or working combination becomes valuable, if not essential, to a national party leader. In fact, the condition of things is not wholly unlike that of England in the middle of last century, when a great borough-monger like the Duke of Newcastle was a power in the country, who must be not only consulted and propitiated at every crisis, but even admitted to a ministry if it was to secure a parliamentary majority. When a crisis rouses the nation, the power of these organization-mongers or vote-owners vanishes, just as that of the English borough-owning magnate was checked on like occasions, because it is only when the people of a State are listless that their Boss is potent. Unable to oppose a real wish of the masses, he can use their vote only by professing obedience while guiding it in the direction of the men or the schemes he favours.

This remark suggests another. I have remarked that among statesmen of the first of the two types described there are always ability and integrity sufficient for carrying on the regular business of the country. Men with those still higher gifts which European nations look for in their prime ministers (though they do not always find them) have of late years been rare. The Americans admit the fact, but explain it by arguing that there has been no crisis needing those gifts. Whether this is true may be doubted. Men of constructive statesmanship were surely needed in the period after the Civil War : and it is possible that a higher statesmanship might have averted the war itself. However, I am giving the view the Americans take. When the hour comes, they say, it will bring the man. It brought Abraham Lincoln. When he was nominated by the famous convention of 1860 his name had been little heard of beyond his own State. But he rose at once to the level of the situation, and that not merely by virtue of strong clear sense, but by his patriotic steadfastness and noble simplicity of character. If this was luck, it was just the kind of luck which makes a nation hopeful of its future, and inclined to overlook the faults of the methods by which it finds its leaders.

Part 4

PUBLIC OPINION

Chapter 1

The Nature of Public Opinion

In no country is public opinion so powerful as in the United States : in no country can it be so well studied. Before I proceed to describe how it works upon the government of the nation and the States, it may be proper to consider briefly how it is formed, and what is the nature of the influence which it everywhere exercises upon government.

What do we mean by public opinion? The difficulties which occur in discussing its action mostly arise from confounding opinion itself with the organs whence people try to gather it, and from using the term, sometimes to denote everybody's views,— that is, the aggregate of all that is thought and said on a subject, — sometimes merely the views of the majority, the particular type of thought and speech which prevails over other types.

The simplest form in which public opinion presents itself is when a sentiment spontaneously rises in the mind and flows from the lips of the average man upon his seeing or hearing something done or said. Homer presents this with his usual vivid directness in the line which frequently recurs in the *Iliad* when the effect produced by a speech or event is to be conveyed : "And thus any one was saying as he looked at his neighbour." This phrase describes what may be called the rudimentary stage of opinion. It is the prevalent impression of the moment. It is what any man (not every man) says, *i.e.* it is the natural and the general thought or wish which an occurrence evokes. But before opinion begins to tell upon government, it has to go through several other stages. These stages are various in different ages and countries. Let us try to note what they are in England or America at the present time, and how each stage grows out of the other.

A business man reads in his newspaper at breakfast the events of the preceding day. He reads that Prince Bismarck has announced a policy of protection for German industry, or that Mr. Henry George has been nominated for the mayoralty of New York. These statements arouse in his mind sentiments of approval or disapproval, which may be strong or weak according to his previous predilection for or against protection or Mr. Henry George, and of course according to his personal interest in the matter. They rouse also an expectation of certain consequences likely to follow. Neither the sentiment nor the expectation is based on processes of conscious reasoning—our business man has not time to reason at breakfast—they are merely impressions formed on the spur of the moment. He turns to the leading article in the newspaper, and his sentiments and expectations are confirmed or weakened according as he finds that they are or are not shared by the newspaper writer. He goes down to his office in the train, talks there to two or three acquaintances, and perceives that they agree or do not agree with his own still faint impressions. In his counting-house he finds his partner and a bundle of other newspapers which he glances at; their words further affect him, and thus by the end of the day his mind is beginning to settle down into a definite view, which approves or condemns Prince Bismarck's declaration or the nomination of Mr. George. Meanwhile a similar process has been going on in the minds of others, and particularly of the journalists, whose business it is to discover what people are thinking. The evening paper has collected the opinions of the morning papers, and is rather more positive in its forecast of results. Next morning the leading party journals have articles still more definite and positive in approval or condemnation and in prediction of consequences to follow; and the opinion of ordinary minds, which in most of such minds has been hitherto fluid and undetermined, has begun to crystallize into a solid mass. This is the second stage. Then debate and controversy begin. The men and the newspapers who approve Mr. George's nomination argue with those who do not; they find out who are friends and who opponents. The effect of controversy is to drive the partisans on either side from some of their arguments, which are shown to be weak; to conform them in others, which they think strong; and

to make them take up a definite position on one side.   This is the
third stage.   The fourth is reached when action becomes necessary.   When a citizen has to give a vote, he votes as a member
of a party ; his party prepossessions and party allegiance lay hold
on him, and generally stifle any individual doubts or repulsions
he may feel.   Bringing men up to the polls is like passing a
steam roller over stones newly laid on a road : the angularities
are pressed down, and an appearance of smooth and even
uniformity is given which did not exist before.   When a man
has voted, he is committed : he has thereafter an interest in
backing the view which he has sought to make prevail.   Moreover, opinion, which may have been manifold till the polling, is
thereafter generally two-fold only.   There is a view which has
triumphed and a view which has been vanquished.

In examining the process by which opinion is formed, we
cannot fail to note how small a part of the view which the
average man entertains when he goes to vote is really of his own
making.   His original impression was faint and perhaps shape-
less : its present definiteness and strength are mainly due to
what he has heard and read.   He has been told what to think,
and why to think it.   Arguments have been supplied to him
from without, and controversy has imbedded them in his mind.
Although he supposes his view to be his own, he holds it rather
because his acquaintances, his newspapers, his party leaders all
hold it.   His acquaintances do the like.   Each man believes and
repeats certain phrases, because he thinks that everybody else on
his own side believes them, and of what each believes only a
small part is his own original impression, the far larger part
being the result of the commingling and mutual action and
reaction of the impressions of a multitude of individuals, in
which the element of pure personal conviction, based on individual
thinking, is but small.

Every one is of course predisposed to see things in some one
particular light by his previous education, habits of mind,
accepted dogmas, religious or social affinities, notions of his own
personal interest.   No event, no speech or article, ever falls upon
a perfectly virgin soil : the reader or listener is always more or
less biassed already.   When some important event happens,
which calls for the formation of a view, these pre-existing habits,
dogmas, affinities, help to determine the impression which each
man experiences, and so far are factors in the view he forms.

But they operate chiefly in determining the first impression, and they operate over many minds at once. They do not produce variety and independence : they are soon overlaid by the influences which each man derives from his fellows, from his leaders, from the press.

Orthodox democratic theory assumes that every citizen has, or ought to have, thought out for himself certain opinions, *i.e.* ought to have a definite view, defensible by arguments, of what the country needs, of what principles ought to be applied in governing it, of the men to whose hands the government ought to be entrusted. There are persons who talk, though certainly very few who act, as if they believed this theory, which may be compared to the theory of some ultra-Protestants that every good Christian has or ought to have, by the strength of his own reason, worked out for himself from the Bible a system of theology. But one need only try the experiment of talking to that representative of public opinion whom the Americans call " the man in the cars," to realize how uniform opinion is among all classes of people, how little there is of that individuality in the ideas of each individual which they would have if he had formed them for himself, how little solidity and substance there is in the political or social ideas of nineteen persons out of every twenty. These ideas, when examined, mostly resolve themselves into two or three prejudices and aversions, two or three prepossessions for a particular leader or section of a party, two or three phrases or catchwords suggesting or embodying arguments which the man who repeats them has not analysed. It is not that these nineteen-twentieths are incapable of appreciating good arguments, or are unwilling to receive them. On the contrary, and this is especially true of the working classes, an audience is usually pleased when solid arguments are addressed to it, and men read with most relish the articles or leaflets, supposing them to be smartly written, which contain the most carefully sifted facts and the most exact thought. But to the great mass of mankind in all places, public questions come in the third or fourth rank among the interests of life, and obtain less than a third or a fourth of the leisure available for thinking. It is therefore rather sentiment than thought that the mass can contribute ; and the soundness and elevation of their sentiment will have more to do with their taking their stand on the side of justice, honour, and peace, than any reasoning they can apply to the sifting of the multifarious facts thrown before them, and to the drawing of the legitimate inferences therefrom.

It may be suggested that this analysis, if true of the uneducated, is not true of the educated classes. It is less true of that small class which in Europe specially occupies itself with politics; which, whether it reasons well or ill, does no doubt reason. But it is substantially no less applicable to the commercial and professional classes than to the working classes; for in the former, as well as in the latter, one finds few persons who take the pains, or have the leisure, or indeed possess the knowledge, to enable them to form an independent judgment. The chief difference between the so-called upper (including the wealthy part of the commercial classes) and humbler strata of society is that the former are less influenced by sentiment and possibly more influenced by notions, often erroneous, of their own interest. Having something to lose, they are more apt to imagine dangers to their property or their class ascendency. Moving in a more artificial society, their sympathies are less readily excited, and they more frequently indulge the tendency to cynicism natural to those who lead a life full of unreality and conventionalisms.

The apparent paradox that where the humbler classes have differed in opinion from the higher, they have often been proved by the event to have been right and their so-called betters wrong (a fact sufficiently illustrated by the experience of many European countries during the last half-century), may perhaps be explained by considering that the historical and scientific data on which the solution of a difficult political problem depends are really just as little known to the wealthy as to the poor. Ordinary education, even the sort of education which is represented by a university degree, does not fit a man to handle these questions, and it sometimes fills him with a vain conceit of his own competence which closes his mind to argument and to the accumulating evidence of facts. Education ought, no doubt, to enlighten a man ; but the educated classes, speaking generally, are the property-holding classes, and the possession of property does more to make a man timid than education does to make him hopeful. He is apt to underrate the power as well as the worth of sentiment ; he overvalues the restraints which existing institutions impose, he has a faint appreciation of the curative power of freedom, and of the tendency which brings things right when men have been left to their own devices, and have learnt from failure how to attain success. In the less-educated man a certain simplicity and openness of mind go some way to compensate for the lack of knowledge. He is more apt to be influenced by the authority of leaders ; but as, at least in England and America, he is generally shrewd enough to discern between a great man and a demagogue, this is more a gain than a loss.

While suggesting these as explanations of the paradox, I admit that it remains a paradox. But the paradox is not in the statement, but in the facts. Nearly all great political and social causes have made their way first among the middle or humbler classes. The original impulse which has set the cause in motion, the inspiring ideas that have drawn men to it, have no doubt come from lofty and piercing minds, and minds generally belonging to the cultivated class. But the principles and precepts these minds have delivered have waxed strong because the masses have received them gladly, while the wealthiest or so-called educated classes have frowned on or persecuted them. The most striking instance of all is to be found in the early history of Christianity.

The analysis, however, which I have sought to give of opinion applies only to the nineteen men out of twenty, and not to the twentieth. It applies to what may be called passive opinion— the opinion of those who have no special interest in politics, or concern with them beyond that of voting, of those who receive or propagate, but do not originate, views on public matters. Or, to put the same thing in different words, we have been considering how public opinion grows and spreads, as it were, spontaneously and naturally. But opinion does not merely grow; it is also made. There is not merely the passive class of persons ; there is the active class, who occupy themselves primarily with public affairs, who aspire to create and lead opinion. The processes which these guides follow are too well known to need description. There are, however, one or two points which must be noted, in order to appreciate the reflex action of the passive upon the active class.

The man who tries to lead public opinion, be he statesman, journalist, or lecturer, finds in himself, when he has to form a judgment upon any current event, a larger measure of individual prepossession, and of what may be called political theory and doctrine, than belongs to the average citizen. His view is therefore likely to have more individuality, as well as more intellectual value. On the other hand, he has also a stronger motive than the average citizen for keeping in agreement with his friends and his party, because if he stands aloof and advocates a view of his own, he may lose his influence and his position. He has a past, and is prevented, by the fear of seeming inconsistent, from departing from what he has previously said. He has a future, and dreads to injure it by severing himself ever so little from his party. He is accordingly driven to make the same sort of compromise between his individual tendencies and the general tendency which the average citizen makes. But he makes it more consciously, realizing far more distinctly the difference between what he would think, say, and do, if left to himself, and what he says and does as a politician, who can be useful and prosperous only as a member of a body of persons acting together and professing to think alike.

Accordingly, though the largest part of the work of forming opinion is done by these men—whom I do not call professional politicians, because in Europe many of them are not solely occupied with politics, while in America the name of professionals must be reserved for another class,—we must not forget the reaction constantly exercised upon them by the passive majority. Sometimes a leading statesman or journalist takes a line to which he finds that the mass of those who usually agree with him are not responsive. He perceives that they will not follow him, and that he must choose between isolation and a modification of his own views. A statesman may sometimes venture on the former course, and in very rare cases succeed in imposing his own will and judgment on his party. A journalist, however, is almost invariably obliged to hark back if he has inadvertently taken up a position disagreeable to his *clientèle*, because the proprietors of the paper have their circulation to consider. To avoid so disagreeable a choice a statesman or a journalist is usually on the alert to sound the general opinion before he commits himself on a new issue. He tries to feel the pulse of the mass of average citizens ; and as the mass, on the other hand, look to him for initiative, this is a delicate process. In European countries it is generally the view of the leaders which prevails, but it is modified by the reception which the mass give it ; it becomes accentuated in the points which they appreciate ; while those parts of it, or those ways of stating it, which have failed to find popular favour, fall back into the shade.

This mutual action and reaction of the makers or leaders of opinion upon the mass, and of the mass upon them, is the most curious part of the whole process by which opinion is produced. It is also that part in which there is the greatest difference between one free country and another. In some countries the leaders count for, say, three-fourths of the product, and the mass for one-fourth only. In others we may find these proportions reversed. In some countries the mass of the voters are not only markedly inferior in education to the few who lead, but are more modest, more disposed to look up to their betters. In others the difference of intellectual level between those who busy themselves with politics and the average voter is far smaller. Perhaps the leader is not so well instructed a man as in the countries first referred to ; perhaps the average voter is better instructed and more self-confident. Where both of these phenomena coincide, so that the difference of level is inconsiderable, public opinion will evidently be a different thing from what it is in countries where, though the Constitution has become democratic, the habits of the nation are still aristocratic. This is the difference between America and England.

CHAPTER 2

Government by Public Opinion

WE talk of public opinion as a new force in the world, conspicuous only since governments began to be popular. Statesmen, even in the last generation, looked on it with some distrust or dislike. Sir Robert Peel, for instance, in a letter written in 1820, speaks with the air of a discoverer, of "that great compound of folly, weakness, prejudice, wrong feeling, right feeling, obstinacy, and newspaper paragraphs, which is called public opinion."

Yet opinion has really been the chief and ultimate power in nearly all nations at nearly all times. I do not mean merely the opinion of the class to which the rulers belong. Obviously the small oligarchy of Venice was influenced by the opinion of the Venetian nobility, as the absolute Czar is influenced now by the opinion of his court and his army. I mean the opinion, unspoken, unconscious, but not the less real and potent, of the masses of the people. Governments have always rested and, special cases apart, must rest, if not on the affection, then on the reverence or awe, if not on the active approval, then on the silent acquiescence of the numerical majority. It is only by rare exception that a monarch or an oligarchy has maintained authority against the will of the people. The despotisms of the East, although they usually began in conquest, did not stand by military force but by popular assent. So did the feudal kingdoms of mediæval Europe. So do the despotisms of the Sultan (so far, at least, as regards his Mussulman subjects), of the Shah, and of the Chinese Emperor at this moment. The cases to the contrary are chiefly those of military tyrannies, such as existed in many of the Greek cities of antiquity, and in some of the Italian cities of the Renaissance, and such as exist now in the so-called republics of Central and South America. That even

288

the Roman Empire, that eldest child of war and conquest, did not rest on force but on the consent and good-will of its subjects is shown by the smallness of its standing armies, nearly the whole of which were employed against frontier enemies, because there was rarely any internal revolt or disturbance to be feared. Belief in authority, and the love of established order, are among the strongest forces in human nature, and therefore in politics. The first supports governments *de jure*, the latter governments *de facto*. They combine to support a government which is *de jure* as well as *de facto*. Where the subjects are displeased, their discontent may appear perhaps in the epigrams which tempered the despotism of Louis XV. in France, perhaps in the sympathy given to bandits like Robin Hood, perhaps in occasional insurrections like those of Constantinople under the Eastern Emperors. Of course, where there is no habit of combination to resist, discontent may remain for some time without this third means of expressing itself. But, even when the occupant of the throne is unpopular, the throne as an institution is in no danger so long as it can command the respect of the multitude and show itself equal to its duties.

In the earlier or simpler forms of political society public opinion is passive. It acquiesces in, rather than supports, the authority which exists, whatever its faults, because it knows of nothing better, because it sees no way to improvement, probably also because it is overawed by some kind of religious sanction. Human nature must have something to reverence, and the sovereign, because remote and potent and surrounded by pomp and splendour, seems to it mysterious and half divine. Worse administrations than those of Asiatic Turkey and Persia at this moment can hardly be imagined, yet the Mohammedan population show no signs of disaffection. The subjects of Darius and the subjects of Theebaw obeyed as a matter of course. They did not ask why they obeyed, for the habit of obedience was sufficient. They could, however, if disaffected, have at any moment overturned the throne, which had only, in both cases, an insignificant force of guards to protect it. During long ages the human mind did not ask itself—in many parts of the world does not even now ask itself—questions which seem to us the most obvious. Custom, as Pindar said, is king over all mortals and immortals, and custom prescribed obedience. When in any society opinion becomes self-conscious, when it begins to realize its force and

question the rights of its rulers, that society is already progress-
ing, and soon finds means of organizing resistance and compelling
reform.

The difference therefore between despotically-governed and
free countries does not consist in the fact that the latter are
ruled by opinion and the former by force, for both are generally
ruled by opinion. It consists rather in this, that in the former
the people instinctively obey a power which they do not know
to be really of their own creation, and to stand by their own
permission ; whereas in the latter the people feel their supremacy,
and consciously treat their rulers as their agents, while the rulers
obey a power which they admit to have made and to be able to
unmake them—the popular will. In both cases force is seldom
necessary, or is needed only against small groups, because the
habit of obedience replaces it. Conflicts and revolutions belong
to the intermediate stage, when the people are awakening to the
sense that they are truly the supreme power in the state, but
when the rulers have not yet become aware that their authority
is merely delegated. When superstition and the habit of submission have vanished from the whilome subjects, when the
rulers, recognizing that they are no more than agents for the
citizens, have in turn formed the habit of obedience, public
opinion has become the active and controlling director of a
business in which it was before the sleeping and generally forgotten partner. But even when this stage has been reached, as
has now happened in most civilized States, there are differences
in the degree and mode in and by which public opinion asserts
itself. In some countries the habit of obeying rulers and officials
is so strong that the people, once they have chosen the legislature
or executive head by whom the officials are appointed, allow
these officials almost as wide a range of authority as in the old
days of despotism. Such people have a profound respect for
government as government, and a reluctance, due either to
theory or to mere laziness, perhaps to both, to interfere with its
action. They say, "That is a matter for the Administration ;
we have nothing to do with it ;" and stand as much aside or
submit as humbly as if the government did not spring from their
own will. Perhaps they practically leave themselves, like the
Germans, in the hands of a venerated monarch and a forceful
minister, giving these rulers a free hand so long as their policy
moves in accord with the general sentiment of the nation, and

maintains its glory. Perhaps while frequently changing their ministries, they nevertheless yield to each ministry, and to its executive subordinates all over the country, an authority great while it lasts, and largely controlling the action of the individual citizen. This seems to be still true of France. There are other countries in which, though the sphere of government is strictly limited by law, and the private citizen is little inclined to bow before an official, the habit has been to check the ministry chiefly through the legislature, and to review the conduct of both ministry and legislature only at long intervals, when an election of the legislature takes place. This was the case in Britain down till a recent period. Although the people ruled, they ruled not directly, but through the House of Commons, which they chose only once in five, six, or seven years, and which might, at any given moment, represent rather the past than the present will of the nation.

I make these observations for the sake of indicating another form which the rule of the people may assume. We have distinguished three stages in the evolution of opinion from its unconscious and passive into its conscious and active condition. In the first it acquiesces in the will of the ruler whom it has been accustomed to obey. In the second conflicts arise between the ruling person or class, backed by those who are still disposed to obedience, on the one hand, and the more independent or progressive spirits on the other ; and these conflicts are decided by arms. In the third stage the whilome ruler has submitted, and disputes are referred to the sovereign multitude, whose will is expressed at certain intervals upon slips of paper deposited in boxes, and is carried out by the minister or legislature to whom the popular mandate is entrusted. A fourth stage would be reached if the will of the majority of the citizens were to become ascertainable at all times, and without the need of its passing through a body of representatives, possibly even without the need of voting machinery at all. In such a state of things the sway of public opinion would have become more complete, because more continuous, than it is in those European countries which, like France, Italy, and Britain, look chiefly to parliaments as exponents of national sentiment. The authority would seem to remain all the while in the mass of the citizens. Popular government would have been pushed so far as almost to dispense with, or at any rate to anticipate, the legal modes in which the majority speaks its will at the polling booths; and this informal but direct control of the multitude would dwarf, if it did not supersede, the importance of those formal but occasional deliverances made at the elections of representatives. To such a condition of things the phrase, "Rule of public opinion," might be most properly applied, for public opinion would not only reign but govern.

The mechanical difficulties, as one may call them, of working such a method of government are obvious. How is the will of the majority to be ascertained except by counting votes? how, without the greatest inconvenience, can votes be frequently taken on all the chief questions that arise? No country has yet surmounted these inconveniences, though little Switzerland with its *Referendum* has faced and dealt with some of them. But what I desire to point out is that even where the machinery for weighing or measuring the popular will from week to week or month to month has not been, and is not likely to be, invented, there may nevertheless be a disposition on the part of the rulers, whether ministers or legislators, to act as if it existed; that is to say, to look incessantly for manifestations of current popular opinion, and to shape their course in accordance with their reading of those manifestations. Such a disposition will be accompanied by a constant oversight of public affairs by the mass of the citizens, and by a sense on their part that they are the true governors, and that their agents, executive and legislative, are rather servants than agents. Where this is the attitude of the people on the one hand and of the persons who do the actual work of governing on the other, it may fairly be said that there exists a kind of government materially, if not formally, different from the representative system as it presented itself to European thinkers and statesmen of the last generation. And it is to this kind of government that democratic nations seem to be tending.

The state of things here indicated will be illustrated by what I have to say in the following chapters regarding opinion in the United States. Meanwhile a few remarks may be hazarded on the rule of public opinion in general.

The excellence of popular government lies not so much in its wisdom—for it is as apt to err as other kinds of government— as in its strength. It has often been compared to a pyramid, the firmest based of all buildings. Nobody can be blamed for obeying it. There is no appeal from its decisions. Once the principle that the will of the majority, honestly ascertained, must prevail, has soaked into the mind and formed the habits of a nation, that nation acquires not only stability, but immense effective force. It has no need to fear discussion and agitation. It can bend all its resources to the accomplishment of its collective ends. The friction that exists in countries where the laws or institutions handed down from former generations are incompatible with the feelings and wishes of the people has disappeared. A key has been found that will unlock every door.

On the other hand, such a government is exposed to two dangers. One, the smaller one, yet sometimes troublesome, is the difficulty of ascertaining the will of the majority. I do not mean the difficulty of getting all citizens to vote, because it must be taken that those who do not vote leave their will in the hands of those who do, but the difficulty of obtaining by any machinery yet devised a quite honest record of the results of voting. Where the issues are weighty, involving immense interests of individual men or groups of men, the danger of bribery, of force, and still more of fraud in taking and counting votes, is a serious one. When there is reason to think that ballots have been tampered with, the value of the system is gone ; and men are remitted to the old methods of settling their differences.

The other danger is that minorities may not sufficiently assert themselves. Where a majority has erred, the only remedy against the prolongation or repetition of its error is in the continued protests and agitation of the minority, an agitation which ought to be peaceably conducted, carried on by voice and pen, but which must be vehement enough to rouse the people and deliver them from the consequences of their blunders. But the more complete the sway of majorities is, so much the less disposed is a minority to maintain the contest. It loses faith in its cause and in itself, and allows its voice to be silenced by the triumphant cries of its opponents. How are men to acquiesce promptly and loyally in the decision of a majority, and yet to go on arguing against it ? how can they be at once submissive and aggressive ? That conceit of his own goodness and greatness which intoxicates an absolute monarch besets a sovereign people also, and the slavishness with which his ministers approach an Oriental despot may reappear in the politicians of a Western democracy. The duty therefore of a patriotic statesman in a country where public opinion rules, would seem to be rather to resist and correct than to encourage the dominant sentiment. He will not be content with trying to form and mould and lead it, but he will confront it, lecture it, remind it that it is fallible, rouse it out of its self-complacency. Unfortunately, courage and independence are plants which a soil impregnated with the belief in the wisdom of numbers does not tend to produce : nor is there any art known to statesmen whereby their growth can be fostered.

Experience has, however, suggested plans for lessening the risks incident to the dominance of one particular set of opinions. One plan is for the people themselves to limit their powers, *i.e.* to surround their own action and the action of their agents with restrictions of time and method which compel delay. Another is for them so to parcel out functions among many agents that no single one chosen indiscreetly, or obeying his mandate over-zealously, can do much mischief, and that out of the multiplicity of agents differences of view may spring which will catch the attention of the citizens.

The temper and character of a people may supply more valuable safeguards. The country which has worked out for itself a truly free government must have done so in virtue of the vigorous individuality of its children. Such an individuality does not soon yield even to the pressure of democratic conditions. In a nation with a keen moral sense and a capacity for strong emotions, opinion based on a love of what is deemed just or good will resist the multitude when bent on evil : and if there be a great variety of social conditions, of modes of life, of religious beliefs, these will prove centres of resistance to a dominant tendency, like rocks standing up in a river, at which he whom the current sweeps downwards may clutch. Instances might be cited even from countries where the majority has had every source of strength at its command—physical force, tradition, the all but universal persuasions and prejudices of the lower as well as of the higher classes—in which small minorities have triumphed, first by startling and then by leavening and convincing the majority. This they have done in virtue of that intensity of belief which is oftenest found in a small sect or group, not because it is small, but because if its belief were not intense it would not venture to hold out at all against the adverse mass. The energy of each individual in the minority makes it in the long run a match for a majority huger but less instinct with vitality. In a free country more especially, ten men who care are worth a hundred who do not.

Such natural compensations as this occur in the physical as well as in the spiritual and moral world, and preserve both. But they are compensations on which the practical statesman cannot safely rely, for they are partial, they are uncertain, and they probably tend to diminish with the progress of democracy. The longer public opinion has ruled, the more absolute is the authority of the majority likely to become, the less likely are energetic minorities to arise, the more are politicians likely to occupy themselves, not in forming opinion, but in discovering and hastening to obey it.

CHAPTER 3

How Public Opinion Rules in America

IT was observed in last chapter that the phrase "government by public opinion" is most specifically applicable to a system wherein the will of the people acts directly and constantly upon its executive and legislative agents. A government may be both free and good without being subject to this continuous and immediate control. Still this is the goal toward which the extension of the suffrage, the more rapid diffusion of news, and the practice of self-government itself, necessarily lead free nations; and it may even be said that one of their chief problems is to devise means whereby the national will shall be most fully expressed, most quickly known, most unresistingly and cheerfully obeyed. Delays and jerks are avoided, friction and consequent waste of force are prevented, when the nation itself watches all the play of the machinery and guides its workmen by a glance. Towards this goal the Americans have marched with steady steps, unconsciously as well as consciously. No other people now stands so near it.

Of all the experiments which America has made, this is that which best deserves study, for her solution of the problem differs from all previous solutions, and she has shown more boldness in trusting public opinion, in recognizing and giving effect to it, than has yet been shown elsewhere. Towering over Presidents and State governors, over Congress and State legislatures, over conventions and the vast machinery of party, public opinion stands out, in the United States, as the great source of power, the master of servants who tremble before it.

For the sake of making clear what follows, I will venture to recapitulate what was said as to the three forms which government has taken in free countries. First came primary assemblies, such as those of the Greek republics of antiquity, or those

296

of the early Teutonic tribes, which have survived in a few Swiss cantons. The whole people met, debated current questions, decided them by its votes, chose those who were to carry out its will. Such a system of direct popular government is possible only in small communities, and in this day of large States has become a matter rather of antiquarian curiosity than of practical moment.

In the second form, power belongs to representative bodies, Parliaments and Chambers. The people in their various local areas elect men, supposed to be their wisest or most influential, to deliberate for them, resolve for them, choose their executive servants for them. They give these representatives a tolerably free hand, leaving them in power for a considerable space of time, and allowing them to act unchecked, except in so far as custom, or possibly some fundamental law, limits their discretion. This is done in the faith that the Chamber will feel its responsibility and act for the best interests of the country, carrying out what it believes to be the wishes of the majority, unless it should be convinced that in some particular point it knows better than the majority what the interests of the country require. Such a system has long prevailed in England, and the English model has been widely imitated on the continent of Europe and in the British colonies.

The third is something between the other two. It may be regarded either as an attempt to apply the principle of primary assemblies to large countries, or as a modification of the representative system in the direction of direct popular sovereignty. There is still a legislature, but it is elected for so short a time and checked in so many ways that much of its power and dignity has departed. Supremacy is not with it, but with the people, who have fixed limits beyond which it cannot go, and who use it merely as a piece of machinery for carrying out their wishes and settling points of detail for them. The supremacy of their will is expressed in the existence of a Constitution placed above the legislature, although capable of alteration by a direct popular vote. The position of the representatives has been altered. They are conceived of, not as wise and strong men chosen to govern, but as delegates under specific orders to be renewed at short intervals.

This is the form established in the United States. Congress sits for two years only. It is strictly limited by the Constitution, which is a fundamental law placed out of its reach, and by the co-existence of the State governments, which the Constitution protects. It has (except by way of impeachment) no control over the Federal executive, which is directly named by and responsible to the people. So too the State legislatures sit for short periods, do not appoint the State executives, are hedged in by the prohibitions of the State constitutions. The people frequently legislate directly by enacting or altering a constitution. The principle of popular sovereignty could hardly be expressed more unmistakably. Allowing for the differences to which the vast size of the country gives rise, the mass of the citizens may be deemed as directly the supreme power in the United States as the Assembly was at Athens or Syracuse. The only check on the mass is that which they have themselves imposed, and which the ancient democracies did not possess, the difficulty of changing a rigid constitution. And this difficulty is serious only as regards the Federal Constitution.

As this is the most developed form of popular government, so is it also the form which most naturally produces what I have called government by public opinion. Popular government may be said to exist wherever all power is lodged in and issues from the people. Government by public opinion exists where the wishes and views of the people prevail, even before they have been conveyed through the regular law-appointed organs, and without the need of their being so conveyed. As in a limited monarchy the king, however powerful, must act through certain officers and in a defined legal way, whereas in a despotism he may act just as he pleases, and his initial written on a scrap of paper is as sure of obedience as his full name signed to a parchment authenticated by the Great Seal or the counter-signature of a minister, so where the power of the people is absolute, legislators and administrators are quick to catch its wishes in whatever way they may be indicated, and do not care to wait for the methods which the law prescribes. This happens in America. Opinion rules more fully, more directly, than under the second of the systems described above.

A consideration of the nature of the State governments as of the National government will show that legal theory as well as popular self-confidence gives birth to this rule of opinion. Supreme power resides in the whole mass of citizens. They have prescribed, in the strict terms of a legal document, the form of government. They alone have the right to change it, and that only in a particular way. They have committed only a part of their sovereignty to their executive and legislative agents, reserving the rest to themselves. Hence their will, or in other words, public opinion, is constantly felt by these agents to be, legally as well as practically, the controlling authority. In England, Parliament is the nation, not merely by a legal fiction, but because the nation looks to Parliament only, having neither reserved any authority to itself nor bestowed any elsewhere. In America, Congress is not the nation, and does not claim to be so.

The ordinary functions and business of government, the making of laws, the imposing of taxes, the interpretation of laws and their execution, the administration of justice, the conduct of foreign relations, are parcelled out among a number of bodies and persons whose powers are so carefully balanced and touch at so many points that there is a constant risk of conflicts, even of deadlocks. Some of the difficulties thence arising are dealt with by the Courts, as questions of the interpretation of the Constitution. But in many cases the intervention of the courts, which can act only in a suit between parties, comes too late to deal with the matter, which may be an urgent one ; and in some cases there is nothing for the courts to decide, because each of the conflicting powers is within its legal right. The Senate, for instance, may refuse the measures which the House thinks necessary. The President may veto bills passed by both Houses, and the Houses may not have a two-thirds majority to pass them over his veto. Congress may urge the President to adopt a certain course of action, and the President may refuse. The President may propose a treaty to the Senate and the Senate may reject it. In such cases there is a stoppage of governmental action which may involve loss to the country. The master, however, is at hand to settle the quarrels of his servants. If the question be a grave one, and the mind of the country clear upon it, public opinion throws its weight into one or other scale, and its weight is decisive. Should opinion be nearly balanced, it is no doubt difficult to ascertain, till the next election arrives, which of many discordant cries is really the prevailing voice. This difficulty must, in a large country, where frequent plebiscites are impossible, be endured, and it may be well, when the preponderance of opinion is not great, that serious decisions should not be quickly taken. The general truth remains that a system of government by checks and balances specially needs the presence of an arbiter to incline the scale in favour of one or other of the balanced authorities, and that public opinion must therefore be more frequently invoked and more constantly active in America than in other countries.

Those who invented this machinery of checks and balances were anxious not so much to develop public opinion as to resist and build up breakwaters against it. No men were less revolutionary in spirit than the heroes of the American Revolution. They made a revolution in the name of Magna Charta and the Bill of Rights : they were penetrated by a sense of the dangers incident to democracy. As an able American writer says, "the prevalent conception of popular opinion was that it was aggressive, revolutionary, unreasoning, passionate, futile, and a breeder of mob violence." We may presently inquire whether this conception has been verified. Meantime be it noted that the efforts made in 1787 to divide authority and, so to speak, force the current of the popular will into many small channels instead of permitting it to rush down one broad bed, have really tended to exalt public opinion above the regular legally-appointed organs of government. Each of these organs is too small to form opinion, too narrow to express it, too weak to give effect to it. It grows up not in Congress, not in State legislatures, not in those great conventions which frame platforms and choose candidates, but at large among the people. It is expressed in voices everywhere. It rules as a pervading and impalpable power, like the ether which, as physicists say, passes through all things. It binds all the parts of the complicated system together and gives them whatever unity of aim and action they possess.

There is also another reason why the opinion of the whole nation is a more important factor in the government of the United States than anywhere in Europe. In Europe there has always been a governing class, a set of persons whom birth, or wealth, or education has raised above their fellows, and to whom has been left the making of public opinion together with the conduct of administration and the occupancy of places in the legislature. The public opinion of Germany, Italy, France, and England has been substantially the opinion of the class which wears black coats and lives in good houses, though in the two latter countries it has begun of late years to be affected by the opinion of the classes socially lower. Although the members of the English Parliament are increasingly controlled by their constituents, still the influence which plays most steadily on them and permeates them is the opinion of a class or classes and not of the whole nation. The class to which the great majority of members of both Houses belong (*i.e.* the landowners and the persons occupied in professions and in the higher walks of commerce) is the class which chiefly forms and expresses what is called public opinion. Even in these days of vigilant and exacting constituencies one sees many members of the House of Commons the democratic robustness or provincial crudity of whose ideas melts like wax under the influence of fashionable dinner-parties and club smoking-rooms. It is a common complaint that it is hard for a member to "keep touch" with the opinion of the masses.

In the United States public opinion is the opinion of the whole nation, with little distinction of social classes. The politicians, including the members of Congress and of State legislatures, are, perhaps not (as Americans sometimes insinuate) below, yet certainly not above the average level of their constituents. They find no difficulty in keeping touch with outside opinion. Washington or Albany may corrupt them, but not in the way of modifying their political ideas. They do not aspire to the function of forming opinion. They are like the Eastern slave who says "I hear and obey." Nor is there any one class or set of men, or any one "social layer," which more than another originates ideas and builds up political doctrine for the mass. The opinion of the nation is the resultant of the views, not of a number of classes, but of a multitude of individuals, diverse, no doubt, from one another, but, for the purposes of politics far less diverse than if they were members of groups defined by social rank or by property.

The consequences are noteworthy. One is, that statesmen cannot, as in Europe, declare any sentiment which they find telling on their friends or their opponents in politics to be confined to the rich, or to those occupied with government, and to be opposed to the general sentiment of the people. In America you cannot appeal from the classes to the masses. What the employer thinks, his workmen think. What the wholesale merchant feels, the retail storekeeper feels, and the poorer customers feel. Divisions of opinion are vertical and not horizontal. Obviously this makes opinion more easily ascertained, while increasing its force as a governing power, and gives the people, that is to say, all classes in the community, a clearer and stronger consciousness of being the rulers of their country than European peoples have. Every man knows that he is himself a part of the government, bound by duty as well as by self-interest to devote part of his time and thoughts to it. He may neglect this duty, but he admits it to be a duty. So the system of party organizations already described is built upon this theory ; and as this system is more recent, and is the work of practical politicans, it is even better evidence of the general acceptance of the doctrine than are the provisions of Constitutions. Compare European countries, or compare the other states of the New World. In the so-called republics of Central and South America a small section of the inhabitants pursue politics, while the rest follow their ordinary avocations, indifferent to elections and pronunciamentos and revolutions. In Germany, and in the German and Slavonic parts of the Austro-Hungarian monarchy, people think of the government as a great machine which will go on, whether they put their hand to or not, a few persons working it, and all the rest paying and looking on. The same thing is largely true of republican France, and of semi-republican Italy, where free government is still a novelty, and local self-government in its infancy. Even in England, though the fifty-six years that have passed over her since the great Reform Act have brought many new ideas with them, the ordinary voter is still far from feeling, as the American does, that the government is his own, and he individually responsible for its conduct.

15. *Anton Chekhov,* ST. PETER'S DAY AND OTHER TALES. For the first time in English, here is a hilarious collection of early Chekhov stories and sketches. Resembling Dickens, Gogol and the Keystone Kops in their comic method, these stories will undoubtedly consolidate Chekhov' growing reputation as a major comic writer. Translated by Frances H. Jones. *A Putnam Capricorn Original.* 224 pp. $1.25 (Hardcover, $2.50).

16. *Thomas Nashe,* THE UNFORTUNATE TRAVELLER, OR JACK WILTON. Edited, with an Introduction, by John Berryman. Illustrated by Michael Ayrton. "The first novel in English" is the claim that has been made for this wonderful book. Published in 1594, it displays Nashe's madly inventive prose style, which has been compared to the style of Joyce's FINNEGANS WAKE, and Nashe's uncanny ability to create marvellously alive personalities. Of the first importance in the history of the novel. *A Putnam Capricorn Original.* 128 pp. $1.15 (Hardcover $2.50).

17. *Simone Weil,* WAITING FOR GOD. With an Introduction by Leslie Fiedler. T. S. Eliot said of it, "This book, by the late Simone Weil, is almost too important to be included in one's list of preferred reading for one year only." Andre Gide said, "It is clear that Mlle. Weil is the most truly spiritual writer of this century." 240 pp. $1.25.

18. *Robert M. Coates,* THE EATER OF DARKNESS, by the author of THE HOUR BEFORE WESTERLY. It is difficult to describe this superb novel adequately, but it can be said that it is written in an experimental style resembling that of the early Dos Passos and the style of the Nighttown scene in ULYSSES. It was originally published in Paris more than thirty years ago, and it has been called every-

thing from "a great comic adventure" to "the first surrealist novel in English." Completely revised for this edition by Mr. Coates, it contains an introduction by him giving in detail the circumstances of its composition and his intentions in writing it. *A Putnam Capricorn Original.* 128 pp. $.95.

19a, and 19b. *James Viscount Bryce*, THE AMERICAN COMMONWEALTH. Completely edited, abridged and introduced by Louis Hacker, Professor of Economics, Columbia University, and former Dean of the School of General Studies. A completely new edition of this great work on the American system of government. Always mentioned in the same breath with De Tocqueville's earlier work, Lord Bryce's superb study of the American commonwealth has been edited for Capricorn by a distinguished American scholar and historian for the present age. *A Putnam Capricorn Original.* 2 vols. $1.35 each (Hardcover, 1 vol. $5.00).

20. *George Moore*, CONFESSIONS OF A YOUNG MAN, A famous book by a most unusual man, this memoir concerns Moore's life in the Paris of the Nineties, when he lived a rich and crowded existence in his apartment in the *Rue de la Tours des Dames* (an unusually appropriate name), "with all its charming adjuncts, palms and pastels, my cat, my python, my friends, blonde hair and dark." It also details Moore's friendships with the Decadent and Symbolist writers, and with Manet, Degas and Renoir. This account sums up the artistic life of the Nineteenth Century, and was a prime influence on Ezra Pound, T. S. Eliot and James Joyce. 288 pp. $1.25.

OTHER CAPRICORN BOOKS

1. *John Dewey*, ART AS EXPERIENCE. 384 pp. $1.35.

2. *Rainer Maria Rilke*, NOTEBOOKS OF MALTE LAURIDS BRIGGE. 256 pp. $1.15.

3. *Alfred Adler*, WHAT LIFE SHOULD MEAN TO YOU. 320 pp. $1.25.

4. *Clive Bell*, ART. 192 pp. $1.25.

G. P. PUTNAM'S SONS

210 Madison Avenue • New York 16, N. Y.